CW00694326

The Heart of Buddhist Philosophy: Diṅnāga and Dharmakīrti

The Heart of Buddhist Philosophy: Diṅnāga and Dharmakīrti

Amar Singh

with Foreword by

Prof A.K. Warder

Munshiram Manoharlal Publishers Pvt. Ltd.

ISBN 81-215-0121-0
Reprinted 2004
First published in 1984

Printed in India.
Published by Munshiram Manoharlal Publishers Pvt. Ltd.,
Post Box 5715, 54 Rani Jhansi Road,
New Delhi 110 055.

In loving memory
of
my best friend
Late Prof. Rāhula Sāṅkṛtyāyana
the discoverer of
original works of
Dharmakīrti

Contents

Foreword

This piece of research is a very important contribution to the understanding of Buddhist philosophy and to the history of Indian philosophy generally. It is the first comprehensive study of the crucial problem of the philosophical position of Dharmakīrti, i.e. which school of Buddhism he was affiliated to, and of his predecessor Diṅnāga. The prevailing view at present is that these two philosophers were 'idealists', or more precisely that they belonged to the Buddhist 'Vijñānavāda' School (known also as 'Yogācāra'). Amar Singh challenges this view on the basis of a comprehensive examination of the primary sources, most of which are in Sanskrit (all were originally in Sanskrit, some now are available in Tibetan or Chinese translations only). Much has been published on this problem before, but it has been limited to the study of separate aspects of a complex problem, such as the study of particular texts. Since Stcherbatsky, the pioneer among modern scholars to study the works of Diṅnāga and Dharmakīrti, believed, though with serious reservations, that these philosophers were 'idealists', many scholars working in the field more recently have simply followed him, taking it for granted that they are idealists and then interpreting their works accordingly. A thorough investigation was long overdue, especially as many old texts have come to light since Stcherbatsky wrote, half a century ago, but it was a big task, not a matter that could be settled in the introduction to a translation of a text but one demanding a full scale monograph and several years' full-time study. It is this full scale monograph which Amar Singh now offers.

The key to the problem of the affiliation of Diṅnāga and Dharmakīrti is the relationship of the former to a certain 'Vasubandhu'. Buddhist traditions which are generally accepted describe Diṅnāga as a pupil of 'Vasubandhu'. Indeed it is the fact that one Vasubandhu was clearly a follower of the Vijñānavāda School, in his writings intended to establish its special views, that has led many scholars to assume that Diṅnāga also followed this School in general, although he does not uphold its special views and seems at times to go against them, or at least to be making a revision of them (hence Stcherbatsky's opinion that he started a new 'critical' school). However, it is now clear that there were at least two Buddhist philosophers named Vasubandhu during the period with which we are concerned. In particular there was one, the author of the *Abhidharmakośabhāsya*, who upheld the views of the Sautrāntika School. No doubt Mahāyānist tradition, and Modern-Mahāyānist Buddhists (especially in Japan), maintain that he was afterwards converted to the Mahāyānist Vijñānavāda, but that is improbable legend, propaganda in favour of one's own school. The kernel of this thesis is therefore the relationship of three Buddhist philosophers, Vasubandhu, Diṅnāga and Dharmakīrti, and whether they followed one school without serious modification of their views or 'conversion' to Mahāyāna.

In his First Chapter, Singh has investigated this relationship very thoroughly and effectively, on the basis of sifting out all the relevant primary evidence. He has established clearly the philosophical relationship of Diṅnāga's works to the *Abhidharmakośabhāṣya*. The fact that Diṅnāga actually wrote a commentary, the *Marmapradīpa*, on this Sautrāntika work seems to clinch the matter of his affiliation. This commentary is not an independent or critical work, with reference to Vasubandhu's text, but rather a summary of it. Again, the fundamentally important discussions by Diṅnāga on 'sensation' (*pratyakṣa*, sometimes translated 'perception') in his *Ālambanaparīkṣā* and *Pramāṇasamuccaya* seem to be dependent on those in the *Abhidharmakośabhāṣya* and therefore to be based on the Sautrāntika standpoint.

In his Second Chapter, Singh has examined the arguments used by modern scholars to establish the position of Diṅnāga and Dharmakīrti. For example, a careful reading of the *Ālambanaparīkṣā* shows that Diṅnāga accepted 'atoms' as real, as capable of producing effects, though denying that they can become objects of consciousness (*ālambanas*). This is consistent with Sautrāntika, not with Vijñānavāda. Similarly, the *Santānāntarasiddhi* of Dharmakīrti appears to be a Sautrāntika critique of Vaibhāṣika doctrine, not a Vijñānavāda work. The argument that all Dharmakīrti's works are written merely at the *saṃvṛti* level (do not deal with questions of ultimate truth or reality but only with superficial appearances) is refuted by pointing out categorical statements in these works which are inconsistent with such an interpretation. This interpretation itself, of course, concedes that to a Vijñānavāda philosopher these works do appear to be at the *saṃvṛti* level and to express a view which is not his own, not Vijñānavāda nor Mahāyānist but that of some early school of Buddhism, such as the Sautrāntika. But the author of these works, Dharmakīrti, clearly indicates that in his own view he is discussing philosophy at the 'ultimate' (*paramārtha*) level. Thus Amar Singh appears to establish conclusively that Dharmakīrti is not a Mahāyānist or Vijñānavādin.

This is a serious and illuminating contribution to an important and complex problem. It is not to be expected that all scholars in the field will immediately accept its conclusion. But it is to be expected that those who doubt Singh's conclusion will have to look more closely at the evidence of the primary sources. Even if they arrive at a different conclusion, Singh's contribution will have been of fundamental importance in bringing about more serious investigations than have been made in the past, in showing how the problem should be tackled.

A.K. Warder

University of Toronto
11 October 1978.

Preface

The purpose of this book consists in investigating and determining the real philosophical standpoint of Dharmakīrti.

Since the renaissance of Buddhist studies in the West and in the East, this question has been a subject of serious controversy and calls for a thorough examination. This research has been made in an attempt to clarify confusing situations and to ascertain the reality.

In the scholarly world there persists a fixed attitude, with a few exceptions that Dharmakīrti along with Diṅnāga and Vasubandhu II belong to the Mahāyāna Vijñānavāda school.

The discussion as set out by certain prominent scholars is supposed to be concluded and others follow them unquestioningly. Here an attempt has been made to re-investigate the question on the ground of some substantial evidence.

During the course of my study of the recently discovered original texts of Dharmakīrti and some important commentaries, there appeared a doubt regarding this prevalent view, and after a comprehensive survey a hypothesis came into existence: that he is a Sautrāntika, not a Viñānavādin. The present thesis is a thorough investigation of this hypothesis.

Historically, Dharmakīrti's epistemology and philosophy have influenced Buddhist and non-Buddhist philosophical schools and some of the later exponents have utilized it for their own philosophical expositions and have incorporated it into their own traditions.

Therefore, the author has mainly relied on the internal evidence of the original writings of Dharmakīrti and those expositors who appear to be faithful to him. The internal philosophical consistency of a school generally remains unaltered and a misinterpretation can easily be pinpointed on this very ground. The internal evidence is of three kinds: epistemological, which covers the views of Dharmakīrti on the nature of valid cognition, sources of valid cognition, criterion of valid cognition, perceptions, limits of knowledge, etc.; the ontological, which reveals his views on physical and mental reality, illusion, etc.; and the axiological, which shows his ethical code, the goal and the path in relation (identity, causal and negation) to the school it belongs to.

The prevalent *controversy* regarding Dharmakīrti's philosophical standpoint demonstrates the doubtful nature of the issue. The *examination* of the controversy reveals the invalid, inconsistent, contradictory and illogical natures of wrong views. The threefold (epistemological, ontological. axiological) *evidence* drives the author to the following conclusion.

Firstly, the *epistemological evidence*: the definition of cognition, criterion of right cognition, theory of correspondence, means of right cognition, importance of direct cognition, two means of valid cognition and limit of valid cognition; secondly, the *contological evidence*: two realities, atomism, non-eternalism, nature of reality, negation of eight kinds of consciousness, store-house consciousness and solipsism; and thirdly, the *axiological evidence*: the theory of the four noble truths, three intrinsic natures of reality, ethical radicalism which positively proves Dharmakīrti's philosophical standpoint along with Diṅnāga and Vasubandu II as that of a Sautrāntika.

The conclusion reviews the implications for an understanding of Diṅnāga and Dharmakīrti and of the history of philosophy in India from the 5th century onwards. In the beginning the author was not confident in receiving any recognition to his critical work and non-traditional conclusions. He was rather afraid of displeasing great scholars by criticising their views. But it was for his surprise to receive a warm recognition from many prominent scholars as Y. Kajiyama, M. Nagatomi, A. Wayman, P.S. Jaini, S. Ruegg, T. Vetter, etc. In the course of personal discussions of their respective criticism with some of these scholars, they seemed to be agreed with my conclusions. Prof. A.K. Warder was first to be convinced by this evidence and he made due revisions in the second edition of his book *Indian Buddhism* (vii-viii, 448). During my lecture tour in Singapore, Malaysia and Thailand, this research received an interesting response from the scholars of the Theravāda philosophy. In India, I presented these findings to a conference of Buddhist scholars at Bodhagaya (Dec. 1982) for examination. Some scholars were really stimulated by this research and called for a 'Workshop on Sautrāntika Philosophy' in Sāranāth (April, 1983) to examine my thesis and to collect some material on Sautrāntikas. The author had to undergo a critical period of questioning and ultimately convinced Prof. Jagannath Upādhyaya and Rāmaśaṅkara-Tripāthi who have been teaching Dharmakīrti as a Vijñānavādin and collecting some material on Sautrāntikas, along with many Tibetan Geshes and foreign scholars who were really hopeful to find new material on Sautrāntikas vis-a-vis Diṅnāga and Dharmakīrti. Prof. R.C. Pandey has also translated the whole of *Pramāṇavārttika* (in press) having been fully convinced with this new evidence. This is, indeed, an interesting recognition of a piece of research work by scholars whose views are critically examined. It shows their love for truth and faithfulness to reason. I offer my sincere respect to all these great scholars.

Dharmakīrti who is regarded as a Kant of India by Stcherbatsky, could not receive any recognition of his works from contemporary scholars. In the very beginning of Pramāṇavārttika Dharmakīrti expresses his grief for feeble-mindedness (*mandadhīḥ*) of scholars, filled with the filth of jealousy (*irṣāmala*). He died as a desperate philosopher thinking that his works will be annihilated along with his own body (*svadehe jarām*). The disappearance of the Sautrāntika works and tactful inclusions of almost all Sautrāntika Ācāryas into Vijñānavāda (Idealism) make me to suspect a tactful foul play against these critical philosophers. The author expresses his deepest sympathy for these suppressed, neglected, and forgotten ones, hoping that some one will further explore this lost treasure of critical philosophy of India. Dharmakīrti's maxim "nothing is possible by single (cause) but by collection of (causes) everything is possible" (*na kiñcid ekasmāt sāmgryā sarva sambhava, PV.* 2/536 ab), is also true in respect of this book. The work was far more difficult than I had first expected, and it was the kind help of my teachers, colleagues, and friends which enabled me to present my work in its present form.

First of all, I wish to thank Prof. Anthony K. Warder for his patient supervision, active interest and creative discussions which eventually led to the arguments and conclusions presented in this thesis. I have acquired through his affectionate guidance the training of intellectual freedom and the disciplines of Buddhist Psychology (*Abhidharma*) and Indian Epistemology (*Pramāṇavidyā*) which last is the predominant instrument (*sādhakatamaṃ karaṇaṃ*) for the thesis.

I am indebted also to Prof. B.K. Matilal for his graduate course in Vedantic and Buddhist Idealism, teaching *Mādhyamikakārikas* and for his valuable and stimulating discussions. I also thank Prof. T. Venkatacarya for the graduate course in Indian Linguistics (*Mahābhāṣya*), Prof. C.D.C. Priestley for his *Vigrahavyāvartanī*, Prof. Shoro Katsurā for his Tibetan, *Abhidharmakośabhāṣya* and *Vijñāptimātratāsiddhi*, Prof. M. Fujimoto for *Pramāṇasamuccaya* and *Santānāntarasiddhi*, and Prof. A. Urquhart of the Department of Philosophy for his graduate course in Modern Logic. I am highly indebted to Prof. H.G. Herzberger and Prof. J.G. Slater, Department of Philosophy for their valuable criticism and suggestions.

I also wish to thank all the prominent scholars whose views are examined and referred to, for their valuable pioneer research work in this field, and particularly Prof. Y. Kajiyama of the Kyoto University, for suggesting many new channels which are critically examined in this book.

Many thanks to the University of Toronto for its financial assistance which is very foundation of this work.

Amar Singh

New Delhi
22 February 1984

Abbreviations

Abk.	*Abhidharmakośa*
AbkB	*Abhidharmakośabhāṣya*
AAV	*Abhidhammathavikāsinī*
AMS	*Abhidkhammamūlaṭīkā*
AbD	*Abhidhamadīpa*
AbS	*Abhidharmasamuccaya*
AP	*Ālambanaparīkṣā*
ATV	*Ātmatattvaviveka*
AVS	*Arthaviniścayasūtra*
Buddh. phil	*Buddhist philosophy Theory and Practice*
BSOAS	*Bulletin of the School of Oriental and African Studies*
BL	*Buddhist Logic*
CCB	*Central Conception of Buddhism*
DAT	*Dīghanikāyaaṭṭhakathāṭikā*
Dig. on Per	*Dignāga on Perception*
DNCV	*Dvādaśāraṃnayacakra-Tṛtti*
Hetu	*Hetubindu*
HIP	*History of Indian Philosophy*
HBT	*Hetubinduṭīkā*
IHQ	*Indian Historical Quarterly*
JAS	*Journal of Asiatic Society*
MV	*Madhyanta-vibhāga*
MSL	*Mahāyānasūtralaṅkara*
Moha	*Mohavicchedanī*
MK	*Mādhyamikakārikā*
NB	*Nyāyabindu*
NBT(V)	*Nyāyabinduṭīkā (Vinītadeva)*

NBT(D)	*Nyāyabinduṭīkā (Dharmottara)*
Nyāyavatāra	*Nyāyavatāravārttikavṛtti*
PS	*Pramāṇasamuccaya*
PSV	*Pramāṇasamuccayavṛtti*
PV	*Pramāṇavārttika*
Pvin	*Pramāṇaviniścaya*
PVV	*Pramāṇavārttikabhāṣya*
PVST	*Pramāṇavārttika-svavṛtti*
Prasannapadā	*Mādhyamikavṛttt*
PM	*Pramāṇamīmāṃṣā*
PPP	*Prajñaparamitāpindārtha*
Pradīpa	*Dharmottarapradīpa*
RAS	*Royal Asiatic Society*
Spuṭārtha	*Abhidharmakośavyāhyā*
SP	*Sambandhaparīkṣā*
SS	*Santānāntarasiddhi*
SVK	*Ślokavārttikakāśikā*
SVV	*Ślokavārttikavāyakhyā*
TrimB	*Triṃśikābhāṣya*
TS	*Tattvasaṃgraḥ*
TSP	*Tattvasaṃgraḥapañjikā*
VisM	*Visuddhimagga*
Vib	*Vibhāvinī*
VPV	*Vibhāṣāprabhāvṛtti*
VV	*Vigrahavyāvartanī*
WZKM	*Wiener Zeitschrit für die kunde des Morgenlandes*
WZKSO	*Wiener Zeitschrift fur die kunde des Sud-uad Ost-Asiens*
Yogasthana	*Śrāvakabhumau naiṣkarmya bhumi*
YA	*Yogāvatāṛa*
YAU	*Yogāvalāropadeśa*

Introduction

The origin of this research goes back to the discovery of some original manuscripts of the Sanskrit texts[1] of Dharmakīrti's works, unearthed by Rāhula Sāṅkṛtyāyana, from a Tibetan monastery. Early in this century, Vasubandhu, Diṅnāga and Dharmakīrti were merely legendary names, except they were traced in the writings of non-Buddhist critics. Rāhula Sāṅkṛtyāyana mentions:

> "Only a few decades ago, Vasubandhu, Diṅnāga and Dharmakīrti were mere legendary names, which we only heard, when the long forgotten tomes of the old masters were dusted on ceremonial occasions."[2]

Fortunately, I had a golden opportunity to study Dharmakīrti's magnum opus *Pramāṇavārttika* (*PV*) under Prof. Rāhula Sāṅkṛtyāyana's guidance in Śrīlaṅka during 1960-63. In the course of various discussions, he used to doubt the prevalent idealistic interpretation of Dharmakīrti's philosophical standpoint, but he was not yet sure about Dharmakīrti's school of affiliation. He passed away in 1963, leaving all the responsibilities in my hands. I first met this great scholar in my hometown of Agra, India in 1959, when he came to deliver a series of lectures on Buddhist Philosophy. I had had eight years of special training in Brahmanic logic and Mahāyāna Philosophy under A.K. Chatterji, the disciple of T.R.V. Murti. I began to debate with Sāṅkṛtyāyana on logical questions. Seeing my interest in this difficult subject, he invited me to Śrīlaṅkā where he was a professor of Buddhist Philosophy. He told me about his meeting with

[1]See Bibliography.
[2]*Pramāṇavārttika* (*PV*), Preface, pp. 8-9; see Bibliography.

T. Stcherbatsky, who invited him to Russia after the discovery of some of the texts of Dharmakīrti. For two years, he stayed in Russia and worked there with Stcherbatsky and followed his interpretation on Dharmakīrti's philosophical standpoint.

The Russian scholar, Stcherbatsky, who was the greatest orientalist of his time, discovered and discussed Diṅnāga's and Dharmakīrti's works mainly from Tibetan sources. Winternitz mentions this astonishing discovery of Stcherbatsky:

> "Translations of Diṅnāga's works on logic are to appear shortly, by Prof. Stcherbatsky who wrote to me about it on 26th April, 1929 in the following words: 'You will be astonished to find among the Indians, especially Diṅnāga, a comprehensive system of critical philosophy. It has long been my conviction that we here have before us a most excellent achievement of the Indian mind, this conviction has now grown stronger than ever before, and I hope to be in a position to present it clearly'."[1]

Rāhula Sāṅkṛtyāyana, though influenced by Stcherbatsky's attempt of including Dharmakīrti under Idealism, used to tell me about the following important points in the writings of Dharmakīrti:

1. Dharmakīrti could not get any recognition from the contemporary Buddhist scholars. He begins his *PV* in the desperate situation of the intelligentsia of that time, suffering through the defilements of jealousy (*īrṣyā mala*) and weak intelligence (*mandadhī*). Why was this and why did he die a desperate philosopher who could not find anyone to understand his writings?

2. The doctrine of causal efficiency (*arthakriyākāritva*) does not seem to be a Vijñānavādin Doctrine.

3. The concept of *svalakṣaṇa* as ultimate reality does not fit with the Vijñānavāda.

4. Dharmakīrti denied the concept of omniscience of the Buddha. It was a break with traditional ideas.

And so we continued to examine the philosophical positions of Dharmakīrti. But because of the non-availability of some important missing links, we could not decide his real philosophical position. Before his death, Rāhula Sāṅkṛtyāyana handed over all his material on Dharmakīrti to me and asked me to find out the reality, as his

[1] *A History of Indian Literature*, II, p. 363.

last wish. But, for the following reasons, I was not able to decide:

1. Many important missing links were not yet discovered.
2. The commentators had different opinions on this issue.
3. The Sanskrit text of the *Abhidharmakośabhāṣya* was not yet published.
4. The influence of the authority of Stcherbatsky was strong all over the world and I had no courage to question the views of such an intellectual giant.
5. Both Stcherbatsky and Sāṅkṛtyāyana believed that there was only one Vasubandhu, who was a Vijñānavādin, and that Diṅnāga was his direct disciple. It was very hard to investigate this complex issue.
6. There were some complex passages in *PV*, which on the surface look Vijñānavādin in nature.
7. The subject-matter and language of Dharmakīrti was extremely difficult.

In spite of these difficulties, I continued to try to fulfil Sāṅkṛtyāyana's last wish. In Śrīlaṅkā, I had an opportunity to discuss these complex subjects with, K. N. Jayatilleke. W.S. Karunaratne, G.P. Malalasekhara, S.B. Shastri. Once P.S. Jaini visited Vidyālaṅkāra University and I discussed with him some of the problems about Dharmakīrti. He upheld the view of only one Vasubandhu who changed his position, and mentioned Frauwallner's new thesis that there were two Vasubandhus, which Jaini attempted to refute. I was very curious about this new thesis. I also met Paranavitana who showed me the photocopies of some Sanskrit *ślokas* from Diṅnāga's *Pramāṇasamuccaya* (collection of his theories on the valid source of cognition), he found in a cave in Śrīlaṅkā carved on a rock. But since the complete original text was not available (only some fragments published by Randle), it was hard to identify them for certain.

While studying the Pāli *Sutta Piṭaka*, *Abhidhamma Piṭaka*, and *Vinaya Piṭaka*, as well as various commentaries by Buddhaghosha and Sinhālese authors, I found a striking similarity of epistemology and logical analysis between Dharmakīrti's doctrine and the Pāli *Sutta Piṭaka* and the *Abhidhamma Piṭaka* (which latter was my second field of interest). I thought, at that time, that Dharmakīrti might be following early Buddhism, or was quite independent, or might have tried to reconcile the doctrines of all Buddhist philosophical schools. But I was getting sure that there is nothing in common with Vijñānavāda. In spite of this confusing state, I did not give up hope. I then returned to India.

In 1967, I got an opportunity to work as co-director in the Institute of Indology of New Delhi where Dharmendranatha Shastri has been preparing his monumental thesis on a comparative study of the school of Diṅnāga and Nyāya-Vaiśeṣika, for publication. I also discussed this issue with Profs. A.K. Chatterjee, T.R.V. Murti, R.C. Pandey, D.N. Shastri, Ven. Jagdishakassapa, but they also believed Dharmakīrti was an idealist. By that time some Tibetan monks, expelled by the Chinese invasion, set up a monastery in Sikkim and I thought of exploring Tibetan tradition on Dharmakīrti.

I got an opportunity as a Sanskrit teacher in the monastery of H.H. Lāmā Karmapā and stayed there for one year (1969-70). I studied Tibetan and with the help of some learned Lāmās I collected information about Dharmakīrti's system as understood in Tibet. Their view about Dharmakīrti was controversial. Some called him a Svātantrika or a Sautrāntika and others considered him to be a combination of Yogācāra-Sautrāntika. Generally his philosophy was included under Śāntarakṣita and Kamalaśila's Svātantrika Mādhyamika Yogācāra system. This Tibetan account made me more doubtful. I thought of going to the West to learn the techniques of critical research. Among the Western scholars with whom I discussed this problem were: in London, A. Kunst; in Holland, J. Gonda, and later. Tilmann Vetter; in New York, I met Alex Wayman in Columbia University. Fortunately, I came to know about A.K. Warder teaching at University of Toronto and visited him. It will be interesting to cite the discussion which led to the discovery of the truth about Dharmakīrti's philosophical standpoint. Warder asked a question, "Do you think that the terms *ālambana* (object of consciousness), *vastu* (reality), *viṣaya* (sense object) *svalakṣaṇa* (particular), *gocararūpa* (range), *dharma* (element or mental object), all have similar meaning or different?" I answered him, "I think sometimes they have almost similar meaning." He replied, "This is not true. The term *ālambana* connotes the object of consciousness while *viṣaya* is the object of senses. At one time, I also held this view that these words are synonyms, now I am positive of the different meanings of these terms. For example, Diṅnāga criticized *ālambana* in *Ālambanaparīkṣā* as not being external, but did not criticize the *viṣaya* or *svalakṣaṇa*."

At the same time, other professors such as C. D. C. Priestley and S. Katsura were also teaching at the University of Toronto.

I was happy to see the possibility of finding a solution after my seven years of constant search to find out the reality about Dharmakīrti.

At the University here, I could find an opportunity to re-study Dharmakīrti's work, Diṅnāga's works, and pre-Diṅnāga logic, *Abhidharmakośabhāṣya*, and the works of Yogācāra Vijñānavāda, and the *Mādhyamikas*. During two years of constant critical training of mind and critical analysis of the original texts the difficulties mentioned above faded away, one by one in the following way:

1. The important missing links such as Vaibhāṣika works (*Abhidharmadīpa, Vibhāṣaprabhāvṛtti*), Vijñānavādin's works, etc. were found and thoroughly studied.
2. The commentators of Dharmakīrti could be criticized on the ground of internal evidence and logic.
3. The *Abhidharmakośabhāṣya* was published and the Sautrāntika doctrines, which were not clearly known before, became known.
4. Stcherbatsky's and doubtful statements made me doubt the authority of this great scholar.
5. By this time my knowledge of Dharmakīrti's difficult passages was quite clear.
6. The positions of Diṅnāga and Vasubandhu also became clear.
7. Two years of constant training in critical techniques of research made me confident of reaching a definite conclusion.

After a thorough investigation of the nature of the object, or sense-datum (*svalakṣana*), I discovered that Dharmakīrti and Diṅnāga both believed in the ultimate reality of the sense-datum which consists of assemblages of atoms (*aṇusañcaya*), a typical doctrine mentioned by the Sautrāntika Vasubandhu in his *Abhidharmakośabhāṣya*. Diṅnaga was explaining and defending the Sautrāntika Vasubandhu's doctrines from critics. Diṅnāga in turn was attacked by Brahmanical and Jaina critics and Dharmakīrti was explaining and defending his position from the critics by giving new logical arguments.

As Diṅnāga and Dharmakīrti were the commentators and defenders of the Sautrāntika Vasubandhu's doctrines, it was possible that they were following this Vasubandhu, who seemed to be different from the Vijñānavāda Vasubandhu, whose disciples they were considered to be by some ancient and modern scholars. It appeared to be the root-cause of the confusion and I have to go deep into this highly complex issue. Frauwallner's exciting thesis of two Vasubandhus gave me a clue to solve this problem.

I also considered the possibility that Dharmakīrti may not have belonged to any school and may have been quite independent, as it was theoretically possible that a commentator could have been quite independent, being neither Yogācāra nor Sautrāntika.

But this hypothesis did not work as I found that Diṅnāga was not only a commentator but a defender also. The same was the case with Dharmakīrti. I then made a thorough survey of Diṅnāga's works, which doubtless are based on the *Abhidharmakośabhāṣya* and *Vādavidhāna* of the Sautrāntika Vasubandhu, and found that Diṅnāga was defending Vasubandhu's doctrines in intellectual debates.

A commentator from another school, who does not identify himself with the doctrines of the original philosopher, would not be likely to enter into such an intellectual fight with Vasubandhu's opponents.

The study of some fragments of the *Vādavidhāna* (collected by Prof. Frauwallner from *NVTT.*) uncovers the fact that the Sautrāntika Vasubandhu is criticizing Gautama (Akṣapāda) and Vatsyāyana's method of logic and debate. Diṅnāga comments on the *Vādavidhāna* and *Abhidharmakośabhāṣya* and further attacks Brahmanic logic (Nyāya) along with Vaiśeṣika, Sāṃkhya and Mimāṃsā. Diṅnāga is again attacked by Uddyotakara, Kumārila, and Jaina logicians. Dharmakīrti comments on Diṅnāga's main work (*PS.*) and writes different independent treatises to defend his doctrines by a serious intellectual counter-attack on Diṅnāga's critics. This peculiar situation of the development of Indian critical philosophy from a religious founder to original philosophers, then to commentators and defenders, forces a researcher to classify a philosopher in terms of schools. As Diṅnāga and Dharmakīrti are commentators and defenders of the Sautrāntika Vasubandhu, they are then Sautrāntikas. I made a thorough survey of the characteristics of this school and recorded the main doctrines of the Sautrāntikas as found in *Abhidharmakośabhāṣya* etc.,

1. Acceptance of knowledge and verifiability of knowledge on the ground of non-contradiction (*avisaṃvāda*).

2. Acceptance of causal efficiency (*arthakriyākāritva*) as the criterion to judge the validity of sensation and inference.

3. Its emphasis on sensation (*pratyakṣa*) as the criterion of the validity of inference.

4. Correspondence (*sādṛśya or sārūpya*) between the object (*svalakṣaṇa*) and its mental image as the criterion of valid knowledge.

5. The division of phenomenal reality (*samvṛtisatya*) and the ultimate reality (*paramārthasatya*) is quite different from other systems.

6. The doctrine of the assemblage of atoms (*aṇusañcayavāda*) as

ultimate reality.

7. The doctrine of momentariness (*anityavāda*) not believing in durability (*sthiti*) even for a moment.

8. The nature of the particular object (*svalakṣaṇa*).

9. The nature of imagination (*kalpanā*) and illusion (*bhrānti*),

10. No single cause but assemblage of causes (*kāraṇasaṃghāta*) in the form of causes, conditions and result (*hetu-pratyaya-phala*) as the producer of everything.

11. The doctrine of non-causal destruction (*ahetukavināśavāda*).

12. Unity of mind and mental factors (*cittacaittābhedam*).

13. The rejection of eight types of consciousnesses (*aṣṭavijñāna*) (acceptance of six kinds of consciousnesses).

14. The rejection of store-consciousness (*ālayavijñāna*).

15. Acceptance of the existence of other streams of thought or refutation of Solipsism (*santānāntarasiddhi*).

16. Sixteen descriptions of four noble truths (*caturāryasatya*), emphasis on non-eternal, disgusting, and non-ego (*anitya*, *duḥkha*, *anātman*) and refutation of wrong ethical concepts and practice.

I found striking similarity of these doctrines in the writings of Dharmakīrti, Diṅnāga, and Sautrāntika Vasubandhu. The hypothesis that the three of them were Sautrāntikas appeared to be probable on the ground of evidence and logic.

It was an inference from an effect to cause (*kāraṇa-kārya*), based on internal evidence. A thorough comparison of these doctrines made me more and more certain about the hypothesis of their belonging to the Sautrāntika school. I also made a comparison with the *Sūtrapiṭaka* (some Sanskrit, the rest Pāḷi) and the *Arthaviniścayasūtra*, etc. which also proved similarity of these doctrines to the *Sūtra*.

I still did not rest and made a thorough survey of the writings of Buddhist and non-Buddhist critics of Sautrāntikas, such as Vaibhāṣikas, Yogācāra Vijñānavādins, Mādhyamikas, and the Nyāya, Vaiśeṣika, Mīmāṃsā, Jainas, etc.

It was amazing to find that some reliable critics such as Pārthasārathi, Uddyotakara, Vācaspatimiśra, Mallavādin, Siṃhasūri, etc. called Vasubandhu, Diṅnāga, and Dharmakīrti Sautrāntikas and opponents of Vijñānavādins.

A thorough survey of commentators of Dharmakīrti revealed the fact that some of them try to include him under Vijñānavāda, some under Mādhyamika-Yogācāra (Prajñākaragupta) some try to reconcile Sautrāntika and Yogācāra (Vinītadeva-Manorathanandin, etc.)

and some (Dharmottara, Arcaṭa, Durvevakamiśra, Mallavādin) criticize Vinītadeva and others for misinterpretation of Dharmakīrti's standpoint. They categorically called Dharmakīrti and Diṅnāga's doctrines Sautrāntika doctrines. This also strengthened the probability of my thesis.

But the problem was not yet over. The following were the serious difficulties still standing in the way:

1. Some of the old commentators of Dharmakīrti were to be examined.

2. Some of the great modern scholars' views on this issue were to be examined.

It was not an easy task to examine the findings of these ancient and modern scholars for whom I had great regard.

Many times I thought to quit research on such a complex and polemic issue, where one has to enter into the delicate task of examining these authorities.

But as I have studied Dharmakīrti's seven works many times and the internal evidence in my favour was very strong, I took courage to examine them. I also found controversial statements in the writings of these great scholars, which made me doubtful about their authority. But my main strength was internal evidence and training in Indian and Western logic, which made me unhesitant regarding any authority which contradicts evidence and logic.

The first necessity, I thought, was of a logical methodology which can remove wrong views and ascertain correct views. After a long time of research, one idea struck my mind—that Dharmakīrti's epistemology and logic can as well be used as a research methodology. Some rules for research also came into light. These rules are common sense axioms, but neglection of them caused many serious mistakes.

For research methodology, I have applied the method of analysis of epistemological, ontological, and axiological evidence, based on the method of agreement and difference (*sādharmya-vaidharmya-anvaya-vyatireka*).

The original and commentarial pieces of internal evidence revealing these three-fold philosophical doctrinal proofs are analyzed to judge Dharmakīrti's real philosophical standpoint. In the case when some of the ancient and modern commentators have interpreted Dharmakīrti to satisfy their own philosophical interests, it is difficult to find the reality until a thorough study of the original source is undertaken and the possibilities of misinterpretations are checked.

External evidence was found to have different manifestations in different periods. Historically, Dharmakīrti's epistemology and philosophy have influenced Buddhist and non-Buddhist philosophical schools, and as stated above, some of the later exponents have utilized it for their own philosophical expositions and have included it under their own schools. In order to be careful about correct interpretation, the following rules were outlined and followed:

(i) A document must be the original work of the writer concerned. Interpolations must be excluded. Sometimes it is possible that we have interpolations not by Dharmakīrti, but due to later teachers or some other error which may have been included in his writings. Sometimes two or more persons of the same name may cause grave confusion. It is not hard to find cases in the history of Indian philosophy where some books written by others were assigned to philosophers of great repute, whereas in reality they were forgeries. The long lists of apocryphal writings of famous authors in Tibetan prove this tendency.

(ii) Writings in the original Sanskrit are more authentic than translations. For example, Dharmakīrti's own exposition in Sanskrit will be of greater authenticity than the Tibetan translations. It is found sometimes that the translators do not fully understand the meaning of the original Sanskrit, or they may not translate it correctly because of language ambiguities. Sometimes, because of their predisposition or liking for a particular philosophical viewpoint, or because they belong to a particular school of philosophy, they may make a mistake in translation. Such examples of distortion are found in Tibetan and Chinese translations when they are compared with the original Sanskrit.

(iii) There must be a thorough investigation of all the similar documents related to the issue in the same book or in other books written by the same author.

(iv) The terms used must be cognized in the sense intended by the author. It is generally found that a particular author used a certain term in a particular connotation. Thus, such terms as *ālambana*, *artha*, *viṣaya*, *vijñapti*, *grāhya-grāhaka* are used by various authors with different meanings. With the evolution of language, the meaning of terms also undergoes some changes. Particularly, a four-fold possibility of changes is well known. Extension in meaning, contraction in meaning, super-evaluation and devaluation of the meaning. Without being aware of these possibilities, one cannot penetrate into the genuine connotation of the terms used by Dharmakīrti or any other philosopher. The meaning of the terms should be determined by comparing the meaning with that of the same term used in the same text in different places and in other books by the same author.

(v) Care should be taken in identifying the opponent's thesis (*pūrvapakṣa*) and the answer (*uttarapakṣa*-anti-thesis) on a particular issue expressed by the author. When new ideas and schools of thought have sprung forth, some commentators of a later period have interpreted a refutation by an author of the school as the views of the said school itself. But in fact, the original author might have expressed the view, not as a view belonging to a particular school, but as a possible objection.

For instance, the commentator Vinītadeva seems to have a strong tendency of this sort. Therefore, he has deprived us of the original viewpoint of the author and has created confusion and complexity, rather than clarification. This misapprehension can be checked through the author's own usage of the same argument in other chapter of the same book and in his other books, external and internal inconsistencies, etc.

(vi) Care should also be taken against any hasty assumption about a philosopher for example as belonging to Mahāyāna or early Buddhism. Sometimes a particular author may, in fact, not have belonged to the Mahāyāna trend of thought, but may have been arbitrarily interpreted as Mahāyānist and the whole of his philosophy misrepresented because of this grave mistake in the very beginning.

(vii) The authority of ancient or modern commentators or scholars, if contradicted by evidence or logic, should be doubted and examined,

The real credit for the present research goes to Rāhula Sāṅkṛtyāyana who made three painful adventurous trips to Tibet and discovered Dharmakīrti's original Sanskrit works and published them (Bib. Notes). But he edited them in a hurry; consequently various mistakes have occurred. He also divided *Pramāṇavārttika* in subheadings, on the basis of Manorathanandin's commentary, which sometimes create confusion and misdirect a reader. The revised editions by Dwarikadass Shāstri are well polished but the division of headings is the same. I think one should not mix any of one's personal understanding in the body of an original text, because later the readers follow and interpret it in the same direction. However, Rāhula Sāṅkṛtyāyana's discovery has unearthed a great treasure of Indian analytical philosophy which will be remembered throughout the centuries to come.

Scherbatsky's research in this field is of paramount value. Long before Rāhula Sāṅkṛtyāyana's discovery, he translated Dharmakīrti's *Santānāntarasiddhi* along with Vinītadeva's *ṭīkā* on it, from Tibetan into Russian (1922), from his previously published Tibetan edition (1916). His monumental work, *Buddhist Logic* (1932) is the greatest contribution to the Buddhist epistemology and logic in particular and towards the understanding of Indian analytical philosophy in general. This work and many other works on Buddhism reveal his painstaking efforts and comprehensive study in this field.

Stcherbatsky's exploration of Indian critical philosophy is the greatest contribution of presenting the "most excellent achievement" of Indian minds to the West. His comprehensive study of Indian Critical Philosophy through Tibetan and Sanskrit sources ranks him as the greatest orientalist of his time. It was his valuable writings which made me analyse and examine the particular issue of Dharmakīrti's philosophical position. Stcherbatsky himself seems to be puzzled by the controversial accounts about Vasubandhu, Diṅnāga, and Dharmakīrti's philosophical positions and made some controversial statements which led me to investigate this enigma. Stcherbatsky was misled by Vinītadeva's idealistic commentary on *SS* and the lack of sufficient evidence and non-availability of missing links were the main reasons which are responsible for his controversial assertions. Therefore, I have critically examined the wrong commentary of Vinītadeva and other Vijñānavādin commentators of Dharmakīrti. Hence, this thesis should not be considered as destructive criticism of Stcherbatsky and other scholars mentioned. The present author has expressed, as a student to his teachers, his gratitude by analysing and examining the critical issues suggested and left by them for future investigation.

As Vinītadeva calls Dharmakīrti an Idealist (Vijñānavādin) in his short commentary on *Santānāntarasiddhi* (*SS*), Stcherbatsky took it for granted and presented Dharmakīrti as an Idealist and later partially Sautrāntika. When I examined *SS*, keeping apart from the commentary of Vinītadeva, several times, I found the facts to be contrary. It was not really the fault of this greatest orientalist of his time, but of Vinītadeva who misdirected this great scholar. Therefore, I had to examine for the first instance, this very root-cause of all misunderstandings. Stcherbatsky, as I was told by Sāṅkṛtyāyana and as is also clear through Stcherbatsky's attempts to compare

Dharmakīrti's philosophy with that of Kant, Hegel, Bradley, etc., liked Idealism. He also believed in the theory of only one Vasubandhu. These factors led him to call Dharmakīrti an Idealist in the main and a critical realist (Sautrāntika) in general. He could not accept the views of Ṭippaṇakāra, Dharmottara, Pārthasārathimiśra, Vācaspatimiśra, Udayana, etc. who called Vasubandhu (II), Diṅnāga, and Dharmakīrti's philosophical standpoint that of the Sautrāntika. Stcherbatsky would have thought the reconciliation of both these standpoints will solve this complex problem. But I found that Idealism (Vijñānavāda) and Critical Realism (Sautrāntika) are two contrary systems; except that there are some general similarities of definitions of traditional psychological findings of the Ābhidharmikas as a whole. I also found that there have been serious intellectual fights between these two schools on epistemological and ontological issues. The *Viṃśatikā* (The establishment of Idealism in 20 verses), *Triṃśikā* (Same in 30 verses) clearly manifest the serious differences between Vijñānavādins and Sautrāntikas. I also found Vācāspatimiśra, as translated by Stcherbatsky himself, bringing into light this serious conflict between Vijñānavādins and Sautrāntikas. I also found a conflict between Vijñānavādins and Sautrāntikas (*Vijñānavādin-Sautrāntikayaḥ kalaha*) in the *Śāstradīpikā* (vv. 22-27) of Pārthasārathimiśra. Both these critics put forward Diṅnāga and Dharmakīrti as opponents of Vijñānavāda. In the *Bhāmatī* and *Prameyakamalamārtanda,* the argumentation of the Sautrāntikas is used to refute Vijñānavādin doctrines in general and solipsism in particular. Thus, the theory of the reconciliation of both (V-S) in Dharmakīrti, as a solution of this enigma, seemed to be non-factual.

In India, the great scholars who undertook the serious task of exploration of various fields of these difficult subjects are: Rāhula Sāṅkṛtyāyana, the discoverer of some of Dharmakīrti's texts, Satkari Mukerjee, *Buddhist Philosophy of Universal flux* and translation of the portion of Dharmakīrti's *PV*, Dalasukh Malvaniya, ed *Svārthānumāna-pariccheda, Dharmottarapradīpa*, Acarya Narendradeva, *Buddha dharma-darśana*, (in Hindi), Baldeva Upādhyāya, *Bauddhadarśanamīmāṃsā* (in Hindi), S.N. Dasgupta, *History of Indian Philosophy*, Umeśa Miśra, *A History of Indian Philosophy*, N.C. Shah, *Akalaṅka's Criticism of Dharmakīrti's Philosophy*, S. C. Vidyabhusana, *History of the Medieval School of Indian Logic*, Muni Jambuvijaya reconstructed many portions of *PSV* into Sanskrit, ed. *Dvādaśāranayacakra*, and P.S. Jaini ed. *Abhidharmadīpa*, criticized Frauwallner's thesis. These are the prominent scholars who discussed Dharmakīrti and allied subjects.

Among Japanese scholars, H. Kitagawa, *A Study of Indian Classical Logic—Diṅnāga's System*, trans. of *Santānāntarasiddhi*, M. Hattori, *Diṅnāga on Perception*, H. Sakarube an Abridgement of *Abhidharmakośa* ascribed to Diṅnāga in Japanese, Y. Kajiyama, trans. *Santānāntaradūṣaṇa*, article. 'The Atomic Theory of Vasubandhu', S. Katsura, *A Study of Harivarman's Tattvasiddhi*, unpublished thesis.

Among European scholars, are: la Vallée Poussin, trans. *Abhidharmakośabhāṣya*, E. Lamotte, ed. *Karmasiddhiprakaraṇa*; *Histoire du Bouddhisme Indienne*. Ruegg, *La Théorie du Tathāgathāgarbha et du gotra*, etc., Eric Frauwallner, ed. *Sambandhaparīkṣā*, articles on Diṅnāga and Dharmakīrti's works, Tilmann Vetter, *Erkenntnisprobleme bei Dharmakīrti's Philosophie*, trans, *Pratyakṣapariccheda* of *Pramāṇaviniścaya*, Schmithausen, article 'Sautrāntika voraussetzungen im Tiṃśatikā' und Triṃśika'. In North America they are, Alex Wayman, (*Śrāvakabhūmi manuscript* criticized Frauwallner's thesis), A.K. Warder, article 'Earliest Indian Logic', 'Concept of the Concept', 'Objects', discussed Dharmakīrti's seven works in *Indian Buddhism*. This is a short account of the valuable contributions of these authors in this field.

The categorisation of philosophers as belonging to different schools used in this dissertation should not be considered as an imposition on the facts, but an examination of a real situation. Because of the peculiar historical development of Indian philosophy, ancient and modern scholars were bound to classify these philosophers in terms of schools established by original philosophers who wrote fundamental texts to expand and establish certain points of view (*Siddhānta*). The organization in schools was inherent in the method of teaching. The commentators, followers, and defenders of their schools are categorized by contemporary critics. It also does not imply that there was no further evolution in Indian philosophy.

Sometimes, an original philosopher breaks through the traditional schools; in that case he establishes a new school of interpretation or introduces a new school of philosophy. Dharmakīrti, Diṅnāga, and Vasubandhu (II) were Buddhist monks following a particular Vinaya (rules of discipline) and philosophical school. Therefore, because of peculiarity of the development of Indian philosophy, it was necessary to classify commentators as belonging to a particular school.

Because of this fact, I had investigated the school of Dharmakīrti.

Undoubtedly, there is emergence of some new arguments to defend the views of Diṅnāga and Vasubandhu (II). Many new explanations of the concept of negation (*anupalabdhi*), causal efficiency (*arthakriyākāritva*), sense-data (*svalakṣaṇa*), illusion (*bhrānti*), etc. have occurred but they are based on Sautrāntika doctrines of Diṅnāga and Vasubandhu (II).

It will be useful if a short summary of the book is presented. The first part of the first chapter is devoted to defining and exploring the origins of the Sautrāntika movement of Indian Critical Philosophy. The Sautrāntika was a critical revolt against Buddhist (Sarvāstivāda) and non-Buddhist metaphysics. They criticized any metaphysical entity which contradicts empirical experience, including the evidence of constant change (law of universal flux). Very little is known about this tradition. But I have solely relied on *Abhidharmakośabhāṣya* (*AbkB*). and *Sphutārthā* for the Sautrāntika doctrines. I have listed 24 topics of the Vaibhāṣikas critically examined by the Sautrāntika Vasubandhu. I have also given the Sautrāntika and Vaibhāṣika account of epistemological and logical doctrines on the ground of Tibetan tradition. I have not gone into details because some of these doctrines are already mentioned and discussed by others. This is only intended as an introduction to my main thesis on Dharmakīrti.

The last part of this chapter deals with the serious problem of identification of Vasubandhu (II). The problem is very complex and of decisive importance for the philosophical affiliation of Diṅnāga and Dharmakīrti, as it is presumed by most scholars that the Sautrāntika Vasubandhu was converted to Yogācāra Vijñānavāda and that Diṅnāga was his disciple and Dharmakīrti followed Diṅnāga. Therefore the three of them were supposed to belong to the Vijñānavāda school. I have analyzed and examined this polemic issue in detail. The examination of this root-cause of misinterpretation will clarify the original thesis of Eric Frauwallner, who changed it later because of some new reasons. I have not only analysed the reasons of the scholars, such as P. S. Jaini, Alex Wayman, S. Anacker who opposed Frauwallner's thesis, but the reasons of the change of Frauwallner's thesis are also analysed and examined.

B.K. Matilal stimulated me to analyse the similarity and differences of definitions of Abhidharma concepts in *AbkB.* and *Viṃśatikā Triṃśikā* which look similar and might prove one authorship. I have analysed and examined in detail the topic of mental factors (*caitasikas*) in these treatises.

The second chapter is devoted to giving an account of the present situation existing in the scholastic world about Dharmakīrti's philosophical standpoint. A thorough survey of different views on the affiliation of Dharmakīrti disclosed six different opinions :

A. Vijñānavāda (Idealism)
B. Sautrāntika-Vijñānavāda
C. Vaibhāṣika
D. Mādhyamika
E. Svatantra Vijñānavāda
F. Sautrāntika

I have analysed the reasons which lead these scholars to put forward different views.

The last part of this chapter is the detailed critical examination of the reasons which lead these great scholars to have controversial viewpoints. It should not be considered as personal criticism but the criticism of wrong views and wrong directions of ancient commentators. The first five views (A-E), are based on insufficient evidence and wrong reasons. The last one (Sautrāntika) appears to be correct and verifiable on the ground of evidence and logic.

In the third chapter, I have adduced the internal evidence which confirms the fact that Dharmakīrti's philosophical standpoint is that of the Sautrāntika. Dharmakīrti's doctrines are derived from Vasubandhu (II) and Diṅnāga who were also Sautrāntikas.

Fourth chapter is the critical examination of the ultimate reality (*svalakṣaṇa*) in the Sautrāntika school as well as in other schools of Buddhist philosophy. It provides us with a historical, psycho-physical, and epistemological survey of this central philosophical subject. At the same time, it is the critical examination of Stcherbatsky's contrary views on *svalakṣaṇa*. His idealistic interpretation of Dharmakīrti is incorrect while the Sautrāntika interpretation is correct.

Another important question is to be clarified. What are the implications of the present work?

It is hard to calculate all the implications of a piece of research work. To find truth and to ascertain reality about Dharmakīrti's philosophical position is the main motive behind this work; but it may bring about the following effects or changes:

1. This is the first attempt to study Dharmakīrti and his school in different perspectives of critical philosophy (Sautrāntika) about which hitherto very little is known.

2. It is important also to our understanding of Dharmakīrti's philosophy itself: the assumption that Dharmakīrti was a Vijñānavādin (Idealist) has tended to influence our interpretation of a philosophy which on the face of it, has little in common with Idealism. It may stimulate modern research scholars in this field to be curious about this new finding.

3. It is the first attempt to study Dharmakīrti's seven books together as a consistent whole.

4. The belief that Dharmakīrti was a Vijñānavādin seems to have arisen primarily from the idea that was the philosophical lineage to which Dharmakīrti belonged. Therefore, I have also investigated the highly complicated issue of the doctrinal affiliations of Diṅnāga and Vasubandhu, which gives weight to my conclusion and clears out various cobwebs. This may be the first criticism of erroneous views prevailing in the modern Scholastic world.

5. If the thesis is correct, then the history of the Buddhist Indian philosophy from 5th century onward has to be re-written. Also new studies and translations are implied of all the works of Diṇnāga, Dharmakīrti, and their successors.

6. Dharmakīrti not only provides the method of mental freedom from erroneous views but also give us key to achieve all human goals (*sarva puruṣārtha*) mundane or supra-mundane (*laukika-lokottara*), negative or positive (*heya-upādeya*). It will be very useful to know Eastern techniques of epistemological and logical analysis of human cognition, in respect to what human beings strive for. Stcherbatsky's assertion that these critical philosophers were the best of Indian minds may be true in respect to its practical application.

7. Linguistically, it reveals the importance of philosophical meanings rather than terminological or etymological meanings. On this ground, various misinterpretations of many important texts of Dharmakīrti and of others are eliminated, for the first time. It may change the prevalent interpretation of those texts and part of texts.

8. Religiously, it explains the importance of logic and epistemology for religious purification. Any authority either of scripture or of a person should be doubted if it contradicts direct cognition (*pratyakṣa*) and inference (*anumāna*). It may be utilised to eliminate wrong views about the original teachings of the Buddha from the Buddhist world as a whole and Indian Buddhism in particular.

9. Philosophically, Sautrāntikas brought into light empirical methods of examining metaphysical entities and maintained that

reality is ever dynamic. They called it sense-data, assemblage of atoms, an event, a burst of energy, etc. It may be interesting to study this emergence of critical philosophy in fifth century India.

In the end, I wish humbly to make a clarification of my own position. The training of my mind through epistemology, logic, and Eastern and Western critical philosophy made me believe in the principles of empirical analysis of human cognition. This attitude made me accept Sautrāntika, psychological, epistemological and logical analysis of valid and invalid knowledge, illusion and reality. My position is similar to that of Dharmakīrti.

The following are my conclusions:

1. Valid knowledge exists and is verifiable through successful activity.

2. Knowledge is purposive and applicable to attain human goals.

3. Non-contradiction and causal efficiency are the two criteria of the validity of knowledge.

4. Valid cognition could only be achieved and verified through direct cognition (*pratyakṣa*) and indirect cognition (*anumāna*). Matters which transcend these two methods of verification are doubtful and no definite conclusion can be reached. On these issues, one should suspend any judgments either positive or negative. It is the limit of valid cognition.

4. Correspondence (*sārūpya*) between the objects and knowledge is the sole criterion of truth or falsity of a cognition.

5. The ultimate reality of sense-data is beyond all doubts. Thus, the unique event is ever-dynamic, self-destructive energy manifesting itself in the form of assemblages of atoms, which stimulates our different senses and fulfills human goals.

6. Every event is happening due to different causes, conditions, and results. I also believe, in accordance with the methods of scientific research, in the laws of probability and the law of relativity. One can only be certain of the knowledge which leads to a successful activity, other remains probable, depending on different causes and conditions. Thus, the present thesis is also subject to this limitation and I leave it open for further investigation on the grounds of evidence and logic.

CHAPTER 1

The Sautrāntika Tradition

Who were the Sautrāntikas? What were the conditions which gave rise to this movement? What was the method of their investigation?

The very term Sautrāntika connotes the meaning "An adherent of the *Sūtrapiṭaka*". Yaśomitra has clearly defined it: "Who are the Sautrāntikas? Those who recognise the *Sūtrapiṭaka*, not the *Śāstra*, as valid are the Sautrāntikas" (*kaḥ sautrāntikārthaḥ? ye sūtrapramāṇikāḥ, na tu śāstrapramāṇikās te sautrāntikāḥ*).* It is well known that the *Sūtrapiṭakā* consists of the original dialogues of the Buddha, who revealed his doctrinal views and methodology in the form of dialogues. The Sautrāntika movement was a revolt against the Vaibhāṣika Ābhidharmikas, who introduced a new kind of literature, a new kind of doctrine, a new terminology, and a new methodology in Buddhism. This tendency was long ago noticed by the scholars of the *Sūtrapiṭaka*. The *Vibhaṅga* classified two trends of thought running side by side, viz: *Suttantabhājanīya* (analysis according to Sūtra), and *Abhidhammabhājanīya* (analysis according to Abhidharma). Suttantikas were aware of the emergence of these new doctrines.

Yaśomitra regards all seven books of the Sanskrit Ābhidharmikas as written by seven different authors, not as the words of Buddha as stored in the *Sūtrapiṭaka*. On the question of the Sautrāntika Abhidharma, Yaśomitra mentions that the *Arthaviniścayasūtra*, etc. which are part of the *Sūtrapiṭaka*, contain all the Abhidharma analysis done by the Buddha himself (*naiṣa doṣaḥ sūtraviśeṣā eva hi arthaviniścayādāyo' bhidharma-saṃjñāḥ, eṣu dharmalakṣaṇaṃ varṇyate*)** Candrakīrti clearly differentiates the Sautrāntikas as propounders of the

* *Abhidharmakośavyakhyā*, (*sphuṭārtha*) ed. by Unrai Wogihara, p. 15.

**ibid, p. 15.

theory of reality of 'present-time' (*vartamāna-kāla*) only, and as considering past (*bhūta*) and future (*anāgata*) as not real, but conventional (*atha sautrāntikamate atītānāgataśūnya anyad aśūnyam*).**

The whole account of Vasubandhu's criticism of the *tri-adhvan* (triple-time) doctrine can easily be understood through the following diagram:

Vaibhāṣika-Sautrāntika
Controversy on Time (*Kāla*)

	Propounder	*Position*	*Example*
1.	Bhadanta Dharmatrāta	*Bhāvānyathika* change of state	Form—gold & ornament Quality-milk & yogurt
2.	Bhadanta Ghoṣaka	*Lakṣaṇānyathika* change of characteristic	Man in love with one woman becomes detached from others
3.	Bhadanta Vasumitra	*Avasthānyathika* or *kāritrānyathika* change of position or change of activity	If a token is placed in the unit column, it means 1, and if the same token is placed in the tens column, it means 10.
4.	Bhadanta Buddhadeva	*Anyathānyathika* change of relation	One woman is a daughter and a mother at the same time.

Vasubandhu's criticism: The first one in the same as the Sāṃkhya theory of transformation (*pariṇāmavāda*). The second one implies intermixture of time (*adhvasaṃkara*) which makes it illogical; because rising for love for one proves only the possession (*prāpti*) of love for other women, which is not possible in an inanimate entity like time. The fourth one includes all three in one which is logically impossible. Vasubandhu praises the third view; because of application or position, the triple division of time is determined. When it is not yet functioning, it is future; while functioning, it is present; and when it has ceased to function, it is past. Thus, the reality (efficacy) of the present (*vartamāna*) is accepted by Sautrāntikas. But Vasubandhu criticizes Vasumitra's division of reality and efficacy (*kāritra*). The following are the other ontological topics of the

**M. vṛtti*, p. 444.

vaibhāṣikas, critically examined by Vasubandhu II on the ground that they involve contradictions with the information of the senses (*pratyakṣa*) and the *Sūtrapiṭaka: kāla* (time), *asaṃskṛta*, (uncomposed), *pratisaṃkhyānirodha* (intellectually discriminative cessation), *apratisaṃkhyānirodha* (intellectually non-discriminative cessation), *sthiti* (durability), *āyu* (age), *ākaśa* (space), *dravya* (substance), *prāpti* (possession), *aprapti* (non-possession), *vijñapti* (making of consciousness), *paramaṇu* (atom), *nirodha* (cessation), *skandha* (aggregate), *dhaṭu* (element), *āyatana* (sense-sphere), *caitasika* (mental factor), *sahabhūhetu* (co-existing cause), *sabhāhetus* (co-part cause), *saṃprayuktahetu* (applied cause), *sarvatragahetu* (universal cause), *vipākahetu* (resultant cause), *nirvāṇa* (salvation), *rūpa* (form).

The epistemological difference between the Vaibhāśikas and the Sautrāntikas is well preserved in Tibetan tradition.* For example, the Vaibhāṣika finds three kinds of valid sensation (*pratyakṣa*): sensory (*indriya*), mental (*mānasa*), and yogi (*yogin*). It does not recognise self-consciousness (*svasaṃvedana*). It finds inference (*anumāna*) valid but not recognition, error, doubt, and uncertainty.

On the other hand, the Sautrāntika recognises a fourth kind of sensation, self-consciousness (*svasaṃvedana pratyakṣa*) and finds it valid. It finds valid the following:

1. *pratyakṣa*-four kinds; includes *svasaṃvedana pratyakṣa.*
2. *anumāna* (inference)-based on universal (*sāmānya*); two kinds: *svārthānumāna* (inference for oneself), *parārthānumāna* (inference for others), when one points out impermanence and when one makes the statement "sound is impermanent". Diṅnāga in *PS* and Dharmakīrti in *PV* describe these divisions. The list of the invalid cognitions is the same.

The above Tibetan account indicates the affiliations of Vasubandhu II, Diṅnāga, and Dharmakīrti. This summary of the difference between the Vaibhāṣika and the Sautrāntika on ontological and epistemological matters reveals the difference in their critical attitude. The validity of sensory cognition and the recognition of inference allowed the Sautrāntikas to use inductive and empirical techniques to put an end to the growth of dogmatic philosophy and metaphysics.

The ancient name for this movement, as shown by Vaibhāṣika works, is Dārṣṭāntika, which is highly significant. In Sanskrit, *dṛṣṭa* means seen or empirically observed, and *antika* connotes conclusive

*Translated. by Herbert V. Guenther, *Buddhist Philosophy*, pp. 78-88.

or an end (not requiring any other further source to prove it). It should not be confused with the term *upamā* (simile), which is not invariable conditioned by observed fact or sensory cognition and may be purely speculative, poetical, or fictitious; but *dṛṣṭānta* is bound to be a perceived fact which is also the sole criterion to test the truth or falsity of an inference.

The *Sūtrapiṭaka* clearly reveals the fact that the Buddha used the method of *dṛṣṭānta* to convince an opponent or a questioner. His method consisted in providing an observed particular example which is well known in the world, then establishing a universal law on that ground, such as "whatever is produced is subject to decay" (*yat kiñcidudayātmakaṃ nirodhadharmakaṃ sarvaṃ tad*).* This method was definitely inductive (known to unknown, particular to universal) in nature as opposed to the deductive, authoritarian, or revelatory methods of past and contemporary Vedic, Śramaṇa and Ājīvaka philosophers.

The Dārṣṭāntikas followed the Buddha's method of the *dṛṣṭānta*, as preserved in the Sūtrapiṭaka, to cope with the doubtful, conflicting, confusing, and uncertain doctrines of Vaibhāśika Abhidharma.

History reveals that at the time when the Dārṣṭāntikas set forth this revolution, the condition of Ābhidharmika doctrines, introduced by different individual philosophers, was highly controversial and there was no way to decide which one was the correct one. In this stage of doctrinal turmoil within Buddhism, the Sautrāntikas adopted the neutral method of empirical example and logic to decide facts and to remove conflicting and doubtful doctrines. The application of *dṛṣṭānta* became the central point in this movement which later terminated in logical and epistemological investigations.

At a later stage, the Dārṣṭāntikas favoured the name "Sautrāntika" for their system, for the following reason: only the *Sūtra* was agreed to contain the doctrine taught by the Buddha himself.

The Sautrāntika was not a movement against Dārṣṭāntikas, but merely a new name. The Vaibhāṣikas frequently use these names as synonyms and the Tibetan tradition confirms it. Yaśomitra also reveals the same fact that the Dārṣṭāntikas are the Sautrāntikas.*

**Dīghanikāya* (Pāli), 3.10.45 ref. in *PV.*, 1/286d; *Madhyānta-Vibhāga* (*MV*) 1.7.16 and *Pramāṇavārtikavṛtti*, (*PVV*)., p. 97.

**Dārṣṭāntikāḥ Sautrāntikāḥ, Dārṣṭāntikāḥ Sautrāntikaviśeṣāḥ, Sphuṭārthā*, pp. 400-17; *Sūtranikāyācāryāḥ Abhidharmakośabhāṣya* (*AbkB*)., 2/226.

It is also worth noting that in the beginning, the Sautrāntika was not a different school, but only a movement launched by individual monks called "sūtradharas" or "bahuśrutiyas" who were well versed in the *Sūtrapiṭaka* and disagreed with the Vaibhāṣikas, *Jñānaprasthāna* and *Vibhāṣā* known as *Śāstra*. Particularly, some of the Kāśmīra Vaibhāsikas revolted against the arbitrary introduction of new speculative elements in the Ābhidharma tradition.

There have been two turning points in the development of logic in Buddhism. The first development occurred at the time when Buddhism was divided into the "eighteen schools", each claiming faithfulness to the Buddha's original teachings. There was no common basis to decide which school made the correct interpretations. Doubts, confusions, and schisms, plus dogmatism became extensive in Buddhism until they were checked by the genius of such logicians as Moggaliputtatissa, who established the sound criteria of formal logic and the *Sūtrapiṭaka*. The *Kathāvatthu* seems to be the first Buddhist work preserved which makes use of formal logic, as shown by A.K. Warder.* The application of logical terms such as *vādayutti* (debate), *vacanasodhana* (distribution of terms), *attha-mukhaniggaha* (eight-fold-refutation), *atthamukhavādayutti* (eight openings of debate), *dhammajaya* (victory of Dharma), *anulomapāpanā* (normal consequent), *saṃsandanā* (checking), *lakkhaṇayuttikathā*—(definition-judgment discussion), *paññattānuyoga* (examination of concepts), *patilomathapanā* (reverse antecedent), *lakkhaṇa* (characteristic), *upanayana* (application) *nigamana* (conclusion), etc. reveals a sound formal logical methodology. This methodology continued to evolve in the Ābhidharmika systems such as *Pañcavijñānakāyapāda*, etc. frequently referred to by Vasubandhu II, Diṅnāga, and Dharmakīrti. The wrong views prevalent in this early period were examined on the ground of *yutti* (logic) and *Suttāhāra* (adducing the *Sūtrapiṭaka* in each controversy).

From this period onward we find two methods of verification:

1. Reason (*yutti*), and
2. *Āgama* (*Sūtrapiṭaka*)

Subsequently, *Āgama* was included under inference, as proven by Dhammapālācārya, a Pāḷi sub-commentator (10th century) who clearly asserts that even *Āgama* does not transcend logic (*āgamo, pi takkavisayaṃ nātikkamatīti*)*.

*"The Earliest Indian Logic", pp. 56-68.
**Dīghanikāya-aṭṭhakathātika* (*DAT*), ed by Lily de Silvā, pp. 191-92.

The second turning point of logical development emerged at the time of the Sarvāstivādin Ābhidharmikas, who introduced a new concept and terminology, as mentioned above, in Buddhism. A class of monks called 'Sūtradharas' sought to defend the original doctrines of the Buddha against revisions in the Abhidharmas and started the Sautrāntika movement.

The Sautrāntikas followed the example of Moggaliputtatissa, but they applied the method of empirical logic rather than formal logic, for two reasons:

(a) Elements of Brahmanic tradition (Sāṃkhya, Vaiśeṣika, Mīmāṃsā) entered into the Vaibhāṣika Ābhidharma and it was not possible to examine them only on the strength of formal logic; examination was sometimes possible only on the ground of empirical logic.

(b) The method applied by the Vaibhāṣikas was not solely scriptural, but semi-empirical in nature and could only be corrected through empirical counter arguments.

Among the Sautrāntika Ācāryas, Bhadanta (Sthavira), Śrīlāta, Guṇamati, Kumāralāta, and Vasubandhu II are famous. Unfortunately, their works, except the works of Vasubandhu II, are entirely lost in Sanskrit (except for a few fragments). The source for our knowledge of their doctriness is Vasubandhu's *AbkB.* and Yaśomitra's *Sphūṭārthā.* Vasubandhu II not only critically commented on *Abk.*, but composed various treatises on empirical logic. His work on the latter subject was continued by Diṅnāga, Dharmakīrti and others. Much has been written about the life histories of these critical philosophers by Stcherbatsky and others. Therefore, I only discuss the controversy about Vasubandhu, the expounder of the critical school.

There is considerable controversy about the life, time, place, and school of the Sautrāntika Vasubandhu, whom I have qualified by the number II throroughout this book, A thorough survey of external, internal, and other related factors, which are discussed below, revealed the fact that this Vasubandhu II is different from the Yogācāra Vasubandhu I, the brother of Asaṃga. Apart from the evidence which establishes this difference, it is surprising to know how the tradition of the conversion of the Sautrāntika Vasubandhu into the Vijñānavādin Vasubandhu is so deeply rooted that (except in the modern era when some doubted it and some supported it) throughout the ages it has mislead scholars and has not been doubted.

Who was the Sautrāntika Vasubandhu? Was he converted to the Mahāyāna Vijñānavāda? Chinese translation of the account of the life of Vasubandhu by Paramārtha became a subject of serious controversy in the 20th century. The writings of different authors reveal that there is a great deal of discrepancy and inconsistency regarding Vasubandhu's life. Why has this been the case?

The author has made a thorough investigation of this controversial issue, and found some internal evidence which proves the thesis that the Sautrāntika Vasubandhu is different from the Vijñānavādin Vasubandhu. The author has found no documentary evidence for their identity, except for the accounts of Paramārtha, Hsüan-Tsang, and Tārānātha, who collected their information through hearsay and legends. Particularly, the absence of any sound documentary evidence in Sanskrit makes one believe these to be mere legends.

Prof. Frauwallner, a great Indologist, doubted these legends and in 1951 put forward a thesis that there were two famous philosophers by the name of Vasubandhu. One was the Vijñānavādin Vasubandhu, Asaṃga's brother, and the other was the Sautrāntika Vasubandhu who remained Sautrāntika till death. This radical thesis was criticized by some modern scholars and requires a thorough re-examination.

Recently, further evidence has been produced by P.S. Jaini, who has edited a manuscript discovered by Rāhula Sāṅkṛtyāyana in Tibet, namely the *Abhidharmadīpa* (*AbD.*) and *Vibhāṣāprabhāvṛtti* (*VPV.*) of an unknown author. Jaini categorically claims that Vasubandhu of *AbkB.* changed his position and embraced Mahāyāna Vijñānavāda.[1] P.S. Jaini has claimed to refute Frauwallner's thesis in the introduction (*AbD.*) and in a separate paper.* But when a thorough investigation of the original text is undertaken, Jaini's conclusion appears to be unsound.

Here is an examination of the grounds of Jaini's conclusion:

1. The term *Vaitulika* (Sophist) used for the Sautrāntikas is Mahāyānistic in nature. "The term *Vaitulika* in this passage most certainly refers to the Vijñānavādin Kośakāra"**

2. *Ayoga śūnyatā* (inconsistent-voidness) is also a Mahāyānistic term.

3. *Tri svabhāva* (triple nature) mentioned in *AbD.* is definitely a Vijñānavādin doctrine.

These are the three grounds which Jaini thinks conclusive to prove the conversion of Vasubandhu. Strangely enough, all these

*BSOAS, XXI, 1958, pp. 48-53.

**ibid., p. 52.

grounds proved to be non-existent when examined carefully.

1. The term *vaitulika* used in the *AbD.* and *VPV.* on various occasions is only to ridicule the logic of the Sautrāntikas, not in the sense of any particular school or in the sense of Asaṃga's *Vaipulya-piṭaka* as Jaini has supposed. The terms *vaināśika* and *vaitulika* are applied to a logician or a 'quibbler' who has no reason of his own (Sophist), generally to the Prāsaṅgika Mādhyamikas, but not to the Vijñānavādins, who themselves disagree with them. Therefore, the term in *AbD.* is used only to ridicule the Sautrāntika Vasubandhu or the Sautrāntika as a whole, and definitely not in the technical sense of Vijñānavādins.

2. The same is true with the term *ayoga śūnyatā* Jaini himself confesses that this term is found neither in the Mahāyāna tradition nor in the Theravāda, but uncritically accepts T. R. V. Murti's interpretation in the sense of Mādhyamikas. In this doubtful situation how can one establish that Vasubandhu has changed his position? The term *ayoga* (*ayukta*) itself means simple inconsistent, indicating that its opponent has argued illogically but not what his standpoint is.

It should also be borne in mind that both these terms are used by an opponent to ridicule Vasubandhu in the same way as we say: "You are heading towards Sophistry or Scepticism". It does not prove that Vasubandhu has welcomed this comment. An opponent's criticism cannot be taken as the doctrine of the person under attack. Even if it is granted, though logic does not permit it, these terms will only suggest that he is criticized perhaps as a Mādhyamika or Lakāyata or Vaitulika or Vaināśika or Ayogaśūnyatāvādin, but not as a Yogācāra Vijñānavādin.[2] If Jaini's interpretation is accepted, then it will imply the falsification of all the legends that he was converted to the Yogācāra Vijñānavāda.

As a matter of fact, the text (*AbD.-VPV.*) refers to and refutes the Mādhyamika view separately.*

If Vasubandhu was regarded as Mādhyamika, then why was his position not incluaed under it? Why is it described and criticized differently and separately? The text clearly asserts: "Dārṣṭāntikas are the Vaitulika people who do not follow reason (*yukti*) and the scriptures, but are arrogant regarding their logic (sophistry)".[3] This is apparently an invective against Vasubandhu and his school, not his

*as *ayogaśūnya-vaitulika-vaināśika*, pp. 257-58.

inclusion under any Mahāyāna school.

Jaini manifests great confidence that: "the term *ayogaśūnyatā* should put at rest any doubt about the real affiliations of the Kośakāra. The term certainly refers to a Mahāyāna doctrine."* Then he himself denies it.** Thereby, he weakens the evidence he gives in support of his argument.

On the other hand, Jaini's self-confidence suggests that *ayogaşūnyatā* is not a technical term for any school. If so, then why did Jaini unquestioningly follow T. R. V. Murti's interpretation which itself has no ground? Jaini does not explain why the Dīpakāra calls Vasubandhu a Sautrāntika throughout his treatise,[4] rather than by the name Vijñānavādin or any other. Jaini has soon recognised the mistake of his absolute assertion of affiliations and holds that the use of the term *ayogaśūnyatā* does not prove the conversion of Vasubandhu, but only that he was leaning towards Vijñānavāda. This shift in emphasis contradicts the whole legend of his conversion. It completely undermines the theory that Vasubandhu was a furious opponent of Mahāyāna before he was converted to Vijñānavāda by his brother Asaṃga. Furthermore, how could the Dīpakāra, who has gone to the length of attacking Vasubandhu personally, still call him a Sautrāntika? All of these points point to one fact that the usage of the terms *Vaitulika* and *Ayogaśūnyatāvādin* for Vasubandhu are mere invectives.

3. The third ground which Jaini regards as very convincing is the term *tri-svabhāva* used by the Dīpakāra to criticize Vasubandhu or other Sautrāntikas. The evidence has been carefully examined. It, too, appears to be a misinterpretation of the term. His translation of this part of the text is correct, but Jaini has wrongly interpreted it. The term *tri-svabhāva* does not mean here the triple division of reality of the Vijñānavādins, but it means the triple division of time (*tri-kāla-svabhāva*) of the Sautrāntikas. The context proves that the Dīpakāra is refuting the Sautrāntika doctrine of time. Jaini translates:

"The Vaitulika deviated from Sarvāstivāda, says-we too imagine three svabhāva: To him we should reply the world is full of such fools . . . these three svabhāva imagined by you have been rejected already . . . this is one more occasion where the Kośakāra shows

**BSOAS*, XX1, 1958, p. 51.
**ibid., p. 52.

his ignorance of (the doctrine of) time".*

The expression "have been rejected already" clearly indicates that he has already refuted it. Nowhere in the available text has he mentioned or refuted the *tri-svabhāva,* imaginary, dependent and real (*parikalpita, paratantra, pariniṣpanna*), but he definitely refutes the *tri-kālasvabhāva* doctrine of the Dārṣṭāntikas, who believe that the three times do not exist in substance, but exist only from a conventional point of view (*dravyātmanā na vidyante prajñaptyātmanā tu saditi*).[5] Similarly, the end of this very passage was mentioned in the *Dīpa* as.** "shows his ignorance of (the doctrine of) time" which positively proves that *tri-svabhāva* here has nothing to do with Vijñānvāda. The similarity of the term and hasty comparison have led Jaini to mistake it as the *tri-svabhāvā* doctrine [of *Tri-svabhāvanirdeśa* and of *Laṅkāvatārasūtra* which he has referred to. But as a matter of fact, this meaning is neither in the text nor in the context. The expression "Vaitulika deviated from the Sarvāstivāda" (*sarvāstivāda-vibhraṣṭa*) only connotes a Sautrāntika or Dārṣṭāntika or Vasubandhu who has deviated from the Sarvāstivāda or the Vaibhāṣika. There is no trace, whatsoever, of substantial evidence which can prove the Sautrāntika Vasubandhu's inclination towards Vijñānavāda.

Wayman has also recently opposed Frauwallner's thesis on the same grounds of paramārtha's account† and has argued that Vasubandhu was converted to Vijñānavāda. Much has been said concerning Paramārtha's account. Here only the main points of controversy will be examined. Frauwallner proposed some of the following grounds for his thesis:

(a) That the second part of the life of Vasubandhu in Paramārtha reads that Vasubandhu declines to answer Saṃghabhadra's criticism of *AbkB.* because he was too old to undertake such a work. "And now we are requested to believe that the old man is converted by his brother and develops yet a far-reaching activity at the service of Mahāyāna".

(b) " . . . I should like to point out that there is not a single word about Asaṅga in the whole of the second part of the biography,

**AbD.*, Introduction, p. 128.

**ibid., p. 282.

†*Analysis of the Śrāvakabhūmi Manuscript,* pp. 19-46.

which treats of the author of the Abhidharmakośa, while on the contrary he plays an outstanding role in the life of his brother Vasubandhu, where his absence would be unthinkable".*

Wayman criticizes these points :

(a) Vasubandhu might have written *AbkB.* at a young age, but has been criticized by Saṃghabhadra in old age after he was converted by Asaṃga and had become famous as a Yogācāra Vijñānavādin and would have said that he was too old to answer him. "After he had attained fame in the latter school, his earlier work, the *Abhidharmakośa*, would gradually attain a circulation and following which it could never have had if he had remained in the Sautrāntika School. Thus, in his old age, works might be written in attempted refutation of his *Abhidharmakośa.* Understandingly, he would not care to debate it".**

(b) "... the attempted refutations of his work occurred years after Asaṅga's death. Of course it was not an old man who was converted to the Mahāyāna. It is simply that the part of the account dealing with Vasubandhu's conversion to the Mahāyāna begins immediately after the part dealing with the *Abhidharmakośa*".†

Wayman's answer does not seem to be based on any sound ground. It appears rather to be but a conjecture which opposes the whole tradition of the conversion. Is there any reason behind this presumption that Saṃghabhadra criticized *AbkB.* only after the conversion of Vasubandhu to Vijñānavāda, or was Vasubandhu's *bhāṣya* not in circulation before, or was he not so famous when he was still a Sautrāntika? Tārānātha's account clearly indicates that soon after Vasubandhu's distribution of his *bhāṣya* to Kāśmīra Vaibhāṣikas he received a hostile response in the form of Saṃghabhadra who came to debate with him. In this case, how can one hold the view that he had no response for his sharp criticism of the Vaibhāṣikas in the beginning, but only after his conversion in old age? The response to a sharp criticism is not usually delayed. The hostile language of Saṃghabhadra and Dīpakāra positively proves that the Vaibhāṣikas were sharply awakened by the critical operation of Vasubandhu (II). Similarly, why do some of the Brahmanic and Jaina philosophers also strongly criticize the Sautrāntika Vasubandhu?

*Ref. by Alex Wayman, p. 24.

**ibid, p. 24.

†ibid, p. 24.

If his *AbkB.* was criticized in old age after conversion, then definitely the critics will not keep quiet in mentioning this weak point. Why should a critic raise his voice against a doctrine which the author himself has discarded? Why does not Vasubandhu himself explain this conversion of viewpoints as happens naturally in the case of doctrinal changes? A person who changes his doctrines (in this case a school) without providing the reason in his later works is either confused or unfaithful to reason. One cannot expect such mistakes from a critical mind like Vasubandhu. It seems to be a mistake to assert that Vasubandhu (II) was not yet famous as an author of *AbkB.* or as a Sautrāntika. Yaśomitra in the very beginning of the *Sphuṭārthā* celebrates his fame as a second Buddha (dvitīya-Buddha) because of his sharp critical analysis in *AbkB.*

Apart from this critical appraisal there is some positive internal evidence:

(i) Diṅnāga, who was a direct disciple of Vasubandhu, refers to *AbkB.* in support of his doctrines in some of his writings. He criticizes the definition of *Vādavidhi*, "Sensation is a cognition (produced) from that object" (*tato rthātvijñānaṃ pratyak-ṣaṃ*), in comparison with *AbkB.* and *Vādayidhāna.** He seems to have *Vādavidhāna* in his hands and was told by Vasubandhu himself that the quintessence (*sāra*) of his view is in *Vādavidhāna.* That is why he relied on it. Why does Diṅnāga refer to the Sautrāntika work (*AbkB.*) of Vasubandhu for reinforcement and not to any of his Vijñānavādin works if he was really converted?

(ii) The recently discovered Jaina treatise (*DNCV.*) of that period brings to light the same fact that the Jaina critics Mallavādin and Siṃhasūri, refer to the Sautrāntika *AbkB.*, to show the contradiction in Diṅnāga's definition of *pratyakṣa.* While criticizing Diṅnāga's concept of illusion, why does a contemporary. Jaina critic compare it with *AbkB.*? Why does Mallavādin criticize the Vijñānavāda's definitions separately soon after he has finished Vasubandhu and Diṅnāga? Does it not suggest that this obscurely known Jaina tradition includes both Vasubandhu and Diṅnāga under the Sautrāntikas?

(iii) Why did Diṅnāga write in defence of *AbkB.*, namely *Abhidarma Kośamarmapradīpa* (light on the essentials of *Abhidharmakośa*)? And why does Vācaspatimiśra call them Sautrāntikas?

Recently new evidence to prove the conversion was produced by E.

******Pramāṇasamuccayavṛtti* **(*PS*) 2/2, Dig. on per., pp. 116-17.**

Lamotté who has translated *Karmasiddhiprakaraṇa* (*KSP*) of Vasubandhu from Chinese into French (*Mēlanges Chinois et Bouddhiques*, 4:15ff). Also the article 'Vasubandhu's Karmasiddhiprakaraṇa and the Problem of the Highest Meditation* by Stefan Anacker has attempted to prove the thesis that the Sautrāntika Vasubandhu was gradually changed his position to Vijñānavāda.** The text clearly mentions the Mahāyāna concept of Bodhisattva in the salutation, refers to *Sandhinirmocanasūtra*, and speaks about *Ālapavijñāna*, etc.

The evidence was thoroughly examined. It also appears to be non-authentic in nature. Following are the reasons which compel one to doubt its validity:

1. The Chinese translation of *KSP.* by Hsüan-Tsang is full of interpolation, as the translator himself has distorted the text. Anacker has rightly pinpointed this distortion of Hsüan-Tsang: "The *Karmasiddhiprakaraṇa* is lost in Sanskrit but exists in translation into Chinese, by Hsüan-Tsang (taisho 1608-1609), and Tibetan, by Visuddhisiṃha Devendrarakṣita.† E. Lamotté has translated the Chinese version into French . . . The Chinese differs from the Tibetan so often that it is almost a new text. These differences may be due to Hsüan-Tsang's practice of inserting his own interpretations into the body of his version".††

In such a doubtful situation, how can one make an unqualified assertion that this treatise is composed by the author of *AbkB.*? Definitely one becomes doubtful whether the Mahāyāna doctrines (mentioned above) are not an interpolation by the translators. That the Tibetan translation, on which Anacker relies, is also absolutely free from interpolations is not established because such cases of distortions have been found when compared with the original Sanskrit.

2. One should also not neglect the fact that there have been four persons by the name of Vasubandhu as discussed by Wayman in detail.

In such a complex situation, how can one be completely sure that *KSP.* is composed by the Sautrāntika Vasubapdhu? Until the original manuscripts are discovered and a thorough comparative survey is undertaken, no one can establish a thesis which seems inconsistent

**Philosophy East and West*, XXII, no. 3, July, 1972.

**On the basis of *KSP.* Anacker attempted to refute Frauwallner's thesis.

†*Tibetan Tripitaka*, Peking/Tokyo edition, 113, p. 295 ff.

††*Philosophy East and West*, 1972, p. 247.

when examined according to its various logical implications and consequences. To establish or alter a thesis on insufficient evidence cannot be justified.

Frauwallner has altered his theses, *On the Date of the Buddhist Master Vasubandhu* (1951), in the third revised edition of *Philosophie des Buddhismus* (1969) in which he has proposed a new thesis of a gradual change in the position of Vasubandhu II, the author of *AbkB.* According to his new thesis, the Sautrāntika Vasubandhu, like Vasubandhu (I), Asaṃga's brother also turned to Vijñānavāda and wrote *Viṃśatikā* and *Triṃśikā*, which still show his Sautrāntika past. The same view is further argued by Schmithausen in his celebrated article 'Sautrāntika voraussetzungen im *Viṃśatikā* und *Triṃśika*'*. Is one then to accept Frauwallner's original thesis?

Certainly, Frauwallner has altered his previous thesis concerning the affiliation of Vasubandhu II and the authorship of *Trimśikā* and *Vimśatikā*. But upon further inquiry, his altered view seems to be inconsistent. The grounds which led him to change his prior thesis are as follows :

1. Soon after the publication of his previous thesis, it was vehemently opposed by such scholars as P.S. Jaini, A. Wayman, and S. Anacker, on the grounds of the evidence of *AbD.*, *Śrāvakabhūmi* and *KSP.*, respectively.

2. The discovery of some more of Diṅnāga's works led him to change his thesis. Prof. Frauwallner has his own particular view about the succession of the writings of Vasubandhu, Diṅnāga, and Dharmakīrti.

3. Schmithausen's explanation of *Viṃśatikā* and *Triṃśikā* as showing Sautrāntika influence also induced Frauwallner to change his previous thesis.

The present author has investigated thoroughly all of these grounds and found them insufficient to establish a new thesis. The following reasons call for serious consideration :

1. It is mainly the opposition of other scholars which induced him to alter his thesis, as is proven by Frauwallner's own statement : "Against this distinction between the brother of Asaṅga and the composer of *Abhidharmakośaḥ*, P.S. Jaini has raised, in a lecture given at the 24th International Congress of Orientalists, Munich, 1957. . .Still further research is, of course, to be made here. But the time for it has not yet come, as important material is yet to be

* *WZKSO*, XI, 1967.

published. The Sanskrit originals enable us to make more exact ascertainment than the Chinese and Tibetan translations. But only a small portion of the Sanskrit works discovered by Rāhula Sānkṛtyāyana has been published. The edition of *Abhidharmakośaḥ*, by Prahlād Pradhān has not appeared, nor has the edition of *Abhidharmadīpaḥ* and *Vibhāṣāprabhāvṛttiḥ* by P.S. Jaini. Also the *Bhāṣyaṃ on the Madhyāntavibhāga*, likewise discovered by Rāhula Sānkṛtyāyana, still awaits publication. Only when these texts are published can the foundation for new successful research be laid".*

Frauwallner himself admits the insufficiency of the available material. Even then he altered his previous thesis and accepted the refutation of the above scholars. The author has already examined the views of P.S. Jaini, A. Wayman, and S. Anacker and found them unsound and unfounded.

Frauwallner has also attempted to establish the order of Diṅnaga's earlier and later works in 'Diṅnāga, sein Werk und seine Entwicklung'** Similarly, he has also attempted to establish a sequence in the writings of Dharmakīrti 'Die Reihenfolge und Entstehung der Werke Dharmakīrti's'† showing a sort of development (in the sense of gradual conversion), and has gone to the extent of assuming that even in a single treatise of Dharmakīrti, the gradual conversion patterns are traceable. For example, he thinks that Dharmakīrti begins his *PV.* as a Sautrāntika and ends as a Vijñānavādin ; "Dharmakīrti geht im Pramāṇavārttikaṃ zunächst vom standpunkt der Sautrāntika aus, dass die Einzeldinge als wirklich betrachten und zeigt erst später, das sie nur schöpfung der Erkenntnis sind."††

Thus, he now holds the opinion that the Sautrāntika Vasubandhu gradually turns to Vijñānavāda, Diṅnāga begins his career as a Vijñāṇavādin and ends as a Sautrāntika (note the reverse process), and Dharmakīrti begins as a Sautrāntika and ends as a Vijñānavādin. Now the question arises whether this thesis is valid or not.

Diṅnāga definitely is the commentator of the Sautrāntika Vasubandhu's *AbkB.* (*Abhidharmakośamarmapradīpa*) and *Vādavidhāna* (*Vādavidhānaṭīkā*) and Dharmakīrti is well known as the Vārttikakāra of Diṅnaga's works (who commented on *PS.*). In this case, neither has changed his philosophical position. In this situation, one cannot

*'Landmarks in the History of Indian Logic', *WZKSO*, 1961, p. 132.

***WZKSO*, III, 1959.

†Asiatica, 1954, Festschrift Friedrich Weller.

††*WZKM*. I, p. 93, ref. 2.

hastily assume that the philosophers have constantly changed their positions.

It is also interesting to note that Frauwallner seems to suggest that Vasubandhu II turned from a Sautrāntika to a Vijñānavādin, Diṅnāga again turned from a Vijñānavādin to a Sautrāntika, and Dharmakīrti turned from a Sautrāntika to a Vijñānavādin. Even then they are supposed to be the commentators of the Sautrāntika Vasubandhu (not of the Vijñānavādin Vasubandhu), and nobody reveals the reasons for the changes.

Historically, as shown above, Buddhist empirical logic appeared against the doubtful doctrines of the Vaibhāṣikas and the Brahmanic attack. Vasubandhu II criticized the Sarvāstivādin Vaibhāṣikas, Sāṃkhya, Vaiśeṣika, Mīmāṃsā, etc. Diṅnāga was again attacked by Uddyotakara in his *Nyāyavārttika* and by Kumārila (*Apohavāda of ŚV.*). In turn, Dharmakīrti criticized Uddyotakara, Sāṃkhya, Vaiśeṣika, Mīmāṃsā, Jainas, etc. and defended Diṅnāga's doctrines through his commentary *Pramāṇavārttika.* Dharmakīrti in turn was criticized by Vācaspatimiśra and Pārthasārathimiśra, who definitely call Diṅnāga and Dharmakīrti Sautrāntikas, and none of them pinpoints their opponents' supposed change of affiliations. It is unlikely that a critic would overlook such a weak point of an opponent, i.e. his inconsistency.

It is also worth noting that the account of the Tibetan historian Tāranātha and Paramārtha's account preserved in Chinese, which are the only sources of the theory of conversion, teach the sudden conversion of these Ācāryas and not the gradual conversion as mentioned by Frauwallner. Thus, the theory of gradual conversion refutes the very sources on which it is supposed to be based.

2. It also appears that Frauwallner's change in his previous thesis was influenced by the discovery of new books (*PPP* and *YA.*), supposedly written by Diṅnāga. These two books are found in the original Sanskrit which contains no name and identified by the name of Diṅnāga according to the Tibetan and Chinese colophons. But when the author examined their authorship, this ascription turned out to be not authentic.

There is not the slightest doubt that these two books are works of Mahāyāna Vijñānavādins. But that they were written by Diṅnāga seems to be incorrect for the following reasons:

(*a*) I-ching, who stayed in Nālandā University at the time when Diṅnāga's works were thoroughly studied there and enumerated the writings of Diṅnāga as mentioned by Frauwallner himself, does not include these books as written by Diṅnāga. The authority of I-ching is reliable because he stayed in Nālanda for nearly ten years. If *PPP* and *YA* were earlier writings of Diṅnāga, why are they not mentioned by him? It makes one convinced that they are not authentic.

(*b*) Similarly, Hsüan-Tsang, who was a Vijñānavādin himself, studied at Nālandā and translated *AP* of Diṅnāga, does not even touch these Vijñānavādin works. It is only in the Sung period 10th century that *PPP* was translated into Chinese as Diṅnāga's work. As far as the date is concerned, we find Haribhadra (late 8th century) referring to *PPP* as by Diṅnāga in his *Abhisamayālaṅkāra-āloka* for the first time. Thus, this work was ascribed to Diṅnāga, or a Diṅnāga, by the end of 8th century.

(*c*) The internal examination of *PPP* uncovers the fact that it is a summary (*pīṇḍārtha*) of the Mahāyāna *Aṣṭasāhasrikā-prajñāpāramitāsūtra* (*APP*) as the text itself reveals (*nirdiṣṭo' ṣṭasāhasryāṃ*, 6-17, *Prajñāpāramitāgranthaste sapiṇḍadarśitā*, 20).

(*d*) The internal examination further indicates that the author of *PPP* believes in sixteen kinds of *śūnyatā* (*ṣoḍaśākāra śūnyatā*, *6*), shows his faith in the triple division of reality, (*kalpita*, *paratantra*, *pariniṣpanna*, 27), non-dual-void (*advayaśūnyatā*, 39), thusness (*tathatā* 1), bodhisattva (8,37), perfection of understanding (*prajñāpārmitā*, *1,55*), which is the typical terminology of the Mahāyāna tradition. But Diṅnāga has not used this kind of terminology anywhere in any of his authentic works. Is it not possible that Diṅnāga only wrote, after these works, on logic and epistemology, and had no chance to use this terminology? It is not likely that an author will forget his previous terminology totally, and there is always an opportunity, even in a book of logic and epistemology, where he could have used them, *e.g. AP*, etc.* Particularly, in the opening *śloka* of *PS* where he salutes the Buddha as manifested logic (*pramāṇabhūta PS*. 1/1), *Sugata*, *Tāyin* (protector) and in his explanation of these terms in his autocommentary, there is enough opportunity to use any of the terms. The complete absence of these Mahāyānistic terms in the opening *śloka* makes one sure that these terms are foreign to Diṅnāga. Neither has Dharmakīrti, who wrote a full chapter on this *śloka* (*Ks*. 287), mentioned these terms. Dharmakīrti uses the terms

*One might expect Diṅnāga to relate his two *prameyas* in *PS* to the three *svabhāvās*, and the nature of the cognitive process (*AP* and *PS*) should have some relation to the Vijñānavādin theory of consciousness.

*Arhat**, *Pratyeka Buddha* (1/140), and *Buddha,* and nowhere *Bodhisattva* or *tathatā,* etc. Even the term *tāyin* (protector) is not used in the sense of Bodhisattva taking the pledge to redeem all sentient beings. But the Buddha is a saviour because he has protected all beings by revealing the knowledge of the four noble truths.** The present author has also examined the misinterpretation of some Mahāyāna commentators on this issue.

(*e*) The language and style of *PPP* clearly reveals the fact that this is not the work of the logician Diṅnāga or any other logician. It is apparently a work by a poet who does not know anything about logic or epistemology. But it is a well-known fact and accepted by Frauwallner that Diṅnāga begins his philosophical career by writing a commentary on 'Method of Debate' (*vādavidhāna*) of the Sautrāntika Vasubandhu. It is unlikely that a philosopher will forget his logic after writing a treatise on logic. For a philosopher who entered the field of logic and epistemology, it is unlikely that his other works will not be affected by his logical methodology. The very terminology of the *PPP* indicates that it is not a work of Diṅnāga, but of someone who has nothing to do with logic.

(*f*) There is another reason which strengthens the argument of the present author. After Diṅnāga's death, his commentator Dharmakīrti and others always raised the question whether there is contradiction in the writings of Diṅnāga or not†, and concluded that there was no contradiction. If *PPP* had been the work of Diṅnāga, the commentators and critics would have definitely discussed it.

(*g*) The case of *YA* also seems to be the same as that of *PPP*. Apart from the above reasons, which are also applicable to *YA*, there are other reasons which indicate that it is not authentic. Frauwallner, on the ground of the Tibetan colophon only, has expressed a firm opinion that *YA* is also an earlier work of Diṅnāga. As far as the text is concerned, it is definitely a work in the tradition of the Mahāyāna Vijñānavāda. But the following reasons make one sure that it is not authentic:

(*i*) Frauwallner on the strength of the Tibetan colophon only made an absolute decision of its being an early work of Diṅnāga (when he belonged to the Vijñānavada). This conclusion seems to be based on insufficient evidence. There is no name of author in the Sanskrit text. One should not neglect the fact that there have been various mistakes

**PV.*, 1/47.

***tāyin vā catuḥ satya prakāśanaṃ*, *PV.*, 1/148-282.

†*PV.*, 2/294; *TS.*, 1328-29.

in Tibetan colophons when they were examined by modern scholars.

(*ii*) There is another work, *Yogāvatāropadeśa* (*YAU*) by the name of Ācārya Dharmendra who has borrowed the whole text (9 ślokas) without mentioning the name of Diṅnāga. It is unlikely that an Ācārya will borrow the whole text of another philosopher without even mentioning his name. Thus the *kārikās* and two small paragraphs may be both by Dharmendra. Durgacaran Chatterji who has reconstructed and translated the text given a strange reason for the omission: "The fact that *Yogāvatāropadeśa* has taken the Yogāvatāra almost in its entirety without mentioning its name and the author clearly points to popularity it earned"*. Firstly, the reason of popularity does not seem to be valid because if *YA*, was popularly known as a work of Diṅnāga, then the borrower would not fail to mention the name of the original author or at least that he was writing only a commentary (fearing its detection). Secondly, if its authorship was popularly known, then I-ching cannot fail to count it under the writing of Diṅnāga and commentators and critics also cannot miss it. Therefore, through some mistake it is ascribed to Diṅnāga in the Tibetan colophon (It happens quite often that miscellaneous minor works are ascribed to famous authors in the Tibetan collections *e.g.* to Nāgārjuna, etc. In India also such ascriptions are found to Śaṃkara, Vararuci, Kālidāsa and so on).

(*iii*) The Tibetan translator of both texts (*YA* and *YAU*), Janārdana, also does not refer the authorship to Diṅnāga. Similarly, the Tanjur index mentions the Yogāvatāra thrice: Mdo, A, ku fols. 145[b]. 6-146[a], 8; and Gi, fols. 192[b]; 8-193[b]: 1. But the text is not available in A.

(*iv*) *YAU* which is the work (*kṛti*) of Dharmendra contains as compared with *YA* only one paragraph at the beginning and one extra paragraph at the end The rest is *YA*. Therefor, there is every possibility that both these texts are one work of Dharmendra, not of Diṅnāga.

(*v*) The internal examination of *YA* discloses that it is a Mahāyāna Vijñānavādin work, as Mahāyāna technical terms such as *tathatāvijñānavajra* (thunderbolt or diamond of *Tathatā*, 3, 6), *grāhya-grāhaka* (subject-object in the Mahāyāna sense, 2), *prajñāpāramitā* (perfection of understanding), *bhūtakōṭi* (used in Mahāyāna only, 6), *gaganagañjasamādhi* (9) are used. But Diṅnāga nowhere in his works (*PS*, *AP*, *Nyāyamukha*, etc.) shows any familiarity with these terms.

**Journal of Asiatic Society of Bengal*, NS., XXIII, 1927, p. 250.

It is not likely that a writer will forget totally those terms and adopt entirely new terminology. Therefore, that *YA* and *PPP* are the works of Diṅnāga is not established.

The other works of Diṅnāga such as *Ālambanaparīkṣā* are accepted by Frauwallner as Diṅnāga's later (Sautrāntika-transitional) writing. *Trikālaparīkṣā* and *Hastavālaprakaraṇa* are not yet discovered in Sanskrit. Frauwallner has given the Sanskrit equivalent of *Trikālaparīkṣā* from Bhartṛhari's *Vākyapadīyam**, but that Diṅnāga copied Bhartṛhari mutatis mutandis is not beyond doubt. It is possible that Diṅnāga had some exchange of philosophical views on the doctrine of time with the contemporary philosopher Bhartṛhari. But there were some differences. For example, the concepts of Brahman and Ātman, which are the very fundamental doctrines of Bhartṛhari are totally foreign to Diṅnāga. Until the original text is discovered, no definite conclusion about its authenticity can be arrived at.

Hastavālaprakaraṇa is assigned (in the Tibetan colophon) to Āryadeva, not to Diṅnāga. F.W. Thomas who has reconstructed the text into Sanskrit** calls it a Mādhyamika work. M. Hattori who has made a survey of Diṅnāga's work, also doubts the Tibetan account in the following words:

> "The classification of Diṅnāga's work in the Tibetan Bstan-ḥgyur is not appropriate. For example, Number 5 (*Hastavālaprakaraṇa*) is hardly recognized as a Prajñāpāramitā treatise. It deals with the problem of reality and unreality of existences from the Sautrāntika point of view."†

The same view is expressed by Stcherbatsky on the extra listed works of Dharmakīrti in the Tibetan colophon.††

All this evidence proves one fact. The fact is that Frauwallner has altered his previous thesis for one which seems less satisfactory.

3. The other ground of Frauwallner's altered thesis is the defence of Schmithausen who has attempted to defend the view that *Viṃśatikā and Triṃśikā* are written by the Sautrāntika Vasubandhu at the time he was gradually turning from the Sautrāntika to the Vijñānavāda.

*Chap. III, sambandhasamuddeśaḥ, 53-85.

***RAS.*, London, April, 1918.

†M. Hattori, *Dignāga on Perception*, p. 10.

††*Buddhist Logic* (*BL*) I, p. 37.

He (Schmithausen) also presents the following reasons for his defence of Frauwallner's altered thesis:

(a) *manas, buddhi, citta* are taken (in *Viṃśatikā*) as synonyms.

(b) the doctrine of residue of actions (*karmaṇo vāsanā*), is a Sautrāntika doctrine.

(c) the doctrine of the special transformation of consciousness (*saṃtānapariṇāmaviśeṣaḥ*) belongs to Sautrāntika.

(d) the absence of the Vijñānavādin doctrines such as *ālayavijñāna, aṣṭavijñāna*, etc., and their absence in the writings of Diṅnāga and Dharmakīrti, which confirms the fact that they were following the *Viṃśatikā* tradition.

All these grounds are supposed to verify the altered thesis that the Sautrāntika Vasubandhu, the author of *AbkB* also turned to Vijñānavāda and wrote *Triṃśika-Viṃśaṭīkā* which still exhibits his Sautrāntika past.

(a) (i) But on the examination of these grounds they appeared to be inadequate:

The synonymity of *manas, citta, vijñāna*, as found in the *Viṃśatikā* is not the doctrine of the *Abhidharmakośa* only, but of all the Sarvāstivādin Abhidharma. Harivarman, whose work *Tattvasiddhi*, was recently studied by S. Katsūra, also indicates the same fact.* The Vijñānavādin Abhidharma also uses the same terminology (*Abhidharmasamuccaya*, 35). How then can one establish a thesis on the grounds of such an overlapping (*vyabhicārin*) reason (*hetu*) ?

(ii) Though the *Abhidharmakośa* does hold the same doctrine of synonymity**, it differs from the *Viṃśatikā* by not including *vijñapti* as its synonym.*** And the language is also not completely the same. Similarly, in the next line, the author of the *Viṃśatikā* explains that *citta* (mind), 'here means' the concomitant of mind (*cittaṃ atra sasaṃprayogaṃ abhipretaṃ*). The terms 'here means' (*atrābhipretaṃ*) indicates in this particular context of the refutation of the external object and the establishment of the doctrine of 'mere mind' (*cittamātra*). Because in the next line the author himself mentions it, 'mere' is used in the sense of the negation of the object (*mātraṃ ity arthapratiṣedhārthaṃ*). This implies that the author is using the term *citta* in this particular context in a limited sense. But in other places

***'*A Study of Tattvasiddhi*', p. 137, University of Toronto, 1974.**

*****cittaṃ mano' tha vijñānaṃ ekārthaṃ, Abk.*, 2/34.**

******cittaṃ manovijñānaṃ vijñaptiśceti paryāyāḥ Viṃ-vṛtti*, p. 1, reconstructed from the Chinese.**

(*Triṃśikā*) he uses it in the broader sense, not in the contrary sense as concluded by Schmithausen.

(iii) Vasubandhu II in his *AbkB* defines clearly the etymologically different meanings of these terms* : "Mind is called *citta* because it selects, *manas* because it thinks, *Vijnāna* because it knows" and Yaśomitra brings out an interesting point, that Sautrāntika as well as Vijñānavādin had the same theory.** Both of these systems have similar connotations for these terms, which goes against the thesis that they exhibit Vasubandhu's Sautrāntika past; because the Vijñānavādin Abhidharma also has a similar theory.†

(iv) Another point should also be borne in mind, that Vasubandhu II has a different opinion about mind: that it is not a separate entity from the six consciousnesses, which is the doctrine of the Vaibhāṣikas and Vijñānavādins†† and Yaśomitra clearly mentions it: "From the Yogācāra point of view, mind element is different from six consciousnesses".††† Diṅnāga (*PS*) and Dharmakīrti* in correspondence with the Sautrāntika tradition, do not regard mind as a separate entity apart from the six consciousnesses (*ṣaḍvijñāna*). Therefore, one should not be confused by the similarity of *Viṃśatikā* and *AbkB*.

(b) The doctrine of 'residue karman' (actions) is also found in Sarvāstivādin as well as the Vijñānavādin Abhidharma. The Sautrāntika Vasubandhu II has criticized in detail the Vaibhāṣika concept of past (*atīta*) and possession (*prāpti*) of action, and explains it on the ground of resultant-consciousness (*vipākacitta*), subtle transformation (*sūkṣmapariṇāma*) of action, and homogeneous immediate condition (*samanantarapratyaya*). It definitely differs from the Vijñānavādin concept of store-consciousness (*ālayavijñāna*), which contains the seed of all action.** In the *Viṁśatikā*, Vasubandhu does not mention these doctrines, not because he disbelieves in them or is influenced by his Sautrāntika past, but because *Viṃśatikā* is an answer to the Sautrāntika*** and the Vaibhāṣika and he therefore had to use their terminology. He uses Vijñānavādin terminology in *Triṃśikā* because

**cinoti ti cittam, manuta iti manaḥ, vijñānātīti vijñānaṃ AbkB.*, 2/34, p. 208.

***Sphuṭārthā*, p. 208.

†*Abhidharmasamuccaya*, 35.

††*AbkB*. 1/17.

†††*yogācāramatena tu sadvijñānavyatirikto'py asti manodhātu, Sphuṭārtha*, p. 52.

**PV*., 2/294.

** *vipākaḥ sarvabījakaṃ, Triṃśikābhāṣya* (*Triṃ B*) p. 2.

****Kārikā*, 7-8.

it is an independent treatise, not a refutation or a reply.

(c) The term *pariṇāma* (transformation) *bīja* (seed) is used in both, the traditions. But Vasubandhu II had a critical approach to this term* which should not be confused with Vijñānavāda or Vaibhāṣika concepts.

The term *vijñānapariṇāma* (transformation of consciousness) is also used in both (*Vij.-Saut.*), but there are substantial differences in their explanation. Vijñānavāda holds the simultaneous transformation of consciousness in the form of the object, as explained by Sthiramati: "The transformation is at the same time as the cessation of the moment of the cause. It is the dependence on itself of an effect different from the moment of its cause"** But the Sautrāntikas do not accept the doctrine that objects are mere transformation of consciousness and *pariṇāma* is of some substance (*dravya*) as discussed by Vasubandhu II in the course of refutation of Sāṃkhya concept of *pariṇāma.****

Thus, it seems to be the similarity of these terms which has been confusing scholars. There is also the possibility that Vasubandhu I, the author of *Viṃśatika and Triṃśika* is referring to these terms in the general sense of the Buddhist Ābhidharmika tradition, not in any specific sense.

It is surprising that Schmithausen arrived at the conclusion that *Viṃśatikā* is influenced by Sautrāntika and *Triṃśikā* is influenced by Vijñānavāda, even though the author is the same. There is no substantial proof that *Viṃśatikā* is a Sautrāntika work. On the contrary, *Viṃśatikā* contains fundamental doctrines of Vijñānavāda such as:

1. The total denial of external objects.
2. The total negation of atoms.†
3. The quotation "*mahāyāne traidhātukaṃ vijñaptimātraṃ vyavasthāpyate*" in the very opening of the treatise removes all doubts of its being a Mahāyāna Vijñānavādin work.
4. The reference to "*Daśabhūmikasūtra*" is to the traditional Mahāyānasūtra favoured by Asaṃga (*Mahāyānasūtrālaṅkāra*).[6]
5. Acceptance of the doctrine of "mere consciousness" (*cittamātra*)††

**AbkB.*, II, 36, pp. 217-18.

***kāranakṣanirodhasamakālaḥ pariṇāmāḥ Trim. B., p.* 16.

****AbkB.* 3/49, p. 509.

†*Viṃśātika.*, 11, 15.

††ibid., 21.

6. Reliance on the analogy of dreams.

7. Clear refutation of the Sautrāntika doctrines, etc., indicates that the author is a Māhāyana Vijñānavādin (Vasubandhu I, Asaṃga's brother) not the Sautrāntika Vasubandhu II.

(d) Then why does *Viṃśatikā* not mention the Vijñānavādin doctrines such as *ālayavijñāna* (store-consciousness), *trisvabhāva* (triple nature of reality), *aṣṭavijñana* (eight consciousnesses) as found in *Triṃśikā*?

The reasons are as follows:

Viṃśatika is not an exposition or summary of the Vijñānavādin doctrines, but only a refutation of Sautrāntika and Vaibhāṣika doctrines. Therefore, the author may not have an occasion to explain his own doctrines, or he would have discussed them in his previous (*Triṃśikā*) work.

The conclusion as arrived at by Schmithausen, that his work represents a different position or one that shows the Sautrāntika influence and the other the Vijñānavāda, is not well founded.

Similarly, Schmithausen's conclusion that Diṅnāga and Dharmakīrti have not referred to these doctrines because they are following Vasubandhu of *Viṃśatikā* (not of *Triṃśikā*) also seem to be unsatisfactory for the following reasons:

(i) Diṅnāga and Dharmakīrti are the followers of the Sautrāntika Vasubandhu II, who himself had no belief in these doctrines and both of his followers are following the Sautrāntika doctrines, Therefore, they have no interest in these Vijñānavādin doctrines. Schmithausen in his article attempted to prove a Vijñānavādin element in Dharmakīrti on the ground that it describes the process of inference from the Vijñānavādin point of view.* In fact, Dharmakīrti does mention the Vijñānavādin doctrines up to *K.*, 397 in the form of thesis and in Kārikā 398 gives the conclusion that this is the doctrine of Yogācārins (*viduṣāṃ*). But the ācārya (Diṅnāga) did not describe it from the Vijñānavādin point of view. It is remarkable that Schmithausen has only referred to Kārika 397 and neglects the concluding Kārikā 398.

(ii) Dharmakīrti neglects the Ālaya doctrine** not because it is absent from *Viṃśatikā* but because he is following the Sautrāntika tradition.

(iii) Why Schmithausen forgets the fact that if Diṅnāga and Dharmakīrti were the disciples of the Vijñānavādin Vasubandhu who

**PV.*, 2/393-397.

***PV.*, 2/522.

wrote *Viṃśatikā* and *Triṃśikā*, they should follow the last work (*Triṃśikā*) of the teacher, not the first one (transition=*Viṃśatikā*). And why do they not refer to those books in any of their writings? The simplest explanation is that they both were following the Sautrāntika Vasubandhu, not the Vijñānavādin Vasubandhu.

(iv) This explanation is strengthened by the absence of such a view as that of Schmithausen in any of the vast commentarial and critical traditions of these two unanimously accepted Vijñānavādin treatises.

(v) If this altered thesis of authorship is accepted, then it will lead to the conclusion that Vasubandhu I wrote practically nothing (except a commentary on (*Madhyāntavibhaṅga*) and Vasubandhu II did the whole writing in old age. Why did Frauwallner accept the view that Vasubandhu II refused to answer Saṃghabhadra's criticism of *AbkB* because of old age? In other words, Frauwallner himself opposes his previous ground.

Thus, all this investigation of Frauwallner's altered thesis drives the present author to the conclusion that Frauwallner's previous thesis was correct, while the altered one is subject to various inconsistencies and illogical implications.

Then why does the treatment of Ābhidharmika definitions seem to be the same in *AbkB* and *Triṃśikā-Viṃśatikā* which appears to prove one authorship? When this question is thoroughly investigated, the conclusion appears to be quite contrary. It is the similarity which has caused this confusion. The definition and division of Ābhidharmika concepts appear to be similar, but in fact they are not. The Ābhidharmika terms and their definitions are almost the same in all traditions, but there are fundamental variations in some of the concepts, definitions, and grounds of division. There is a vast difference in counting the numbers of fundamental *Dharmas* (realities) in Vaibhāṣika, Sautrāntika, and Vijñānavādin Abhidharma. For example, a thorough comparison of the topic of *Caitasikas* in both the treatises *AbkB* and *Triṃśika* suggested the following conclusions:

1 Vasubandhu II in his *AbkB* divides the *Caitasikas* (mental factors) differently from the Vijñānavādin Vasubandhu I (author of *Viṃśatikā* and *Triṃśikā*). This point therefore indicates the fact that Vasubandhu II was different from Vasubandhu I. See the following diagram:

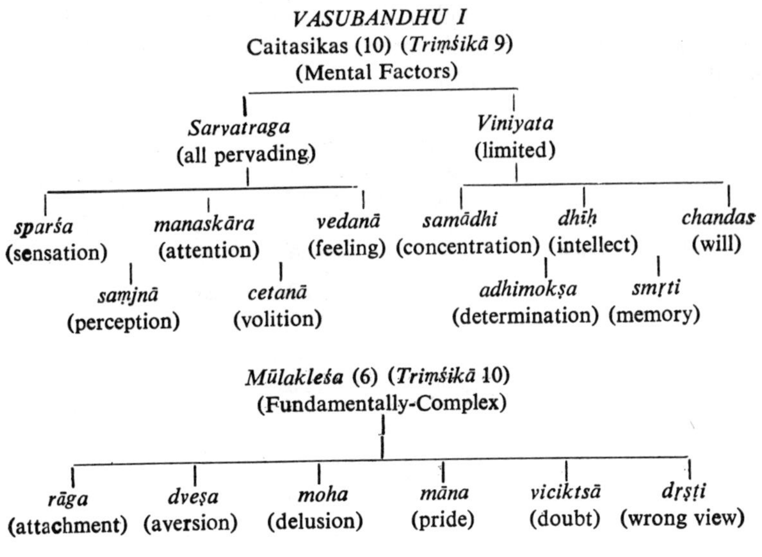

Upakleśa (20) (Triṃśikā 11, 12, 13, 14)
(Sub-Complex)

krodha (anger), *upanāha* (hatred) *mṛkṣā* (hypocrisy), *īrṣyā* (jealousy) *mātsarya* (selfishness), *māyā* (trickery), *śāṭhya* (cheating), *mada* (intoxication), *vihiṃsā* (violence), *pradāsa* (envy), *ahrī* (lack of self-respect), *anapatrāpa* (shamelessness; not fearing blame), *styāna* (stupidity), *audhatya* (vanity or pride), *aśrādhya* (disbelief; lack of confidence), *kauśīdya* (indolence, laziness) *pramāda* (negligence), *muṣitasmṛti* (unmindfulness), *vikṣepa* (confusion), *asaṃprajanya* (non-deliberation).

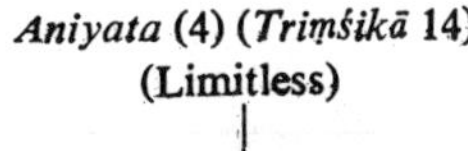

middhaṃ (stupidity; mental derangement), *kaukṛtyaṃ* (anxiety), *vitarka* (reasoning), *vicāra* (*reflection*).

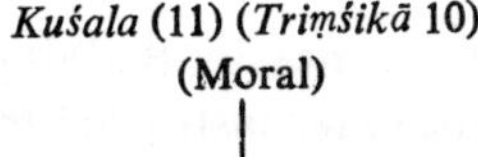

śraddhā (confidence), *vīrya* (energy), *hrī* (self-respect), *apatrāpa* (shame fear of blame) *alobha* (non-greed), *advesa* (non-aversion), *amoha* (non-delusion), *praśrabdhi* (tranquility), *apramāda* (non-negligence), *upekṣā* (equanimity), *ahiṃsā* (non-violence).

10+6+20+4+11=51

On the other hand, Vasubandhu II does not speak of *mūlakleśa* except *kleśa* and *mahopakleśa* (major-complex) eliminating *moha* and dividing *Caitasikas* differently:

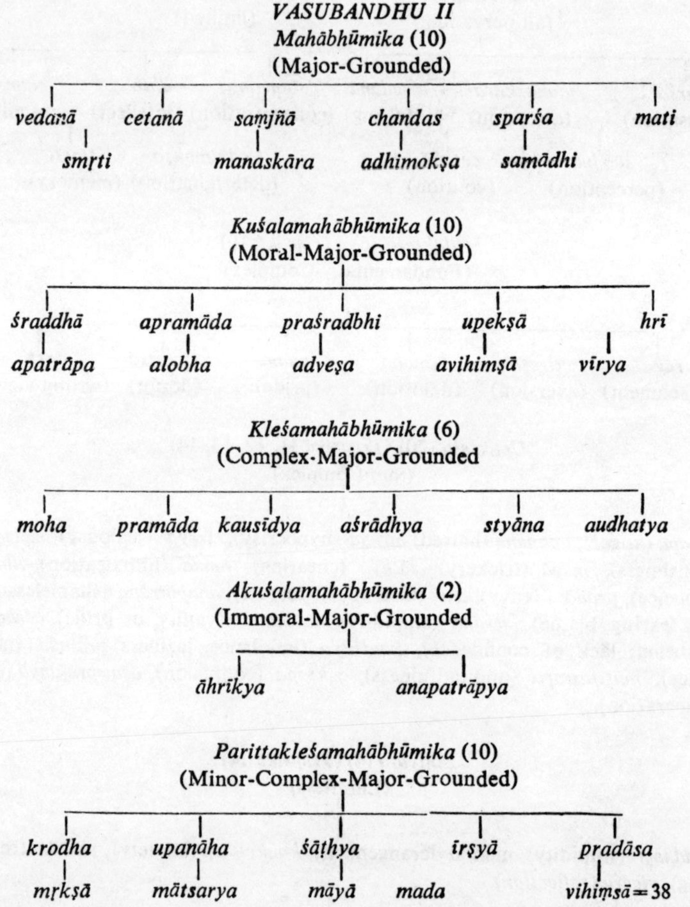

2. Recently one short treatise by Bodhisattva-Vasubandhu (Yogācarā Vasubandhu I has been reconstructed from Chinese to Sanskrit by N. A. Sastri.*

*Ālambanaparīkṣā (AP), p. 113.

It provides us with the list of *Caitasikas* according to Vijñānavāda:

VASUBANDHU I

Sarvatraga	5 (as above)
Viniyata bhūmika	5 (as above)
Kuśala	11 (as above)
Kleśa	6 (as above)
Upakleśa	20 (as above)
Aniyata	4 (as above)
	51

Thus, Bodhisattva Vasubandhu seems to be the same as the author of *Viṃśatikā and Triṃśikā*, while Vasubandhu II is throughout a Sautrāntika who counts only 38 *Caitasikas*. However, Vasubandhu II is aware of the former's classification. On the ground of this different scheme of division one can assert that Vasubandhu II comes later.

In the appendix of *AP*, N.A. Shastri has also given the Tamil tradition which counts Ābhidharmika entities according to different systems. The Sautrāntika counting is the same as that of *AbkB* and it is also includes Diṅnāga and Dharmakīrti under the Sautrāntikas.*

3. Another variation obviously emerges in the definition of *adhimokṣa* (intentness), and *śraddhā* (confidence). *AbkB* after defining *adhimokṣa,* reads "*rucirityanye*" (others define it as 'interest') Who are these others? Yaśomitra clearly refers to Yogācāra (*yathāniścayaṃ dhāraṇeti Yogācāra-cittā*). Similarly, at the occasion of defining *śraddhā,* Vasubandhu mentions others define it as confidence in truth, triple gem, action, and results** which is the definition of Vijñānavādins.† All this evidence indicates that the author of *AbkB* and *Viṃśatika-Triṃśika* are two different persons.

Thus, Dharmakīrti is the follower, commentator, and defender of Diṅnāga while Diṅnāga is the follower, commentator and defender of Vasubandhu's philosophical standpoint. Their affiliation depends on the affiliation of Vasubandhu's school, viz., if they were following the Vijñānavādin Vasubandhu I, then Diṅnāga and Dharmakīrti

*Aruṇandi Sivacāryar, 1275-1325, commentator Jñānaprakāsar *JSVOI*, Tirupati, I, part 2, pp. 176-91.

***satya-ratna-karma-phalābhisaṃpratyaya ity apare, AbkB.*, 2/25.

†*tatra śraddhā karma-phala-satya-ratneṣvabhisaṃpratyayaḥ, Triṃ.B.*, p. 26.

were Vijñānavādins. If they were following the Sautrāntika Vasubandhu, then they were Sautrāntikas.

The Main cause of including Diṅnāga and Dharmakīrti under Vijñānavāda is the conviction that they were following the Vijñānavādin Vasubandhu who was supposed to be a Sautrāntika before. That is why the author had to examine this very important and complex problem. If it is true that there were two famous Vasubandhus belonging to two different traditions, and Diṅnāga and Dharmakīrti were following the Sautrāntika Vasubandhu, then they were definitely Sautrāntikas.

Historically, it is determined (by Frauwallner himself and mostly accepted by modern scholars) that Vijñānavādin Vasubandhu I comes earlier, and the Sautrāntika Vasubandhu later.

Vijñānavāda	*Sautrāntika*	
Vasubandhu I (320-380 AD)	Vasubandhu II	(400-480 AD)
	Diṅnāga	(420-490 AD)
	Dharmakīrti	(600-660 AD)

Because of a mistake in the very beginning, the whole philosophy of these three Sautrāntika philosophers is misinterpreted.

Another important cause which misled scholars is the view of including the logic and epistemology of Dharmakīrti under the phenomenal or worldly or empirical (as the idealists and absolutists call it) in contrast with ultimate reality. This seems to be a misunderstanding. Dharmakīrti's account of *samyagjñāna* (correct knowledge) and the apprehension of ultimate reality (*paramārtha=svalakṣaṇa*) through sensation (*pratyakṣa*) proves that he composed his epistemological treatises having *paramārtha* in mind; that is the attainment of all human goals (*sarva-pursuṣārtha*). Does it eliminate the attainment of Nirvāṇa? On the contrary, *yogi-pratyakṣa* includes the apprehension of *anityatā* leading to knowledge of *duḥkha* and *anātman*. After achieving this stage a Yogin lives moment to moment with reality and dwells in present sensations. This technique was taught by the Buddha himself and is known as *smrt-upasthāna* or *satipaṭṭhāna* (*Pāḷi*). It should not be confused with the mystical or Brahmanical concept of *Yogi-jñāna* or the Jaina concept of *sarvajña* (omniscient). Dharmakīrti has everywhere defined the object of four kinds of sensation as *paramārtha* or *svalakṣaṇa* (*tasya viṣayaḥ svalakṣaṇam*). It means that the object being the one and the same, there is a difference of degree. What all human beings non-conceptually cognize in the first moment of bare sensation, a Yogin can retain all the time my culmination of constant meditation on the four noble truths and *svalakṣaṇa.*

All four kinds of *pratyakṣa* are devoid of imagination and illusion. Thus, the definition is applicable to all of them. If Dharmakīrti wanted to differentiate it, he would have defined it differently (as Naiyāyikas and Jainas, Akalaṅka, etc., have done). His epistemology covers both fields, worldly (*laukika*) and super-worldly (*lokottara=nirvāṇa*), negative and positive (*heya-upādeya*).

Dharmakīrti has not discussed *Nirvāṇa* in detail as the Mahāyānists do, because in the Sautrāntika tradition *Nirvāṇa* is considered only as the "*nirodha*" (cessation) of *duḥkha* (disgust), not something existing by itself. Other evidence is furnished by the beginning of logical treatises at that period in other systems. Gautama, in the very first Sūtra, reveals the purpose of *Nyāyaśāstra* as the realisation of *niḥśreyasa* (*mokṣa*=liberation, NS. 1/1/1). Vātsyāyana and Uddyotakara have explained it in detail. Dharmakīrti's treatises also reveal the same purpose, though it is different from Brahmanic *mukti* or *ātmavāda* and consists of realizing *anitya-duḥkha-anātman*. This intention is also indicated by remembering the Buddha as manifested means of knowledge or logic (*pramāṇabhūta*), which removes the possibility of its being lower.

Indirectly, the criticism by Candrakīrti of the definition of *pratyakṣa* also implies the same fact. Had Diṅnāga written his treatise from a lower or phenomenal point of view, Candrakīrti would not have criticized it, because he accepts even Brahmanical logic from the worldly point of view.

Patañjali in his *Mahābhāṣya* has provided "*lokapratyakṣa*" (*loke dṛśyate*) as the criterion for judging the truth or falsity of a doctrine, a tendency adopted by later logicians who articulated the definition of *pratyakṣa* on this very ground. Another possible cause of misunderstanding is the reliance on secondary sources, particularly non-Buddhistic, to decide the views of the original authors. It appears that some non-Buddhist critics such as Śaṃkarācārya, etc., did not study the original sources of Buddhism and collected information through secondary sources or hearsay. The case of some historians of Indian philosophy such as Mādhavācārya, etc., who apparently misrepresented some of the Buddhist scholars seems to be similar.

REFERENCES

1. This statement is very significant. It proves the authenticity of a tradition that the Kośakāra was a Vaibhāṣika before he became a Mahāyānist." *AbD*, p. 33, sup. 3.
2. *vaitulikasya ayoga-śūnyatāvādinaḥ sarvaṃ nāstīti.* ibid, pp. 257-58.
3. *tadanye vādino dārṣṭāntikavaitulikapaudgalikāḥ na yuktyāgamābhidhāyinaḥ, tarkābhimānāste. mithyāvāditvādete lokāyatikavaināśikanagnāṭapakṣe prakṣeptavyāḥ.* ibid, pp. 258-59.
4. "It is interesting to note that the Adv. here identifies the Kośakāra with the Sautrāntika." ibid, p. 33, sup. 2,
5. *atrapratyavatiṣṭhante dārstāntikāḥ-na brūmaḥ sarvathā atītaṃ na vidyate. kiṃ tarhi? dravyātamanā na vidyate prajñaptyātmanā tu saditi. Tatra pratisamādhiyate.* ibid, p. 278.
6. *yathādaśabhūmike'stamyāṃ bhūmau nirdiṣṭaḥ. Mahāyānsūtralaṅkāra* 7/4, p, 28; *yathā daśabhūmikasūtre.* ibid., 18/54, p. 137).

CHAPTER 2

Examination of Controversy on Dharmakīrti

The following is a short account of the prevailing controversial positions about Dharmakīrti's philosophical standpoint which are examined in this chapter.

A

That he is a Vijñānavādin (Idealist)—This view is expressed by Stcherbatsky[1] and some Japanese scholars[2] and is followed by most of the new scholars. The basis of reasoning behind this theory can be analyzed as follows:

A1 Because in *Santānāntarasiddhi* Dharmakīrti is supposed to call himself an idealist and Vinītadeva's commentary thereon clearly states that Dharmakīrti is a Vijñānavādin (Idealist).

A2 Historical evolution is supposed to prove that:

(*i*) Vaibhāṣtka philosophy emerged first, then Sautrāntika, then Vijñānavāda, and

(*ii*) Vasubandhu was first a Vaibhāṣika, then turned to Sautrāntika and finally embraced Vijñānavāda.[3] Therefore, Diṅnāga and Dharmakīrti were only later exponents of the Vijñānavāda school, and also—

(*iii*) Realism appears first, then Critical Realism which is followed by Idealism. This generally accepted view is supposed to prove that Vasubandhu II, Diṅnāga, and Dharmakīrti are Idealists.

A3 In *Ālambanaparīkṣā* (*AP.*) Diṅnāga is supposed to have completely discarded the reality of the external world and taken the side of Idealism.[4] As Dharmakīrti follows Diṅnāga he is bound to follow the same view.

A4 The theory of self-consciousness (*sva-samvedanavāda*) as described by Diṅnāga and Dharmakīrti is supposed to prove them Idealists.

B

That he is a Yogācāra-Sautrāntika—This is a revised view of Stcherbatsky who thought Dharmakīrti an Idealist, but found Vācaspati, etc. considering him a Sautrāntika. So he altered his view and used the new term Yogācāra-Sautrāntika for Diṅnāga and Dharmakīrti.

B1 The main reason is that fundamentally, Dharmakīrti is an Idealist, but he also follows the Sautrāntikas in many of his doctrines.

B2 Malvaniya argues that Dharmakīrti is an Idealist (Vijñānavādin) in *PV.* and a Sautrāntika in *NB.*

B3 N. C. Shah holds the view that he belonged to Sautrāntika-Yogācāra in the sense that he wanted to verify Idealism, but he has his own independent view and he made his own version of Idealism.

C

That he is a Vaibhāṣika—This view is put forward by Umesha Misra in his *History of Indian Philosophy,* in the following words: "From the treatment of *Pratyakṣa* given in this book, it seems that Dharmakrīti was a Vaibhāṣika and his Nyāyabindu is a work on logic according to the Vaibhāṣika school".[5] He does not explain the reasons behind this viewpoint, but it seems that the study of NB. created a general impression of this sort. Mādhavācārya, the author of *Sarvadarśanasaṃgraha* calls the Sautrāntika an "Indirect Perceptionalist" or "Representationalist" (*bāhyārthānumeyavāda*) and Vibhāṣika a "Direct Perceptionist" (*bāhyārthapratyakṣavāda*). Finding the later view in Dharmakīrti's *NB.* he would have upheld this opinion.

D

That he is a Mādhyamika mystic—This view is expressed by the German scholar Tilman Vetter on the ground that Darmakīrti uses terms like *Śūnyatā* or *Niḥsvabhāva* in his *PV.*, 2/208-15, proving him to be a follower of *Mādhyamika* mysticism.

E

That he is a Svatantra-Vijñānavādin—This view is uphelp by C. D. Sharma in his *Critical Survey of Indian Philosophy* which reads: "These Buddhists are generally regarded as Vijñānavādin and no distinction is made between earlier Vijñānavāda and his later form of Vijñānavāda advocated by these writers. According to us this confusion between the original Vijñānavāda of *Laṅkāvatāra,* Asaṃga, and Vasubandhu and the later development of it by these writers treated in the chapter has caused many contradictions and has, in the main, been responsible for many misunderstandings. It is, therefore, very necessary to treat these writers as belonging to separate schools which may be called 'Svatantra-Vijñānavāda,"[6] This is the only ground expressed by him.

F

That he is a Sautrāntika—The upholders of this view are Satkari-Mukerjee[7], Rāhula Sāṅkṛtyayana[8], Dasgupta, and A. K. Warder. But none of them has so far explained the grounds of this thesis, except the general impression they would have derived through the study of *NB.* and other treatises and the studies of Vācaspatimiśra, etc.

These are the prevalent controversies regarding Dharmakīrti's philosophical position which call for a thorough examination.

Examination here means the re-examination of these previous investigations made by distinguished scholars.

A1

Confusion seems to be created by Vinītadeva because an unbiased study of *Santānātarasiddhi* does not suggest that Dharmakīrti considered himself to be a Vijñānavādin. The following facts should be boserved carefully:

(*i*) The translation of the first Kārikā of *SS.*, which contains the essence of the line of argumentation of the whole book, is doubtful.

The Tibetan rendering of it is as follows:

raṅ lus blo sṅon du' gro ba yi,
bya ba mthoṅ nas gzan la de,
dinz phyir gal te blo śes' gyur
sems tsam la yaṅ tshul' di mtshuṅs.

(if observing in one's own body that one's action is preceded by intellect, one knows there is intellect elsewhere, then this method of reasoning is the same in the case of thought only).

Fortunately, the original Sanskrit of the first *śloka* (verse) is quoted by Rāmakaṇṭha in his *Nareśvaraparīkṣāvṛtti*:

buddhi-pūrvaṃ kriyaṃ dṛṣṭvā svadehe, 'nyatra tad-grahāt,
jñāyate yadi dhīś cittamātre'py eṣa nayaḥ samaḥ.

(If, having seen action preceded by intellection in one's own body, one knows there is intellect elsewhere because of understanding this scheme is the same in the case of thought only).

There is no doubt that the term "*cittamātra*" (Tib. *sems tsam*) which is generally translated as "only consciousness" has occurred in the first *śloka and sūtra.*

(*ii*) It is also worth noting that this first *śloka*, quoted in another Sanskrit work entitled "*Tattvārtharājavārttika*" presents a different reading:

buddhi-pūrvaṃ kriyāṃ dṛṣṭvā svadehe'nyatra tad grahāt,
manyate buddhi-sadbhāvaḥ, sā na yeṣu, na teṣu dhīḥ.

[Having observed action preceded by intellect in one's own body, one thinks there is real existence of intellect elsewhere because of understanding that: this intellect can neither be found here nor there [or: where that (action) is not, there intellect is not].

The first line of this śloka is the same in construction as that found in the *Nareśvaraparīkṣāvṛtti*, but the second line is different, having no "*cittamātra*" term in it. Until the original text is discovered it is not possible to decide which one of these ślokas is the original one. In such a state of insufficient evidence, to make an absolute decision that Dharmakīrti is a Vijñānavādin is not justified.

(*iii*) The Tibetan term "*sems*" (Skt., *citta*) of the first *śloka* is replaced in second, third, and fourth *Sūtras* by the term "*śes pa*" (Skt., *jñāna*) which eliminates the possibility of translating "*citta*" in the sense of Vijñānavāda. The late H. Kitagawa who has translated SS after Stcherbatsky's Russian translation, observed this fact: "In the *saṃtānāntarasiddhi* Dharmakīrti uses this word (*śes-pa=vijñapti*) in a very limited sense; he always means by this word the representations of bodily action of the moment of mind".*

There seems to be no doubt that Vinītadeva, who commented on all the works of Dharmakīrti, except *PV.* and *PVin.*, and the Mongolian Commentator Nag-dhan-hstan bar apparently, as far as the Tibetan is concerned, have mentioned, that Dharmakīrti is representing the views of Yogācāra Vijñānavād which claims that the object of cognition exists inside of us (*śes bya naṅ gi yin par smra ba*) and the opponent of Dharmakīrti is a Sautrāntika who believes that there exist real things outside of us (*phyi don du smra ba*). This distinction by commentators is non-factual and arbitrary. There is no such reading in the text.

Even if we read *cittamātra* in the first verse, it seems more natural to suppose that a Sautrāntika is here trying to convince a Vijñānavā-

*A Study of Indian Classical Logic, p. 409.

din opponent that even if only thought exists there are still other intellects than one's own (though I must say it seems a difficult theory to prove: i.e., if other people's actions are imaginary then how we can observe them unless we imagine them; in which case only our own intellect exists and we are reduced to solipsism.)

(*iv*) It is worth considering that Vinītadeva without any reason, designated Sautrāntikas as the opponents of Dharmakīrti, but in Sūtras 34 to 39 indicated Vaibhāṣikas as the opponents. This kind of classification is rather arbitrary and misleading. This type of mistake, committed by Vinītadeva is also found in his other commentaries[9]. It seems that some of the ancient scholars also wanted to satisfy their Idealistic interest by interpreting other famous scholars as belonging to their own school. Vinītadeva, particularly, has evinced this tendency in his commentary on the *Nyāyabindu* where in two places he attempted to prove that Dharmakīrti's standpoint is a reconciliation of Sautrāntika and Vijñānavāda.

In one place while interpreting the term "*samyagjñāna*" (correct knowledge) Vinītadeva asserts:

eṣa samāsārthaḥ anvayārthaḥ tu samyagjñāna-pūrvikā itiatra avisaṃvādakaṃ jñānaṃ samyagjñānam, artha-kriyāyāṃ yad avisaṃvādakaṃ tad abhrāntaṃ tad eva ca samyagjñānaṃ. anyathā prakaraṇena yogācāranaya-nirāsaḥ syāt. iṣṭaḥ ca prakarṇārambhaḥ sautrāntika-yogācārobhaya-nayānudhāvanārthaṃ tasmād ubhaya-naya saṃgrahād avisaṃvādakaṃ jñānaṃ eva samyagjñānaṃ iti bodhyaṃ. (Recon. from Tib).*

[This is the meaning taking it as a whole, but its meaning in parts (will be stated). In the expression 'preceded by right cognition' (*samyagjñāna-pūrvikā*), right cognition means knowledge which is not contradicted (*avisaṃvādaka*), knowledge which is not contradicted in an action in respect of an object (*arthakriyā*) is non-erroneous (*abhrānta*). That is the right cognition, otherwise the treatise would lead to the repudiation of the Yogācāra view. But this treatise is going to be composed with the intention of explaining the views of both the Sautrāntika and the Yogācāra. Therefore, right knowledge here is to be understood (particularly) as knowledge which is not contradicted, because it covers the views of both.]

In another place, while giving his own interpretation of the term "non-illusory" (*abhrantā*) of the definition of sensation (*pratyakṣa*) he states:

**Nyayabindutika*, (*NBT*(*V*) ed. by Mrinal Kanti Gangopādhyāya, p. 7.

kasmād viśeṣaṇadvayaṃ uktaṃ iti cet? ucyate. timiravato bhrāntajñāna-vyavaccheārthaṃ abhrāntaṃ iti uktaṃ. kalpanāpoḍhaṃ iti ca anumāna-vyavacchedārtham uktaṃ. evaṃ abhrāntatvaṃ prāpaka-viṣaye upādeyaṃ na tu ālambanavisaye. yadi ālambanaviṣaye abhrāntatvaṃ abhyupa-gamyate tarhi atra yogācāra-nayanirāsaḥ syāt. yogācāra hi sarvaṃ ālambanajñānaṃ bhrāntaṃ manyante, tataśca prakaraṇārambhaḥ tannaya-nirākaraṇārthaḥ syāt. iṣṭaḥ ca prakaraṇārambhaḥ sautrāntika-yogācārobhaya-matānudhāvanārthaṃ. prāpaka-viṣaye avisaṃvadaka-lakṣaṇaṃ abhrāntatvaṃ ca ubhayānumataṃ eva. (Recon. from Tib.)* [What is the purpose of mentioning that two expressions qualify (knowledge)? The answer is as follows: The expression "non-illusory" is mentioned to exclude having morbid vision (*timira*), the expression "devoid of imagination" is to exclude inference. However, the expression "non-illusory" is to be understood in respect of (the knowledge that makes one reach (the object), and not in respect of "support" (of a cognition) (*ālambana-viṣaya*). If the expression "non-illusory" is admitted to be in respect of the "support" (of a cognition), it would lead to the repudiation of the Yogācāra view; because in the Yogācāra view, all cognitions (so far as they refer) to any "support" (of a cognition) are false (i.e., no object as underlying a cognition does actually exist). And thus, the composition of the treatise would result in the repudiation of the above view. But the treatise is going to be composed with the intention of explaining the views of both the Sautrāntiko and Yogācāre. The expression "non-illusory" in the sense of "not contradicted" in respert of (the knowledge) that makes one reach object is, however, acceptable to both].**

These interpretations clearly indicate Vinītadeva' forceful inclination towards Idealism. Why would Dharmakīrti be vchement in refuting Sautrāntika in *SS* and yet take the side of the Sautrāntika in *NB* and all his other works? Why is this change not even noticed by Dharmakīrti's critics? Dharmakīrti nowhere expresses this intention. Definitely it is Vinītadeva's own interpretation which has been misleading scholars. Now we can check it against the recently discovered commentary of Durvekamiśra, who criticizes in the following words:

na yogācāranaye lakṣaṇamidam kintu sautrāntikanaya eva.
na ca sarvam vijñānavāde yojayitum śakyam. "tasya viṣayaḥ svalak-

*NBT (V), pp. 7.
**ibid. 7.

*ṣaṇam" ityāderaśakyayojanatvāt, taṣmin kiṃ pratyakṣalakṣaṇam iti kalpanāpoḍhatvameva.**

[This definition (of sensation) is not from the Yogācāra point of view, but only from the Sautrāntika point of view. And (one) cannot make everything consistent with Vijñanavāda. "Its object is particular", etc. can never be consistent with it. What then is the definition of sensation (*pratyakṣa*) in it? Only to be devoid of imagination.]

Had this important commentary of Durveka been discovered at the time of Stcherbatsky, he would never have been misled by Vinītadeva's misinterpretation.

It is also interesting to note that Stcherbatsky himself opposes his own observations.

In one place he asserts: "The solution of the problem of Solipsism by Dharmakīrti in his *Santānāntarasiddhi* is that, from the point of view of absolute reality, there is only one spiritual principle undivided into subject and object, and therefore, no plurality of individual existences. But from the empirical point of view there are necessarily other personalities existing in the world, just as there are external objects existing and cognized by the two sources of our knowledge, sense-perception and inference, as they are characterized in Dignāga's and his own epistemological system. Nevertheless, he himself calls his view idealism (Vijñānavāda and Yogācāra) and maintains that an idealist can speak about other personalities and an external world just as a realist does but for the sake of precision he ought to speak not about others personalities, but about "his representations" of other minds; to speak of other minds is only an abbreviation. Our ideas, in this system, are not cognitions of reality, but constructions or dreams about reality. They are indirect cognitions just as dreams are, since dreams are also conditioned by former real experiences, but feebly recollected in a morbid state of mind."**

But in another place he presents a different observation: "But this raises the following question. Dharmakīrti specifically calls himself an Idealist, for whom 'there exists only the representations': there are no external objects, and 'everything cognizable lies inside us'." On the other hand, he agrees that sensibility gives us true knowledge, that in an individual moment of sensibility, we have sensation of reality, cognition of what is truly real. This would appear to mean

**Dharmottarapradīpa* (*Pradīpa*), p. 44.

***BL*, II, p. 370.

that in these moments of sensibility, our cognition is concerned with the external material world, lying outside us. This is how many understood the teaching of Dharmakīrti. The author of *tippaṇi** speaks directly that on this point, Dharmakīrti digresses from the point of view of later idealism and accepts the viewpoint of the Realists—"The Sautrāntikas".**

The following are further considerations which are sufficient to prove *SS* a Sautrāntika work:

(*a*) The whole text is mainly an answer to the Vaibhāṣikas position that the real existence of other streams of thought may be inferred on the ground of an external reason (*bāhyaliṅga*); while Dharmakīrti proves the same on the ground of an internal reason (*āntarikaliṅga*). The debate is not between a philosopher who denies the existence of an other stream of thought, and one who affirms it; but between two kinds of realists, (Vaibhāṣika-Sautrāntika), who both infer the existence of other streams of thought, but according to different reasons.

(*b*) The opinion that *SS* is written from the conventional standpoint, cannot be supported by evidence. Dharmakīrti has given no indication in the *SS* directly or indirectly that such was his intention. On the contrary, Dharmakīrti strongly advocates, without qualifying it as *samvṛtti* (conventional), the Sautrantīka doctrine of other streams of thought.

(*c*) Dharmakīrti makes no mention of Vijñānavādin doctrines, even when there are occasions to discuss them, such as *ālayavijñāna*, *kliṣṭamanovijñāna*, but refers to the doctrines of dominant cause factor *adhipatipratyaya*, *SS* 63), and subconscious residue (*vāsanāśakti*, *SS* 65) which are well known in the Sautrāntika tradition.

(*d*) The Sautrāntika doctrine of "*arthakriyākāritva*" (*SS* 74-76, 85-86), which Dharmakīrti takes as a criterion to judge the validity of the inference of other minds is the same as in *Hetubindu*, *PV.*, *NB.*, etc.

(*e*) Theory of causation (*kāraṇa*, *SS* 12) is the same that of the other treatises.

(*f*) Dharmakīrti's main opponents are the Vaibhāṣikas as indicated by his refutation of the peculiar doctrines of dreams (*SS* 34, 29) Stcherbatsky states: "The Vaibhāṣikas even denied the existence

**Bibliotheca Buddhica*, XI, pp. 18-19.

***Papers of Stcherbatsky*, trans. by H.C. Gupta, p. 78.

of images in dreams. They tried to prove that even in dreams we somehow perceive real external objects. Thus their theory is ridiculed by Dharmakīrti in his *Santānāntarasiddhi*. The *saṃjā* was considered by them as external (*viṣaya*) to pure consciousness (*Vijñāna*)"* There is no indication of a Sautrāntika being the opponent as stated by Vinītadeva.**

(*g*) Even the perception of Yogins (*SS* 92-93) in regard to others minds is defined as a subtle kind of inference, which is the same as in *PV* 2/258-82, and in *NB* 1/10. It is different from the Vijñānavādin concept (*Viṃśatikā*, 19).

(*h*) Dharmakīrti has also discussed the question of "inference of other minds" (*paracittānumānaṃ*) in his *PV* 2/477-84, in connection with self-conscious sensation (*svasamvedanapratyakṣa*) of the objeet (*artha*) as well as the intellect (*buddhi*) simultaneously on the ground of his theory of correspondence (*sārūpya*). He also answers the objection by giving the example of lamp and pitcher (*dīpaghaṭayoḥ*), which signifies both illuminator and illumined (*prakāśaka-prakāśya=vyañjaka-vyaṅgya*) simultaneously. Dharmakīrti clearly indicates:

paracittānumānam ca na syādatmanyadarśanāt,
*sambandhasya, manobuddhāvarthalingāprasiddhitaḥ.****

[There would not be an inference of other's thought if the relation were not seen in oneself, because the relation between object-reason is not established in the case of mind-intellect.]

Dharmakīrti's answer—

1. Because the matter passes into the light (self-consciousness).†

2. Because the object is cognised through this form (correspondence through self-consciousness),†† such as lamp-pitcher (*dīpaghaṭā*) in which one is the illuminator (lamp), and the other is illumined (pitcher). Similarly, in the connection of knowledge (*jñāna*) and the object (*artha*), one is the illuminator (knowledge) and the other is the illumined (object). In the process of "inference of other streams of thought" the same criterion (correspondence through self-consciousness) should be applied. It is the same as in the *SS*. All this internal evidence indicates that the *SS* is a Sautrāntika work.

**BL.*, II, p. 377.
***PVB.*, 3/193, p. 278.
****PV.*, 2/477.
†*prakāśe rupasamkramāt*, *PV.*, 2/479b.
††*arthastadarūpeṇa prakāśate*, *PV*. 2/482d.

(i) Indirectly, the evidence derived from Ratnakīrti's *Santānāntaradūṣaṇa* (Refutation of other streams of thought) also supports this view. Ratnakīrti (a Sākāravādin Vijñānavādin) following the line of Prajñākaragupta (Mādhyamika Yogācāra) assumes that *SS* is only from the phenomenal (*samvṛtti*) point of view. Yuichi Kajiyama, who has translated Ratnakīrti's work has also put forward the same view. Kajiyama favors the idealistic point of view: "This kind of Sautrāntika's criticism of the Vijñānavāda is found in: *Bhāmatī*... The idealists had much to say against this criticism, but I cannot discuss it in detail."*

He is also of the opinion that Ratnakīrti's opponent is not a Sautrāntika, but a Vijñānavādin though the argument is that of a Sautrāntika as found in the *SS*: "This argument is similar to that of Sautrāntika found in the very beginning of Dharmakīrti's *Saṁtānāntarasiddhi*. But here this proof of the existence of other people's minds is proposed by a Vijñānavādin. In our present work Ratnakīrti's opponent is not a Sautrāntika, but a Vijñānavādin."** These references indicate that Y. Kajiyama, although convinced that the *SS*. is written by a Vijñānavādin, grants that the actual argument is that of a Sautrāntika.

Kajiyama himself has established, in 'The Atomic Theory of Vasubandhu, the author of the *Abhidharmakośa*'† that Vasubandhu of *AbkB*. proves the doctrine of the assemblage of atoms (*aṇusañcayavāda*) and causal efficiency (*arthakriyākāritva*): "This can be understood only when we note that for Vasubandhu the criterion of reality or existence is causal efficiency (*kāraṇabhāva—śakti*). An atom and the aggregate of the same kind of atoms are both real because the two are different not in essence but only in grade."††

Dharmakīrti has used the same line of argumentation in his *SS* (above d), which indicates it to be a Sautrāntika work.

A2

The reasons (generally believed by modern scholars) are based on historical and psychological evolution:

1. The criticism of the Vaibhāṣika gave rise to the Sautrāntika,

*Buddhist Solipsism, *Journal of Indian and Buddhist Studies*, XIII, no. 1, p. 434, 2.

**ibid., 14, pp. 13-14n.

†*Journal of Indian and Buddhist Studies*, pp. 19-25.

††ibid., p. 24.

which in turn led to Vijñānavāda or Vasubandhu's own philosophical stages of evolution.

2. The Vaibhāṣika Vasubandhu became the Sautrāntika Vasubandhu, and who became the Vijñānavādin Vasubandhu through the development of his philosophical doctrines.

3. Realism produces Critical Realism, which produces Idealism.

This view does not seem to represent genuine historical and psychological facts.

The following are the reasons which oppose this particular trend of supposed evolution:

1. Historically, Vijñānavāda appeared after Mādhyamika as a reaction against its extreme position. The Sautrāntika movement was a reaction against the Vaibhāṣikas. Both seem to have different grounds of origin which can be truly understood through the following diagram:

TWO TRADITIONS

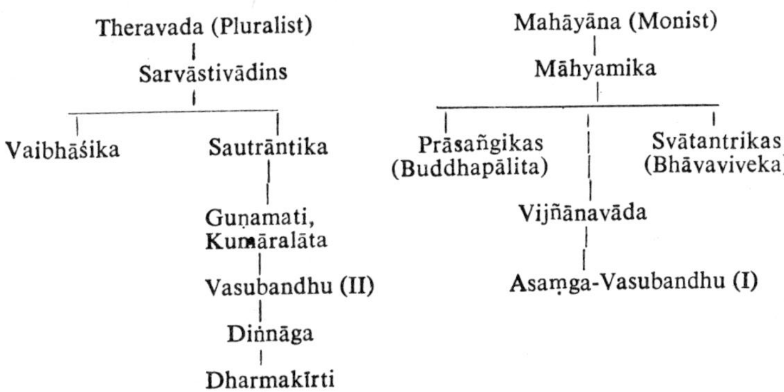

The main reason for the above confusion is the lack of understanding of the two separate trends of evolution and the belief in the theory of only one Vasubandhu who changed his position from Vaibhāśika to Sautrāntrika, and then to Vijñānavāda.

Another ground which strengthens our interpretation is discovered through the critics of Diṅnāga and Dharmakīrti, the Jaina philosophers Mallavādin and Śrī Siṃhasūri who while criticizing Diṅnāga have mentioned *paramāṇu samudāyavāda* or *dausthalyavāda* (doctrine of the assemblage of atoms). They also criticize Vasubandhu (II) as tending to maintain a conceptual or illusory formation of atoms, on the ground that if atoms do not connect but create a gross form by coming nearer, then this appearance which affects the senses is itself either a conceptual formation or an illusory appearance. Had Diṅnāga denied the existence of atoms categorically, this criticism would never have occurred, and Jaina critics would have not compared it with *AbkB*. Similarly, Diṅnāga in *PS*, while criticizing Mādhava's view praises his mode of thinking on atoms: "Therefore, from the dethroning of the view of the older Sāṃkhyas, Mādhava's doctrine ('the possession—by atoms—of each having its own nature') is excellent."* Had Diṅnāga disbelieved in atoms absolutely why, instead of criticizing, does he praise Mādhava's view of the atom, even though he criticizes his doctrines: "(However, the doctrine) that the three (*guṅas*) from that (atom) which possesses only one quality, is not (excellent)."*

This implies that Diṅnāga did believe in atoms, though his conception was different from those of Nyāya, Vaiśeṣika, Vaibhāṣika, and others, but in agreement with that of the Sautrāntika Vasubandhu.**

This thesis is also strengthened by Dharmakīrti's understanding of Diṅnāga's view. Dharmakīrti explained it on the ground that the gross form is not something different from the atom and that atoms always exist not separately, but in a gross "accumulated" or "collective" form (*sañcita* or *samudāya*). If Dharmakīrti denied that there were atoms, then why did he defend it? The only possible answer is that they do believe in "*aṇusamudāya*" and discard the individual atom or combination of atoms as an object of consciousness (*ālambana*). The object of consciousness does not exist in reality, but the object of the senses (*svalakṣaṅa*) does. Consciousness (*vijñāna*) operates on the basis of mental categories, memory, names, etc., and has no corresponding reality, such as a combination of atoms (*aṇusaṃghāta*), substance (*dravya*), universal (*sāmānya* or *jāti*) etc. Aṇusañcayavāda, as criticized by Diṅnāga (*AP.*) is the view of Vāgbhaṭa and others and differs from his own (*aṇusamudāyavāda*. It would appear that it is the predisposed hasty comparison of Diṅnāga with the Vijñānavādin Vasubandhu (I) that has caused this mistaken interpretation. Similarly, the *Sambandhaparīkṣā* of Dharmakīrti can also be misinterpreted as Idealistic in trend. Dharmakīrti examines all kinds of relations and finds them not existing in reality. Nyāya, Vaiśeṣika, Mīmāṃsā, etc. believed in relations like *samyoga* (joining),

**Diṅnāga on Perception*, p. 59.
**ibid., p. 59.

samavāya (inherence), etc. as existing. Dharmakīrti clearly mentions that the atoms are not 'related' to each other.

2. In Chapter 1, I have discussed in detail the identification of Vasubandhu II. Diṅnāga refers to *AbkB* and *Vādavidhānaṃ* of Vasubandhu and never to *Vijñāptimātratāsiddhi* and *Madhyāntavibhaṅgabhāṣya*, etc. Had he been a pupil of Vasubandhu who was converted to the Mahāyāna, *Vijñāvāda* he should have referred to, or relied upon the last works of his master rather than the earlier ones which he must have rejected as belonging to either the Vaibhāṣika or the Sautrāntika schools. The solution of this enigma can consistently be solved only by accepting the fact that the Vasubandhu referred to by Diṅnāga is the second one.

3. The third part of this argument also turns out to be non-factual when analyzed carefully. History does not provide us with a basis to believe that Realism brings about Critical Realism and Critical Realism leads to Idealism. In the evolution of Buddhist philosophy, Sarvāstivāda (Realism) was opposed by Mādhyamika as well as by the early Sautrāntikas simultaneously. Mādhyamika scepticism (particularly the Prāsaṅgika interpretation) brought about the Svātantrikas on one side and the Vijñānavādins on the other. Vijñānavāda was criticized by Mādhyamikas and by various schools of realists. The supposed evolution sometimes seems in this respect to be reversed.

A3

The argument based on *Ālambanaparīkṣā* of Diṅnāga also needs an examination. It is generally presumed that Diṅnāga's Idealistic position is well established by his categorical refutation of the external world in *AP*. The term "*ālambana*" is translated as "object" and the work is taken to refute external objects. As Dharmakīrti follows Diṅnāga, he too is then bound to be an Idealist. But the treatment of *ālambana*, if carefully analyzed, seems to relate to "object" in the sense of the object of consciousness (*vijñānālambana*) not that of the object of the senses (*indriya-viṣaya*—unique particulars=*svalakṣaṇas*).

Diṅnāga in *AP*. accepts the atom as a cause of consciousness but not as its object. He holds:

"*yadyapīndriyavijñapteḥ kāraṇaṃ paramāṇavaḥ,*
atadābhātayā nāsyā akṣavad viṣayo' ṇavaḥ"*

**AP*., 1/1, ref. also in *PVB*., p. 336.

[Though atoms serve as causes of the making of consciousness (*vijñāpti*) through the sense-organs, they are not its actual object (*viṣaya*), because it (consciousness) does not represent the images of atoms as in the case of the sense of sight.]

Diṅnāga further mentions: "Though the atoms of a pot are greater in number and those of a cup less, there exists no distinction whatever amongst the atoms".* All this evidence indicates that Diṅnāga did not deny absolutely the existence of the atom, but only denied the atom as the object of consciousness (*ālambana*).

The verification of this fact is duly found in Diṅnāga's monumental work *PS.*, where he explains his views about atoms on the ground of the Abhidharma tradition. His reference to *AbkB.* and *Vijñānakāyapāda's* doctrine of assemblage of atoms as object of five sensory cognitions (*sañcitālambanā pañcavijñānakāyāḥ*) and his division between *dravya-svalakṣaṇa* (atomic particular), and *āyatanasvalakṣaṇa* (sensory particular) on the same ground proves that he was following the Sautrāntika Abhidharma tradition of Vasubandhu (II) who, though he believed in atoms did not believe in their actual combination. Such a view is quite different from that of the Vijñānavādins, who denied the very existence of atoms. Vasubandhu (I) in his *Viṃśatikā* and *Trimṣikā* particularly and categorically denied all views which accepted atoms. This denial should not be confused with Diṅnāga's view, otherwise it will lead to the view that Diṅnāga himself-committed self-contradiction by refuting his *AP* in *PS.* If so, then why was it not noticed by Uddyotakāra or Vācaspati and why do they call him categorically a Sautrāntika?

In reality Dharmakīrti believed relations to be mere mental categories. He argues that in the case that everything is momentary or in a constant flow no relation is possible between particulars. Dharmakīrti has rightly observed "because of the non-eternality of the things related, no eternal relation is possible" (*saṃbandhīnāṃ anityatvānnasaṃbandhesti nityatā, PV.* 3/232ab). What is real for Dharmakīrti is a burst of energy or flow of atoms (*svalakaṣaṇas*) which are unrelated to each other. But Dharmakīrti, while discussing inference which deals with a universal (*sāmānya*) based on particulars (*svalakṣaṇa*) speaks about three types of mental categories. i.e., characteristics (*lakṣaṇas*) of identity, causality, and non-apprehension (*tādātmya, kārya, anupalabdhi*) which make the definitive indirect cognition

** *AP.*, p. 5.

(*anumāna*) of a particular thing possible.[11] But for the direct cognition (*pratyakṣa*) which is fundamental, no such characteristic is needed. Dharmakīrti's explanation is based on the Sautrāntika Vasubandhu's explanation in *AbkB.* where he criticized different kinds of entities of relation like *nikāyasabhāgatā* (universal), *prāpti* (possession), *vijñapti* (making of consciousness), etc. and explained the process of knowledge from the Sautrantika point of view. Diṅnāga and Dharmakīrti have explained it epistemologically and logically.

A4

Another major ground on which Dharmakīrti is ranked as an Idealist is the theory of self-consciousness (*svasaṃvedanavāda*). It is a fact that Diñnāga and Dharmakīrti have expounded the view that every cognition of an object is always self-conscious, or that knowledge has a double aspect, cognition and cognition of cognition, and does not need any other agent (such as a soul) to make its cognition. It is like a light which reveals other objects and at the same time reveals its own existence and so does not require any other light to reveal it. The knowledge of blue and the knowledge that it is blue are not two different things, but two aspects of one process. Dharmakīrti elaborates on this view in two contexts:

a. while dealing with the four-fold nature of sensation (*pratyakṣa*) and

b. while refuting the Nyāya-Mimāṃsā theory of a difference between a source of valid cognition (*pramāṇa*) and a result of cognition (*pramāṇa-phala*).

Both Stcherbatky and M. Hattori concluded on this ground that Dharmakīrti belonged to Idealism. But they have neglected one important fact; that the Sautrāntika school also had the theory of *sva-samvedanavāda* (self-consciousness)*, and Diṅnāga and Dharmakīrti were epistemologically elaborating this. There is no doubt that the Vijñānavādins also believed in it, and both Diṅnāga and Dharmakīrti agreed with Vijñānavāda on this particular issue. Reconciliation on this particular point is not conclusive in proving a thesis that Diṅnāga and Dharmakīrti belonged to the Vijñānavāda school. This fact of reconciliation, on the contrary, may prove that their fundamental position was sautrāntika, although it also happened to agree with Vijñānavāda on this particular point. In the case that they were

**AbkB.*, II/46, *Sphutārthā*, p. 257.

Vijñānavādins, why did they want to reconcile their position with Vijñānavāda? Why did they not talk of reconciliation on the other issues? An argument for concurrence on one issue implies difference on other issues and two different fundamental positions, It is also interesting to note that the evidence of *PS* and *PV* mentions this reconciliation at the end, i.e., after explaining their own (Sautrāntika) position. Had they been Vijñānavādins their own position would have come first and their reconciliation with that of the Sautrāntika later.

Though Diṅnāga and Dharmakīrti reconciled their position with Vijñānavāda on the unity of *pramāṇa* (source of valid cognition) and *pramāṇa-phala* (result of valid cognition), and on *svasaṃvedanavāda*, (their difference from it was revealed by their doctrine of "*sarūpya*" (correspondence) between the object and self-conscious cognition. The relation of correspondence (*sārūpyaśambandha*) is not mentioned by the Vijñānavādins and can only be possible from the Sautrāntika point of view. This has been accepted and discussed not by the Vijñānavādins, but by the Sautrantika Vasubandhu II, Diṅnāga, and Dharmakırti in detail. Coordination between an object and conscious eognition is quite consistent for them while the Vijñānavādins believed that this object is a mere appearance (*viṣayābhāsa*) of consciousness, and no question of *sārūpyasambandha* arises. Secondly, the Sautrāntikas did not admit the ability (*yogyatā*) of a cognition to cognize own appearance or *svābhāsa* but understood it as not different in meaning from *sārūpya* or *svasaṃvitti*, and because of that they agreed with the Vijñānavadins. Though the evidence of *ŚVV* quoted by M. Hattori itself proves this difference of standpoint, he concludes: "However, Diṅnāga justifies th Sautrāntika view by regarding *sārūpya* (*viṣayākāratā*) as the *pramāṇa* by means of which an external object is cognized.".* But the case may be different, viz. Diṅnāga, after explaining the Sautrāntika viewpoint, may be justifying the Vijñānavāda point of view also. As it is clear by Hattori's reference to *ŚVV*:

*ye'pi sautrāntika-pakṣam evaṃ vyācakṣate bāhyo 'rthaḥ prameyaṃ, vijñānasya viṣayākāratāpramāṇaṃ, svasaṃvittiḥ phalamiti,...idānīṃ, yogācāra-pakṣe' pi...teṣāṃ caitad darśanaṃ bāhyārtho nāsti: vijñānasya viṣayākāratā prameyā; svākāratā pramāṇaṃ, sva-saṃvittiḥ phalaṃ iti.***

**Diṅnāga on Perception*, p. 102, ref. 1.61.
***ŚVV*. p. 139.

[Those who maintain the Sautrāntika position, that the external object is the object of cognition (assemblage of atoms), the form of the object is the validity of consciousness, the self-consciousness is its result...Now in the Yogācāra position also...this is their opinion: There is no external object, the form of an object of consciouness is the object of cognition, the fact of being its own form is the means of knowledge, validity self-consciousness is the result (of cognition).]

And again the Sautrāntika view:

yaditūcyate...dvirūpaṃ ekaṃ eva jñānaṃ svasaṃvittyā viṣayākāraḥ pramāṇaṃ.

[If it is said...two forms are one cognition only, the form of the object is valid through self-consciousness.]

On this Hattori strangely comments:

"Both *ŚVK* and *NR* regard K. 9 as expressing the Sautrāntika thought and K. 10 the Yogācāra view. (As noted above, they reverse the order of K. 9ab. and K. 9cd.). This interpretation, it seems to me, is irrelevant."*

As a matter of fact, the order of Mīmāṃsaka critics is not irrelevant. It is consistent with Diṅnāga's own position in K. 9 and his justification of the Yogācāra view in K. 10. Hattori, prior to this strange comment, quotes Vibhūti who, deriving his views from Devendrabuddhi, the direct disciple of Dharmakīrti, clearly asserts the Sautrāntika view first and its agreement with the Vijñānavāda later:

*Sautrāntika—pramāṇaṃ sārūpyaṃ bāhyo'rthaḥ prameyo'dhigati phalaṃ vyavasthāpyādhunā vijñaptau pramāṇa-phala-vyavasthāṃ nirdidikṣuḥ "sva-saṃvittiḥ..." iti.***

[After establishing correspondence as (its) validity, the object of cognition as the external object, the result as cognition; now in idealism (Vijñānavāda) the valid cognition and result arrangement are described as "self-cognition"...].

This reference goes contrary to Hattori's view of the justification of the Sautrāntika standpoint. The order clearly shows that after establishing the Sautrāntika position, he attempts to agree with the Vijñānavāda point of view on this particular issue only.

The reason behind Hattori's criticism of this order seems to be his firm conviction that Diṅnāga was an Idealist. Of course, there

Dignāga on Perception, p. 103.

**Ibid., p. 102.

are in Diṅnāga's treatise ambiguous passages which are conducive to bringing about conflicting point of view. Diṅnāga mentions '*svābhāsa*' (own-appearance), "*viṣayābhāsa*" (objective-appearance), and "*ubhayābhāsasya sva-saṃvedanaṃ*" (self-consciousness of (both) appearances). There is no doubt that Diṅnāga has used these terms in his *vṛtti* but, nevertheless, this fact is undeniable, that there the meaning may be from the theory of correspondence (*sārūpya*) point of view.

This point is noticed by Dharmottara and Durvekamiśra also. While commenting on "*artha-sārūpyamasya pramāṇaṃ*" (its correspondence with the object is (its) validity) (*NB*, 1/20), Dharmottara clarifies "*tacca sārūpyaṃ sādṛśyaṃ ākāra ityābhāsa ityapi vyapadiśyate.*" [This correspondence is similarity, also described as an "*ākāra*" (form) or appearance (of object) (*viṣayābhāsa*).] Durvekamiśra points out the contradiction in this usage: *nanu cānyatra viṣayābhāsaḥ pramāṇamuktastathā viṣayākāraḥ. iha tu arthasārūpyaṃ tat kathaṃ na vyāghātaḥ ityāśaṅkyāhatacceti, ca yasmādavadhāraṇe vā. ityapyanena śabdena arthasārūpyameva tena tena śabdenābhihitaṃ tato na vyāghāta ityabhiprāyaḥ.**

[In one place, appearance of the object and form of the object is mentioned as *pramāṇa*, here only correspondence with the object, then why is there no contradiction? Creating this doubt, (Dharmottara) answers: "because of that", *ca* means because or it is in the sense of limitation, by this word also only the correspondence with the object is meant by those words, therefore there is no contradiction, this is the meaning].

Therefore, these terms do not indicate Diṅnāga's position as Idealistic. Diṅnāga himself used the term "*tad-rūpa*" (that form) which does not mean *svasaṃvittirūpa*, as interpreted by Hattori, but has the sense of *jñānasthābhāsa-rūpa-viṣayākārarūpa=viṣayākāra* (form of the (object) as understood by Śāntarakṣita and Kamalaśīla:

yady ākāraṃ anādṛtya prāmāṇyam ca prakalpyate,
arthakriyā avisaṃvādāt "tad-rūpo hy arthaniścayaḥ"
ityādi gaditaṃ sarvaṃ kathaṃ na vyāhataṃ bhavet,
vāsanāpākahetūtthastasmāt saṃvāda-saṃbhavaḥ. (*TS.*, 1327-28).

[If, without regard to the form of things, validity were presumed on the ground of mere compatibility with fruitful action, then how would this not contradict such assertions (of yours) as that "the definite cognition of the object has in the form of it (thing)?" As regards the

**Pradipa*, p. 81.

possibility of "compatibility", that can only be the result of the impression (of a previous cognition)].

naiva hi arthakriyā avisaṃvāditva-mātreṇākāramanapekṣya prāmāṇyaṃ kalpanīyaṃ, viṣayākārasyāprāmāṇya prasaṃgāt. tadrūpa iti jñānasthābhāsarūpaḥ 'ādi' śabdena yathā yathā hi arthasyākāraḥ śubhrāditvena sanniviśate tadrūpaḥ sa viṣayaḥ pramīyate ityādikaṃ ācāryīyaṃ vacanaṃ viruddhyata iti darśayati. arthakriyāsamvādastu pūrvārthānubhavavāsanāparipākādeva pramāṇāntarād bhavatītyavaseyaṃ. (TSP)

[Validity cannot be presumed merely on the basis of the compatibility of effective action, without regard to the form; as in that case the cognition in the form of the object itself might have to be regarded as invalid. "In the form of that" means the form that appears in the cognition. By the term "etc.", it is pointed out that such assertions of Ācārya (Diṅnāga) as: "As the form of the object, i.e., white and so on, figures in the cognition, sense obiect is rightly cognised as having the form of that" will be contradicted. As regards "compatibility with effective action", (in the case) in question, it should be understood to be from another means of knowledge, the result of the impression left by previous experiences of objects.]*

This seems to be a consistent understanding of Diṅnāga's Sautrāntika position. Hattori himself seems to be aware of this and comments: "This interpretation shows the Sautrāntika tendency. In fact, Kamalaśīla quotes from the *Vṛtti* the passage explaining the Sautrāntika thought, without referring to Diṅnāga's explanation of the Yogācāra view."[9] Why does Hattori neglect the fact that Diṅnāga's main position was that of a Sautrāntika rather than a Vijñānavādin? Diṅnāga's main ground is the nature of reality and he mentions "*nirvyāpārāḥ sarvadharmā iti*" (all elements are actionless). This view is in conformity with the Sautrāntika Vasubandhu's explanation of a doctrine of momentariness which is consistent with the Sautrāntika tradition rather than with the Vijñānavāda which believes in "*asaṃskṛta dharmas*" (uncomposed elements), and other eternal entities. Let us investigate further the arguments of Śāntarakṣita and Kamalaśīla:

*These translations from *TS* (*P*) are based on G.N. Jha's, but with some corrections, and substituting the equivalents for technical terms used in this book.

[9]*Dignāga on Perception*, p. 103.

na vyavasthāśrayatvena sādhyasādhanasaṃsthitiḥ,
nirākāre tu vijñāne sā saṃsthā na hi yujyate. (*TS.*, 1345).

[The distinction of "probandum and the proof" does not rest upon the substratum of that distinction; cognition being formless, the said distinction cannot be possible.]

nīlasyedaṃ saṃvedanaṃ na pītasyeti viṣayādhigati vyavasthāyā artha-sārūpyaṃ eva nibandhanaṃ, nānyatiti vyavasthāpyavyavasthāpaka-bhāvena sādhyasādhanavyavasthā, notpadyotpādakabhāvena' yasmān, na pāramārthikaḥ kartṛkāraṇādibhāvo'sti kṣaṇikatvena nirvyāpāratvāt sarvadharmāṇāṃ. jñānaṃ hi viṣayākāraṃ utpadyamānaṃ viṣayaṃ paric-chiṇdadiva savyāpāramivābhāti tasmāt sākārameva jñānaṃpramāṇaṃ na nirākāraṃ. (*TSP*).

[The apprehension of blue is not the apprehension of yellow, this distinction in the cognition of sense-objects is based upon the correspondence with the object, nothing else; so that the distinction of probandum and proof is made through the relation of what is distinguished and what distinguishes, not through the relation of the produced; and the producer; because the relation of the acting agent, the instrument and the rest is not real; because all elements being momentary, they cannot have any action. When the cognition is produced in the form of the sense object, it appears to be characterising the sense object, and hence active...Therefore, it is the cognition with a form which is valid, not the formless cognition].

The doctrine of monentariness was the kernel of the Sautrāntika doctrine. On this very ground, they refuted the so-called enternal entities of the Vaibhāṣikas and the Vijñānavādins. Diṅnāga and Dharmakīrti (*yat sat tadanityaṃ*) identified it with reality itself and whatever was not ṁomentary was discarded. Śāntarakṣita and Kamalaśīla further proceeded to clarify the enigma:

viṣayādhigataścātra pramāṇaphalaṃ iṣyate,
svavittir vā pramāṇaṃ tu sārūpya-yogyatāpi vā. (*TS.*, 1343)

[The cognition of the sense object is held to be the "fruit" of the means of cognition, or apprehension of itself (is the fruit), or the means, in this case, consists of correspondence.]

bahye'rthe prameye viṣayādhigamaḥ pramāṇaphalaṃ, sārūpyaṃ tu pramāṇaṃ. svasaṃvittāvapi satyām yathākarāmasya prathanāt. jñānā-tmani tu prameye, svasaṃvittiḥ phalam, yogyatā pramāṇam. (*TSP*)

[When the external object is what is cognised, then the cognition of that sense object is the fruit of the means, and correspondence is the means of the cognition; as even in the case self-cognition, the cognition is of the same form as what is cognised. When the knowledge itself is what is cognised, then the cognition of itself is the fruit, and capability is the means of the cognition.

At the end of chapter "examination of the definition of sensation" (*pratyakṣalakṣaṇaparīkṣā*) Śānlarakṣita clearly differentiates two standpoints; firstly that of the Sautrāntika then of the Vijñānavādins:

kintu bāhyārthasadbhāvavāde sārūpyasaṃbhavaḥ,
dhruvamabhyupagantavya ityarthaṃ sa prakāśitaḥ.
nirbhāsijñānapakṣe hi grāhyād bhede'pi cetasaḥ,
pratibimbasya tādrūpyād bhāktaṃ syād api vedanam.
yena tu iṣṭam na vijñānaṃ arthasārūpyabhājanaṃ,
tasyāyaṃ api naivāsti prakāro bāhyavedane. (*TS.* 1358-60).

[But under doctrine of the reality of the external object, the possibility of sameness of form has to be accepted; that is why it has been mentioned. Under the doctrine, however, of cognition being a mere reflected image, even if the cognition differs from the cognised object, sameness of form belongs to the reflection; and the cognition can be only figurative. Lastly, for one who does not admit the cognition to be the receptacle of the correspondence with the object, there is not even the said method possible for the cognising of the external object].

It indicates that the "*sārūpya saṃbandha*" (relation of correspondence) was the ground of this identity between the object and self-consciousness, though Diṇnāga wanted this point to be agreeable to Vijñānavādins also. But his own position appears to be Sautrāntika, if investigated carefully.

Another ground for Hattori's firm conviction seems to be strengthened by Dharmakīrti's interpretation of Diṅnāga's view on this issue. Hattori asserts that Dharmakīrti criticizes the Sautrāntika theory of *arthasaṃvedana* (cognition of the object) in *PV.*, 2/320-37, and concludes his argument with the following verse:

tasmād dvirūpamastyekaṃ yadevamanubhūyate,
smaryate cobhayākārasyāsya samvedanaṃ phalaṃ. (*PV.*, 2/337)

[Therefore, both of the forms (object and subject) are experienced as one and the recollection of both forms is the result of cognition.]

But when the author investigated carefully the above reference in *PV* he found the facts to be quite contrary.

In *PV.*, 2/320-37, there is no indication that Dharmakīrti is criticizing the Sautrāntika viewpoint, as he definitely does not use this name. However, Manorathanandin does use it and this seems to be the main source of Hattori's and others' misconceptions.

The following points require serious consideration. The kārikā 320 runs as follows:

kārthasamvid yadevedaṃ pratyakṣaṃ prativedanaṃ,
tadarthavedanaṃ kena tadrūpyāt vyabhicāri tat. (*PV.* 2/320).

This kārikā and the following ones up to 324 clearly indicate a kind of "prior thesis" (*pūrvapakṣa*), because Dharmakīrti uses questions: *kārthasamvid*? (what is the cognition of the object?), (*atha so anubhavaḥ kvāsya*? kārika 32la.), (of what experience is this?), (*sarūpayantitat kena*?, kārikā 32lc.), (with what do they correspond?) All these questions followed by an answer and counter objection, and Dharmakīrti remarks "it is considered here" (*tadevedaṃ vicāryate*, kārika 32ld), and again "that very objection is considered" (*saiva pratyāsattir vicāryate*, kārikā 324d). It means that up to kārikā 324, Dharmakīrti introduces logical questions and their implications and then proceeds to examine them one by one in the following kārikās until in kārikā 338, he concludes this by giving the Sautrāntika view first then harmonising it with Vijñānavāda in kārika 339.

There is no doubt that Manorathanandin under kārikā 320 has mentioned that "now not differentiating between cognizer and cognition a Yogācāra asks a Sautrāntika" (*idānīṃ yogācāro vedyavedakabhāvaṃ apaśyan sautrāntikaṃ pṛcchati.*)

This interpretation of Manorathanandin is not consistent with his comments on the following kārikās. It seems that he was inclined to argue that Dharmakīrti's position was that of the Vijnānavāda, a tendency which is apparent by his comments in other places also, but he could not do so because of Dharmakīrti's own comments. The following observation is worth noting:

Manorathanandin under kārikā 338 comments:

yadā bahirarthavāde'pi paro bāhyārtha iṣṭo aniṣṭo vā...tena viṣayasārūpyam pramānamarthasaṃvit phalamuktaṃ.

[When in the doctrine of an external object also the other external object, desired or not desired...therefore correspondence with the sense object is the means of knowledge cognition of the object is the result.]

Then under kārikā 339 he comments:

atha vā vijñānavādepy avirudhamity āha yadā.................tatas ca vijñānavāde'py arthākāraḥ pramāṇaṃ arthasaṃvit phalaṃ aviruddhaṃ.

[or (it is) not contradictory to the Vijñānavāda also......there in Vijñānavāda also the form of the object is the valid source and the cognition of the object as the result is not contradictory.]

It implies that the kārikā 338 is from the Sautrāntika point of view and kārikā 339 from the Vijñānavāda. The usage "*Vijñānavāde'pi aviruddhaṃ*" (not contradictory in the Vijñānavāda also) clearly indicates this justification. Had the Vijnānavāda position been the main position, then it would have been discussed first and then its justification with the Sautrāntika later. Dharmakīrti in kārika 365 states:

tatrātmaviṣaye māne yathārāgādi vedanaṃ,
iyaṃ sarvatra saṃyojyā mānameyaphala-sthitiḥ. (2/365).

[In self-cognition as the criterion, such as the feeling of love, etc., this arrangement of criterion, object (and) result should be applied everywhere (even in Vijnānavāda=Manoratha).]

Monarathanandin comments:

tatra evaṃ sati ātmaviṣaye māne svasaṃvedane pramāṇe yathārāgādivedanaṃ mānameyaphalātmakaṃ iyaṃ mānameya phala-sthitiḥṃsarvatra vijñaptinaye'pi saṃyojyā.

[Then in the case where an internal object is the criterion, self-consciousness is the valid source as in the case of the feeling of love, etc., which has the nature of the criterion the means, as well as the result. This establishing of the object, criterion and the result should be made consistent everywhere even in Vijñānavāda.]

Here also Dharmakīrti wanted, after giving his own position, to justify it as being consistent with the Vijñānavāda, and Manorathanandin had to comment on it as such. It is interesting to note kārika 342, which reads:

yadi bāhyaṃ na vidyeta kasya saṃvedanaṃ bhavet,
yadyagatyā svarūpasya bāhyasyaiva na kiṃ matam. (*PV.*, 2/342).

[If there were no external object, what would there be a cognition of? If it is of its own form (of cognition itself), there being no alternative, (then) is not even that of something external? Shouldn't that be accepted? (Should it not be accepted that even that is of something external?)]

Prajñākaragupta has commented but Manorathanandin has not commented on this important *kārikā* because it contradicts his own interpretation. These kārikās 340, 341, 342 are to show that even the Vijñānavāda has to admit the existence of an external object in this form or another.

Later on Dharmakīrti, after discussing in detail the Vijñānavāda's standpoint on inference (*anumāna*) concludes:

astyeṣa viduṣāṃ vādo bāhyaṃ tvāśriya varṇyate,
dvairūpyaṃ saha-saṃvittiniyamāt tacca sidhyati. (*PV.*, 2/398).

[Though it (above described) is a doctrine of the Vijñānavādins, (Diṅnāga) has described it on the basis of external object, because of the law of simultaneous apprehension both forms (as one) are proved].

Manorathanandin also had to accept it and comments:

evaṃ tarhi vijñānanaya eva sarvavyavasthānaṃ avirodhāt, kathamācāryeṇa bahirartha apekṣayā jñanadvirūpatā uktā, iti āha—astyeṣa sarvavyavasthāsu vijñaptimātratāpratipādako viduṣāṃ nyāyadarśiṇāṃ yogācārāṇām vādaḥ sautrāntikairiṣṭaṃ bāhyamarthamāśriyma jñānasya dvairūpyaṃ ācāryeṇa varṇyate tacca dvairūpyaṃ sahasaṃvedananiyamāt: sahopalambaniyamāt bhede'pi sati tadabhāvāt.

[Even then the idealistic method being non-contradictory in all the cases, why does Ācārya (Diṅnāga) describe two forms of knowledge with regard to the external object? The answer is—indeed this is in all cases the view of mere consciousness propounded by the learned expert in logic, Yogācārins, but Ācārya (Diṅnāga) has described it from the viewpoint of the Sautāntika doctrine of the external object, i.e., because of simultaneous cognition, two forms as one is established; also because of the absence (unreality) of that (duality) though it is divided (it is really one].

This conclusion of Dharmakīrti that the *ācārya* (Diṅnāga) described it from the Sautrāntika point of view was so obvious that even Manorathanandin had to comment upon it as such. He forgets that if the Sautrāntika view is put in the form of *pūrvapakṣa* in the beginning, then how can it become a conclusion at the end? Isn't it possible that he wanted to interpret Dharmakīrti's view as a Vijñānavādin, but was unable to do so because of Dharmakīrti's clear indication? If Dharmakīrti was criticizing the Sautrāntikas, then why is it not mentioned by Prajñākara and others? Why is he establishing the Sautrāntika position in *NB.* and elsewhere?

In other places, Dharmakīrti mentions his view while discussing "*svabhāva*" (natural reason or reason based on identity);

tasmād viṣayabhedo'pi na svasaṃvedanaṃ phalaṃ.
uktaṃ svabhāvacintāyāṃ tādātmyādarthasaṃvidaḥ. (*PV.*, 2/351)

[Therefore, although the objects are different the result is not self-consciousness. This has been stated in the discussion on the "own-nature", because of the identity of the cognition with the object.]

Dharmakīrti's discussion on "*svabhāvahetu*" where he indicates: "This is a tree, because it is an Aśoka", does not indicate that the tree and the Aśoka are different, but merely that there are two aspects of one thing. Vacāspatimiśra has rightly analysed this and clearly calls it a Sautrāntika viewpoint, and refers to Diṅnāga and Dharmakīrti under it.

Dharmakīrti himself lays stress on *sārūpya* (correspondence) as the main ground of this unity in various contexts of discussion in *PV* by the name "*sarūpikā*" (*PV.*, 2/43 d), "*sārūpyanibandhanaṃ*" (*PV.*, 2/334b), and in *NB.* It undoubtedly proves him to be a Sautrāntika. Such evidence proves that Diṅnāga and Dharmakīrti's fundamental position was that of the Sautrāntika.

Stcherbatsky has himself found some critics calling Diṅnāga and Dharmakīrti's doctrine of self-consciousness a Sautrāntika doctrine. He translates and comments on this part of the controversy, between Yogācāra and Sautrāntikas: "Its result is also self-feeling, according to its form the object is determined, just the image is the source of knowledge, through it is cognized". The words *tādrūpyād artha-niśeayaḥ* are reminiscent of *artha-sārūpyaṃ asya pramāṇaṃ. NB*, I, 20, cp. *Tatp.*, p. 34.7 and Kamalaśīla, p. 560.18, *tādrūpyād iti sārūpyāt.* But here the term refers to a coordination between feeling and the ascertainment (*niścaya*) of the object, and evidently also to the subsequent purpositive action, not between the point instant of reality and the image as in the *NB.* Pārthasārathi thinks that the opinion of the Sautrāntikas is here expressed. . ."*

Stcherbatsky further translates and states: "And there is no contradiction of instrument and result (being found) in an undivided self. This, indeed, is either the relation of a function to the possessor of the function or of the conveyed to the conveyor. Indeed, only the axe which is conjoined with trees, etc., by conjunction, by function, is called in common life an instrument. And there is, for sure, no conjunction possessing a body, (a thing) different from the conjoined axe. The relation of conveyed to conveyor also has been surely (*eva*) experienced in a self-luminous cognition and in an external tree suggested by *siṃśapa*. Indeed the tree, for sure, is not something other than the *siṃśapa*, nor the *siṃśapa* (other) than the tree. But in imaginative dealing, just as there is a difference of exclusion, just so between a factor and its possessor, thus no difference whatever, thus the Sautrāntikas. The Sautrāntika-Yogācāras are meant, since Dharmakīrti is quoted. But in the 9th kośa-sthāna Vasubandu speak-

***BL., II, p. 384.**

ing from the standpoint of the Sautrāntikas emits similar views."[8]

The fallacy of misinterpretation seems to be created by Manorathanandin's incorrect identification of *pūrvapakṣa* (anti-thesis) based on his own predilection for the Idealist tendency. But the nature of the fact is such that he could not do it consistently without leaving some weak points which are mentioned above.

B1

Stcherbatsky called Diṅnāga and Dharmakīrti fundamentally Idealists, but when he found certain principles applied by them, and opponents calling them Sautrāntikas, he seems to have altered his opinion and gave a new name "Sautrāntika-Yogācāra" for this system. Therefore, this is examined as follows.

One further question is to be examined here. Is it possible for a philosopher to belong to two opposed schools consistently? The Sautrāntika movement was after the *Kathāvatthu* the second attempt to purify the Buddha's original views about knowledge and reality, etc. from the prevalent confusions of the Sarvāstivādin and the Vaibhāṣika trend of Ābhidharmikas. The earlier Sautrāntikas (Bhadanta Sthavira, Kumāralāta, etc.), also known as Dārṣṭāntikas, used the method of '*dṛṣṭānta*' or empirical observation and its conformity with the *Sūtra Piṭaka*. Any philosophical view which contradicted this criterion was examined and brushed aside. The Sautrāntika Vasubandhu, particularly, critically commented on the *Abhidharmakośa* and criticized the Vaibhāṣika and other views, which were contradicting the above criteria, by introducing methods of logic and debate, and produced a philosopher like Diṅnāga as his successor or expounder. Diṅnāga and later Dharmakīrti, developed epistemological and logical analysis as the only standard to judge reality. They followed the Sautrāntika view of universal flux (*anityavāda* or *santānavāda*) which was found to be provable on the ground of epistemology and logic.

On the other hand, Nāgārjuna on the ground of *pratītyasamutpāda* (dependent origination), or *śūnyatā* criticized the Abhidharma as well as Brahmanic metaphysical foundations. But Nāgārjuna's method was supposed to be a kind of extreme scepticism (particularly its interpretation by Buddhapālita). Asaṃga and Vasubandhu (I) reacted against this extreme tendency and established the Madhyāntavibhaṅga

[8] *BL*,. II, p. 376.

school known as Yogācāra Vijñānavāda. Asaṃga and later his brother Vasubandhu I, in particular criticized the doctrines of the early Sautrāntikas.

There have been constant intellectual fights between these groups on various fundamental epistemological and ontological issues as mentioned by Vācaspatimiśra in detail. The two systems are contrary. Dharmakīrti particularly neglected *ālayavijñāna*, *trisvabhāva*, etc. and his main doctrine of "*svalakṣaṇas*" can never be acceptable from the Vijnānavāda point of view. How then can one assert that they adhered to both schools? The Sautrāntikas were one of the old schools of Buddhism, while the Yogācāras were Mahāyānist. Therefore, they cannot belong to both schools at the same time. It is only in a later period when Vijnānavādin commentators began to assimilate some Sautrāntika doctrines to the Yogācāra that one might speak of some sort of combination of ideas from two schools, but these later trends still belonged fundamentally to one school with merely borrowings from another, adjusted to fit with their own views. But Dharmottara and Durveka vehemently opposed this tendency to reinterpret Dharmakīrti.

One may ask a question: Why do Vijnānavādins attempt to assimilate Sautrāntika ideas? The reason is the epistemology and logic, which was the only weapon to defend and survive in that era. That is why Vigñānavādins had to use it for their own survival. There was no other choice for them, except to use Dharmakīrti's logic for their systems.

Stcherbatsky first seems to be of the opinion that Dharmakirti was an Idealist. When Stcherbatsky found Vācaspati and Udayana calling Dharmakīrti a Sautrāntika, he seemed to change his view and began to call him a Sautrāntika-Yogācāra, as is apparent by his own comments. But in doing so he has really made a contrary statement. The most probable and consistent interpretation is that Vasubandu II, Diṅnāga, and Dharmakīrti were Sautrāntikas, but coincided with Vijñānavāda only on the issue of *sva-saṃvedana*; although this coincidence was only partial because they never forgot their main ground of "*sārupya-saṃbandha*" which is possible only from the Sautrāntika viewpoint. In this case one cannot come to the conclusion that they belonged to both schools, which have contrary doctrines, viz. the Vinjnānavādins were Idealists (total denial of external objects), while the Sautrāntikas were Critical Realists (partial denial of external objects).

If Stcherbatsky's view is accepted then Dharmakīrti has to be called by various other names, as some of his doctrines are in agreement with Vaibhāṣika, (two means of cognition, etc.), and some with Nyāya, Vaiśeṣika, Mīmāṃsā, (*arthakriyā*, etc.). Then it will be implied that we shall name him or his school with a combination of all these names, which will become absurd.

Stcherbatsky himself at one place makes it clear: "According to the Sautrāntikas the direct function of sense perception is the awareness of the presence of something in one's (*grahaṇa*), its indirect function the evoking of its general image in a perceptual judgment (*pratyakṣa-balād utpannena vikalpena adhyasāyaḥ*). The direct function of inference, on the other hand, is the construction of a general image, its indirect function is the ascertainment of the presence of something in our ken...The Yogācāra of the old school and Mādhyamika-Yogācāras reject this theory".* He himself has translated parts of the *Nyāyakaṇikā*, a commentary on the Mīmāṃsā system by Vācaspatimiśra, who particularly deals in detail with the contradiction between Vijnānavāda and Sautrāntika on the issue of "*sva-saṃveda-navāda*". Vācaspati is well known as the neutral expert of all philosophical systems, Brahmanic and non-Brahmanic, and his comprehensive study through original sources makes him more authoritative in rendering correctly the views of the philosophers or philosophical schools. concerned. He refers to Dinnāga and Dharmakīrti as holders of the Sautrāntika view. Stcherbatsky seems to be alarmed by this and makes a strange comment: "Our ideas, in this system, are not cognitions of reality, but construction or dreams about reality. They are indirect cognitions just as dreams are, since dreams are also conditioned by former real experiences, but feebly recollected in a morbid state of mind. Hence Dharmakīrti and Dinnāga are represented here as Sautrāntikas, although in their own opinion they are Yogācāras. They are therefore called Sautrāntika-Yogācāras. Their opponents are the old Yogācāras of Asaṅga's school and later Mādhyamika-Yogācāras."**

One cannot proceed further without pointing out the contrary statement. Vācaspati categorically called Diṅnāga and Dharmakīrti Sautrāntikas. Where Diṅnāga and Dharmakīrti called themselves Yogācāra Vijñanavādins is not to be traced in any of their writings. Some Vijñā-

**BL.*, II, p. 366, n. 2.
**Ibid, p. 370, n. 3.

navādin commentators have created this confusion. Why does Vācaspati present them as opponents of Yogācāra? Nowhere have they expressed "their own opinion" of belonging to Yogācāra. There is no internal evidence, either in the work of Diṅnāga or of Dharmakīrti, that they have called themselves Yogācārins or Sautrāntika-Yogācāra. Even in the later period Buddhists or non-Buddhists also did not use this name, except Vinītadeva who attempted to interpret Dharmakīrti as a Vijnānavādin in "*Santānāntarasiddhiṭīkā*" and in "*Nyāyabinduṭīkā*" to synthesize both views (*ubhayanayavādin*) which has already been examined above.

B 2

The view held by Pandit Dalsukhabhai Malvaniya (*Pradīpa*, Int., XXII-V) that Dharmakīrti was a Vijnānavādin in *PV* and a Sautrāntika in *NB* seems to be incorrect. There is no evidence that Dharmakīrti has mentioned this difference of outlook in any of his seven treatises. Neither do other Buddhists or non-Buddhist expounders or critics mention it. In the case that Dharmakīrti changed his philosophical position in *NB*. he would, directly or indirectly, have explained it himself. If not, then his expounders, or particularly non-Buddhists critics whose main goal was to find inconsistencies, weak points, and contradictions in Dharmakīrti, would never have overlooked this difference. Dharmakīrti himself was highly critical and has criticized the views of Diṅnāga or his own direct teacher Īśvarasena on some minor issues such as "*pakṣadharmatā*" (Īśvarasena)*, and "*virudhāvyabhicārin*"** (Diṅnāga). If Dharmakīrti disagreed on any of the major views he would not have been afraid to point it out as he has done on minor issues. *PV* is fundamentally a commentary on *PS*. with Dharmakīrti's own new arguments. The main doctrines mentioned by Diṅnāga are fully elaborated. In the case of Diṅnāga, he was the expounder of the Sautrāntika Vasubandhu and grounded his views on *Abhidharmakośabhāṣya* and *Vādavidhāna*, etc., with his own original arguments to prove them. He was himself critical in attitude and was not afraid to analyze and criticize his teacher's view on *pratyakṣa*.

In the event that Vasubandhu II changed his position Diṅnāga would not have been silent, or if Diṅnāga had changed his position, then Dharmakīrti would definitely have endorsed or refuted this change of position. In the case that Dharmakīrti changed his position,

*tadetadācāryiyāṃ vyākhyāṃ Īśvarasenākṣiptaṃ, Hetubinduṭīkā., p. 12,
**ayaṃ ca viruddhaṃ Diṅnāgenoktaṃ, NBT., p. 79.

the critics would not have remained silent. The logical explanation of these silences seems to be that the three of them had the same philosophical position (Sautrāntika) and expounded it in relation to different opponents (Buddhist and non-Buddhist) existing in their times. None of them changed their positions.

The view that Dharmakīrti is a Vijñānavādin in *PV* as mentioned by Malvaniya seems to be based on Manorathanandin's wrong division of *pūrvapakṣa* (thesis), and *uttarapakṣa* (anti-thesis) of some passages of *PV.* which have already been examined above, and the assertion: "Darmakīrti has defended the views of Yogācāra in his work like Pramānavārtika very strongly,"* seems to be based on insufficient evidence and wrong interpretation. Though Dharmakīrti agreed with the Yogācāra on the issue of *sva-saṃvedana*, he did not forget the underlying differences and definitely he has not accepted *trisvabhāva* (triple nature of reality), *ālayavijñāna* (store-consciousness) and other fundamental metaphysical doctrines of Yogācāra. It cannot be taken as a strong defence and it also cannot be reconciled with his radical departure in Nyāyabindu. Malvaniya himself points out: "This being the case how is it possible that he left the ideology of Yogācāra and accepted that of Sautrāntika in Nyāyabindu."** The reason he gives is the definition of *svalakṣaṇa* and the like which compel one to conclude that it is not a treatise from the viewpoint of Yogācāra. How then are both of these contrary viewpoints to be explained? It appears that he is of the opinion that the definition of *svalakṣaṇa* in *NB* is different from that in *PV.* But a thorough survey reveals that this is not the case. Diṅnāga mentions *svalakṣaṇa* as the object of sensation *pratyakṣa,* (*PS.*, I/4) and Dharmakīrti has also done so while clarifying it in *PV* :

prāmāṇyam dvividhaṃ viṣayadvaividhyāt. (*PV.*, 2/1ab)
na pratyakṣaparokṣābhyāṃ meyasyānyasya saṃbhavaḥ,
tasmāt prameyadvitvena pramāṇadvitvamiṣyate. (2/63).

[Because of two kinds of objects of cognition, there are two kinds of valid sources of cognition. There is no possibility of any other object of cognition for sensation and non-sensation. Therefore, because of two kinds of objects of cognition, there are two kinds of valid sources of cognition.]

Dharmakīrti thus pinpoints the description of *svalakṣaṇa.* Undoub-

*Introduction, p. xxii.
**Ibid, p. xxii.

tedly, he does not define the term "*svalakṣaṇa*" as directly as he has done in *Nyāyabindu*. This may be because Diṅnāga himself does not define it except as the object of sensation, (*svalakṣaṇaviśayam hi pratyakṣam PSV.*, 1/2). Dharmakīrti's *PV* being a commentary on *PS* does not discuss epistemology independently as is done in *NB*. But one thing is worth noting here, that Diṅnāga refers to the Abhidharma tradition that the eye sees blue, but does not know that "it is blue" (*cakṣurvijñānasamaṅgī nīlamvijānāti no tu nīlamiti· PS.*, I. 4) and that "the *svalakṣaṇas* are described according to the senses not according to substance (atoms)" (*āyatanasvalakṣaṇam praty ete svalakṣaṇaviṣayā na dravyasvalakṣaṇamprati, AbkB.*, 1/10). Thus, he suggests its further explanation in *AbkB.* of Vasubandhu. Dharmakīrti, following the same line, defined it accordingly in *NB*. Therefore it does not indicate any deviation or contradiction or change of views. The definition of *svalakṣaṇa NB* (*yasyasannidhāna*...1/13) is not different in substance from those of *PS* and *PV*. If *PV* is studied carefully it will show the following characteristics of *svalakṣaṇa arthakriyākārin* (causally efficient), *asādṛśya* (dissimilar), *śabdasyāviṣaya* (not the object of words), *indriyaviṣaya* or *pratyakṣaviṣaya* (object of the senses), etc. Darmakīrti has just defined it in *NB* directly which appears to be different from *PV* but in substance it is not.

Dharmakīrti seems to be alarmed by different interpretations of *PV*, even by his own disciple Devendrabuddhi (according to a legend) and expressed grief that the true meaning would disappear with his own body (*svadehejarām*). In such a confusing situation he made concise, precise comments and clarified his view in *NB*, but apparently not because of changing positions. Dharmakīrti was so firm, consistent, and logical in his views that we do not find any discrepancy on the various subjects discussed by him in his seven treatises except some introduction of new arguments or logical proofs. Then how can he be self-contradictory on this issue? If he had wanted any substantial change in his doctrine of *PV* he would definitely have discussed it. Durvekamisra has also attempted to eliminate some such confusing views in his *Pradīpa*. Perhaps the emergence of the view in the mind of Malvania, that he defined "*svalakṣaṇa*" from the Yogācāra point of view in *PV* and from Sautrāntika in *NB.*, is caused by misunderstanding of the text and the facts. It is not an error on the side of modern scholars only, but also of some ancient commentators like Vinītadeva and Manorathanandin, etc. Malvaniya himself seems to be convinced by Durvekamiśra, but he produces (perhaps because of Stcherbatsky's view) a strange interpretation: "In this connection we should note that the Yogācāra believes in the existence of external objects from the standpoint of *samvṛtisatya*, i.e., Empirical Reality, and not from that of *pāramārthikasatya*, i.e., Ultimate Reality. Therefore, the treatment of *pramāṇa*, *prameya*, etc. is empirical in character. Hence, the discussion on logic, etc. is only empirically real. The Ultimate Reality is the subject of self-experience, and is thus indescribable. Discussions regarding *pramāṇa-prameya*, etc. can be carried on on empirical grounds. The Sautrāntika system, which believes in the existence of external objects and undertakes discussion on that very basis, can provide good grounds for the *pramāṇa-prameya* treatment. We can, therefore, maintain that *the pramāṇa-vārtika* deals with the *pāramārthika* standpoint of the system, whereas the *Nyāya-bindu* represents *vyavahārika* viewpoint. It is just natural that the Sautrāntika viewpoint predominates on the *vyavahārika* side. To this extent we can maintain that the *Nyāyabindu* represents the Sautrāntika system."*

This explanation does not seem to be in agreement with a real understanding of Dharmakīrti. If that were the case, then why did the critics of Dharmakīrti refute his logic? If it were only from a worldly (not real) point of view then why did Dharmakīrti defend Diṅnaga's logic from Brahmanical critics like Uddyotakara and Kumārila? He could have just discarded it by claiming that all this *pramāṇya* arrangement was from a worldly point of view, and from a fundamental point of view there is no epistemology and no logic, as is done by some Vedāntins, Mādhyamikas, and Yogācāras who discussed *pramāṇa* from a worldly point of view and relied on either testimony or intuition.

And also, why did Dharmakīrti or his expounders or critics not mention that *PV* is from the higher point of view (Vijñānavāda) and *PB* from the lower (Sautrāntika)? Thus, this does not seem to be correct. This wrong impression may be derived from Dharmakīrti's own statement:

prāmāṇyam vyavahāreṇa, śāstraṃmohanivartanaṃ,
ajñātārthaprakāśo vā svarūpādhigateḥ paraṃ. (*PV*., 1/7).

[Validity (of cognition) depends on applicability, the science is the elimination of delusion, or it reveals an unknown fact through the knowledge of own nature par excellence].

*Ibid, introduction, p. xxii.

But this kārikā is written in order to remove the confusion of of Mīmāṃsakas who believe that knowledge is valid per se (in itself) and does not depend on any other extraneous condition. The kārikā 6 ends with "*svarūpasya svatogatiḥ*", and kārikā 7 is the answer *prāmāṇyaṃ* "*vyavahāreṇa*" that validity depends on successful activity (*artha-kriyā jñānena, tatrārthakriyājñānena prāmāṇyaniścayaḥ* = Manorathanandin). The clear indication is that knowledge in itself cannot determine whether it is real or illusory, but only by its practical application, viz. successful activity. To Dharmakīrti "successful activity" or "causal efficiency" (*arthakriyākāritva*) is the ultimate reality. He clearly holds:

artha-kriyāsamarthaṃ yat tadatra paramārthasat. (*PV.*, 2/3ab).

[Whatever is capable of action towards an object is ultimately real].

pramāṇamavisaṃvādi jñānaṃ; arthakriyāsthitiḥ. (*PV.*, 1/3ab).

[Valid knowledge is not inconsistent and is based on successful action towards an object].

It means that the very definition of *pramāṇa*, or valid cognition, is to be *arthakriyākārin* which is possible through the particular object (*svalakṣaṇa*) which is the real object of the senses (*indriya*) as clarified by Dharmakīrti in *PV.*, 2/1-4, and in *NB. tadeva* (*svalakṣaṇaṃ*) *paramārthasat arthakriyāsāmarthyalakṣaṇatvāt vastunaḥ* (1/14-15).

[Because of having the characteristic of the capability of action towards an object of reality, *svalakṣaṇa* is the ultimate reality].

This description does not leave any doubt as to what Dharmakīrti meant by *prāmāṇyaṃ vyavahāreṇa*. There should also not be any doubt about the fact that Darmakīrti (with Vasubandhu II and Diṅnāga) believes in two kinds of reality:

1. Ultimate or *pāramārthika*
2. Phenomenal or *saṃvṛti*

The first is cognized directly through the senses (*pratyakṣa*) and indirectly through inference (*anumāna*) which is based on the former. The object of the senses is "*svalakṣaṇa*" which is ultimate, and of the latter "*sāmānya*" or generality. There is no indication as far as Dharmakīrti's own position is concerned of a third category by the name "*vyavahāra*" or "*vyavahārasatya.*"

Malvaniya may have had the impression that the Vedāntika or Jaina doctrine of reality was divided into three categories: *pāramārthika*, *Pratibhāsika* and *Vyavahārika* (fundamental, illusory, and worldly). Or, he may have accepted Manorathanandin's alternative comment where he gives a separate interpretation (*atha vā*, p. 7) from the Vijñānavāda point of view. But there seems to be a complete absence of the Vedāntika or Jaina sense and Manorathanandin's alternative interpretation itself seems to be erroneous and the first one correct.

Is there any important problem discussed in *PV* and neglected in *NB*? It is possible that one problem or principle is not fully elaborated on because of different problem tackled in a particular book. *Vādanyāya*, *Pramāṇaviniścaya*, *Hetubindu*, *Santānāntarasiddhi*, *Saṃbandhaparīkṣā*, are written to deal with a particular subject and may not elaborate on subjects like *svalakṣaṇa*, *pratyakṣa* or *sārūpya* in detail and one can easily derive a false conclusion that *PV* and *NB* were works from the Sautrāntika point of view, while the others were from the Vijñānavāda or some other point of view. Only *PV* and *NB* contain the four subject-matters: *Pramāṇa*, *Pratyakṣa*, *Svārthānumāna*, and *Parārthānumāna*, (valid source of cognition, sensation, inference for own-self, inference for others), in accordance with some subject-matters in *PS* and *PV* and the same in a nutshell in *NB*. To speak of discrepancy regarding the definition of *svalakṣaṇa* in *PV* and *NB* is not in correspondence with facts.

It appears that Malvaniya developed this view on the ground of Stcherbatsky's concept of this sort based on his interest in Idealism or Absolutism which believes that all logic is from a lower, empirical, phenomenal, or worldly point of view, and he wrongly applied this treatment to the logic and epistemology of Dharmakīrti, i.e., he also formed logic from the empirical (phenomenal) standpoint while ultimately he believed in the Absolute of the Vijñānavādins. But the case seems to be the contrary. Dharmakīrti rejected, though indirectly, all kinds of metaphysics of Vijñānavāda, including *ālayavijñāna*, *trisvabhāva*, etc. and the so-called Absolute and believed only in empirical knowledge received through the senses as of the highest and fundamental reality. As a matter of fact, the Sautrāntika movement sprang forth as a reaction against the Vaibhāṣikas' unempirical (metaphysical) concepts like "*nikāyasabhāgatā*, *prāpti*, *pratisaṃkhyānirodha*, *apratisaṃkhyānirodha*" (universal, possession, cessation through intellect, cessation not through intellect), etc. criticized by Vasubandhu II from the standpoint of empiricism and the theory of momentariness. For them *pratyakṣa* (sensation) and *anumāna* (inference) were the only source of right knowledge. Dharmakīrti, particularly, suspended judgment regarding the existence of any reality which transcends these two means of cognition (*NB.*, 3/69-95), and identified reality with momentariness (*yat sat tadanityaṃ, NB, arthakriyāsamarthaṃ yat tadatra paramārthasat, PV.*, 2/3). Thus, it leaves no loophole for any mystical entity to enter into its pure empirical chamber. Diṇnāga and Dharmakīrti seem to be radical empiricists who regard only empirical (sensory) knowledge as real. Malvaniya further comments: "*pramāṇavārtika* is more important, since it deals with the Omniscience as well as Dharmakāya of the Buddha. They maintain that the significance of *pramāṇavārtika* does not consist in the fact of its being a treatise on logic, but in its treatment of the fundamental reality of Mahāyāna in the form of the Buddha and his special virtues. The main object of *Pramānavārtika* is to treat of *Dharmakāya, svabhāvakāya, and jñānakāya* of the Buddha." (*Pradīpa*, Introduction, p. xxii)

This comment seems to be not in correspondence with facts when examined and compared with *PV.* It is well known that Dharmakīrti discarded the concept of "omniscience" in *PV* and *NB*. The evidence contradicts the comment that it (*PV*) deals with the omniscience as well as Dharmakāya of the Buddha. There is no doubt that Dharmakīrti (in *PV* as well as in *NB*) discussed "omniscience", not to prove it, but to disprove it. The Buddha is valid (*pramāṇa*) because he is the cognizer of desirable or undesirable facts, not because he is "omniscient" (*na tu sarvasyavedaka, PV.*, 1/34d). Similarly, in *Nyāyabindu* (3/69-85), Dharmakīrti discusses "omniscience" in the form of an example for *sandigdhānekāntika hetvābhāsa* (doubtful uncertain fallacy of reason), and reveals his view, indirectly, against the very concept of "omniscience".

The Buddha was considered as a manifested valid source of cognition (*pramāṇabhūta, PS.*, 1/1), or as the destroyer of the net of imagination (*vidhūtakalpanājalaṃ, PV.*, 1/la), because he had cognized reality. The Buddha nowhere called himself *sarvajña* (omniscient) and did not accept any authorities, including himself, if they contradicted empirical experience. In such a case it will be a blunder to assign a contrary view to Dharmakīrti.

It seems that in some of the original manuscripts and translations of Dharmakīrti's seven works, in the beginning of the treatise, sentences like: *oṃ namaḥ sarvajñāya* (salute to omniscient one), *Mañjuśriyai namaḥ* (salute to Mañjuśrī), etc. have confused many scholars by setting up a wrong impression of Mahāyāna in the very beginning, and the whole system is interpreted accordingly. But in reality these salutations are not part of the main treatise as they vary in different manuscripts and are added either by copiers or by translators or commentators according to the object of their devotion. The terms Dharmakāya, Nirmāṇakāya (which Malvaniya replaced by *Dharmakāya, Svābhāvikakāya*, and *Jñānakāya*) are nowhere found in any of Dharmakīrti's works. Even the term Mahāyāna is foreign to him. This grave mistake which created a misleading set-up of mind in the very beginning is also caused by Dharmakīrti's Vijñānavādin commentators like Karṇakagomin and Manorathanandin, in the commentary of the opening *kārikā* which runs as follows:

vidhūtakalpanājālaṃgambhīrodāramūrtaye
namaḥ samantabhadrāya samantaspharaṇatviṣe. (*PV*., 1/1).

[Salutation to the all blissful (Buddha) who has destroyed the net of imagination, who is the embodiment of the depth of wisdom and compassion, from whom the rays of bliss burst forth in every direction.]

There is no such word as *kāyas* in it, but while commenting on it Manorathanandin and Karnakagomin have undoubtedly taken *vidhūtakalpanājāla=Dharmakāya*, *gambhīra=Saṃbhogakāya*, *udāra=Nirmāṇakāya*, and used the term "*Mahāyāna*" which obviously appears to be a misinterpretation. These commentators were adherents of Vijñānavāda by faith and one should not be surprised if they interpreted a text according to their own assumptions and traditions. It is apparent that *PV* being a commentary on *PS* follows its order of explanation. The first chapter of *PV*, is just a detailed summary on the opening *śloka* of the *PS* and there is no sign of such terms either in *PSV* or in *PV*, Thus, it is not logical that one should make such an absolute decision merely on the authority of later commentators and translators. If it were really their view, somewhere either Vasubandhu II, Diṅnāga, or Dharmakīrti would have mentioned or suggested it. The absolute absence in all three of them of these terms is enough, to prove that it is an interpolation. The three *kāya* doctrine was a typical metaphysical doctrine of the Mahāyānists (Mādhyamika and Vijñānavāda). Contrary to it, the Sautrāntikas criticized it and understood the Buddha to have been an historical human being who destroyed the web of imagination (*vidhūtakalpanājālaṃ*) and embodied depth in wisdom (*gaṃbhīra*) and compassion (*udāra*). The term "*mūrtaye*" means manifestation as in *PS* (*pramāṇabhūtāya*) and there is no trace whatsoever of the mystical supernatural three bodies of the Buddha, which is totally at variance with the historical Buddha's teaching. Diṅnāga and Dharmakīrti mentioned the *svārthasampat* and *parārthasampat* of the Buddha, which contradicts the *trikāya* doctrine and the Mahāyāna tradition.

Dharmakīrti, while explaining this first *kārikā*, brings into light the three characters of ultimate reality, viz. *duḥkha, anitya, anātman* (disgust, non-eternal, no-self) so well known in early Buddhist tradition and well discussed by Vasubandhu in his *AbkB* and by Dharmakīrti in his *PV* which reads:

anityāt prāha tenaiva duḥkhaṃ duḥkhānnirātmatām. (*PV.*, 1/256ab).

[The Buddha taught that because of *anitya* (non-eternal), there is *duḥkha* (disgust) and because of *duḥkha* there is *anātman* (no substance or self)]. This language really differs from the Mahāyāna. Even commentators like Manorathanandin had to quote *Sūtrapiṭaka* in order to clarify it:

Tadyathā—rūpaṃ bhikṣavo nityamanityaṃ vā? anityaṃ bhadanta. Yadanityaṃ tad duḥkhaṃ sukhaṃ vā? duḥkham bhadanta...yadanityaṃ duḥkhaṃ vipariṇāmadharmakaṃ kalpyaṃ nu tadeva draṣṭuḥ—etaṃ mama, eso'hamasmi, eṣa me ātmeti'no hīdaṃ' bhadanta." (*MN.*,3.9.5.5.),

[Such as—"Ye monks, is form eternal or non-eternal? Non-eternal, Blessed one. If it is non-eternal, (then) is it disgusting or non-disgusting? Disgusting, Blessed One...whatever is non-eternal, disgusting, and changing would it be imagined by an observer as: "this is mine", "this I am" "this is myself?" Certainly not, Blessed One."]

If Dharmakīrti was a Mahāyānist Vijñānavādin, then why did he emphasize the three characters of reality? Why was Manorathanandin bound to quote the *Sūtrapiṭaka* instead of any Mahāyāna texts? The logical answer is that Dharmakīrti was not a Mahāyānist, but a follower of the Sautrāntika tradition.

The Sautrāntikas' fundamental and only position in ontology was that everything is non-eternal, and whatever is non-eternal is *duḥkha* (disgusting) and *anātman* (no-self), which is duly elaborated by Dharmakīrti. Similarly, Dharmakīrti believes in only two sources of valid cognition: sensation (*pratyakṣa*), and inference (*anumāna*), neither of which can establish the three *kāyas*.

Thus, how can Dharmakīrti believe in entities which contradict his very foundation? His epistemology seems to be so solid and consistent that even a slight change will contradict the whole system.

The interpreters themselves where baffled by the usage of the term *Samantabhadra** and had to give two interpretations. Karṇakagomin

**samantabhadda* is familiar in Theravāda in connection with conditioned origination well explained by the Buddha e.g., *VbhA.*, p. 132. It is not a Mahāyānist epithet.

comments:

yadā samantabhadraśabdo rudhyā bodhisattvavṛttona gṛhyate tadeyaṃ buddhasya bhagavataḥ pūjā,

[When the term Samantabhadra is not taken according to the usage as Bodhisattva, then it is the respect for the Buddha.] It means that traditionally—the term *samantabhadra* is used for *bodhisattva* (Mahāyāna), but terminologically it means "the Buddha".

Then he further holds:

yadā tu rūḍhirapekṣyate tadayaṃ samantabhadraśabdo mahāyāne bodhisattvavaviśeṣe rūdha iti bodhisattvasya iyaṃ pūja. padārthastu pūrvavad yojya.

[When usage is taken into consideration, then in Mahāyāna the term *samantabhadra* is used in the sense of the respect for a particular Bodhisattva. But terminologically, it should be understood as before (for the Buddha)].

As a matter of fact, Mahāyāna writers generally remember, because of their devotion, particular *bodhisattvas* like Mañjuśrī, Samantabhadra (*bodhisattvaviśeṣa*), Avalokiteśvara, etc., as is done by Karṇakagomin "*suciraṃ śrīmañjunātho vibhuḥ*" (*PVSVT.*, 1/1). But the Sautrāntikas remember only the Buddha, not a *bodhisattva*. That is why Manoratha has to make a comment like Karṇakagomin:

audāryaṃ tu darśabhūmīśvarabodhisattvamāhātmyātiśayah. (*yadyapi*) *kāyatrayaṃ tu badhisatvānāmapyasti*; *prakarṣaniṣṭhāgamanāt tu bhagavatāṃ vyavasthāpyate.* (*PVV.*, *1/1*).

[Benevolence is the excellent virtue of Darśabhūmīśvara Bodhisattva. Though there are three bodies of Bodhisattvas also, yet because of extreme devotion this term (*samantabhadra)* is used for the Buddha.] and before this he mentioned:

yadā tu samantabhadraśabdo rūḍhyā bodhisattvaviśeṣe vartate tadapi pada-vyākhyānam pūrvavadeva.

[Though traditionally the term Samantabhadra is used for a particular Bodhisattva, its terminological explanation should be considered as described before (in the sense of the Buddha].

They were facing difficulties in trying to make it consistent with the *bodhisattva* doctrine. But they could not do so because Dharmakīrti's usage "*namaḥ samantabhadrāya*" is only for the Buddha, not for a *bodhisattva.*

Dharmakīrti himself has explained each and every word of the opening *kārikā* in preceding *kārikā*, for example, *udāra*, is explained as *dayā* (compassion) or *dayāparārthatantratvaṃ* (compassion for others) (*PV.*, 1/284), and *dayayā śreya ācaste* (*PV.*, 1/284) clearly indicates the correct meaning. There is not the slightest hint of the meaning *darśabhūmīśvarabodhisattvamāhātmyātiśaya*, or *nirmāṇakāya* (Manorathanandin) or *udārah=sakalajñeyasakalasatvārthavyāpanāt* (Karṇakagomin). This is contradictory and irrelevant to Dharmakīrti's own meaning. Because of these Mahāyāna cnmmentators, ancient and modern scholars, have been subject to serious misconception.

B 3

N. C. Shah has also expressed the view that Dharmakīrti belonged to the Sautrāntika-Yogācāra school in the introduction of his book *Akalaṅka's Criticism of Dharmakīrti's Philosophy*, but no reasons for his belief are provided. Later on he characterizes Dharmakīrti's system by the new name "own version of Idealism". No reasons for this view are discussed except that Dharmakīrti proves the existence of other minds, according to Stcherbatsky's survey.

He produces in detail Akalaṅka's criticism of Dharmakīrti as an Idealist, but not as a Sautrāṅtika-Yogācāra. In another place he presents Dharmakīrti criticizing the Sautrāntikas on the ground of Manorathanandin's commentary (*PV.*, 2/354-63), which has already been examined. It would have been more consistent if he had ranked him as a pure Idealist, since he treats him exclusively on the ground of Akalaṅka's criticism. If N. C. Shah wanted to establish such a view, he should have consulted Malvaniya's view of the two phases of Dharmakīrti's philosophy. One cannot base an absolute opinion only on the ground of Akalaṅka's criticism, whose main aim is not to find reality, but to ridicule an opponent by imposing his own interpretations and then to show skill in criticizing them. One is bound to consult other works of Dharmakīrti and Diṅnāga to clarify his real position. How the Sautrāntika influenced Dharmakīrti is nowhere clarified. Thus, the whole thesis, though scholarly, appears to be inconsistent on this major issue.

C

Umesha Miśra has really made a daring conjecture by calling Dharmakīrti a Vaibhāṣika and his theory of pratyakṣa, a Vaibhāṣika theory of perception, but he does not explain how he came to this conclusion. In the absence of grounds and reasons, it is hard to examine it.

His ground seems to be Mādhavācārya's division of the Vaibhāṣika and the Sautrāntika views on the external world; the first believing in direct cognition of the external world (*bāhyārthapratyakṣavāda*), and the latter in indirect cognition or cognition through representation (*bāhyārthānumeyavāda*). According to Umesha Miśra, as the *Nyāya-bindu* does not speak of any representation, but of a direct perception of *svalakṣaṇa*, the possibility of representationalism being a Sautrāntika definition is eliminated.*

Umesha Miśra also found the concept of the "relation of correspondence" (*sārpūyasaṃbandha*) accepted by the Vaibhāṣikas. Both of these grounds do not correspond to historical and philosophical facts. Mādhavācārya's classification seems to be non-factual, as observed by Stcherbatsky and others.[12] The Sautrāntikas were not representationalists or bāhyārthānumeyavādins and no original document is available to strengthen this thesis. Either Mādhavācārya himself invented it, or his view was based on some secondary source. This mistake has occurred because of imposing the criticism of critics as the doctrine of the person under attack. In any case, this description of the Sautrāntika position is non-factual and has misled many writers, as the *Sarvadarśanasaṃgraha* became the main source book for non-Buddhists to learn about Buddhism.

The *sārūpyasaṃbandha* was accepted by the Vaibhāṣikas and the Sautrāntikas, but their application of it was quite different. The interesting point is that the Sautrāntika was a movement against the Vaibhāṣika's metaphysical assumptions such as *prāpti*, *nikāyasa-bhāgatā*, etc., as mentioned above. Vasubandhu II has already criticized these. Diṅnāga and Dharmakīrti again refuted them (to gether with *Vaiśeṣika*, *Sāmkhya*, and *Mīmṃasāka* metaphysical doctrines). The confusion seems to be created by the absence of comparative study and the lack of sources for these systems available at that time.

This view, being obviously incompetent and inconsistent as already discussed by previous scholars, is not examined here, but one point really strikes the mind: that Umeshamiśra disagreed with and deviated from the well established generally accepted view of Dharmakīrti's inclusion in Vijñānavāda. There is no doubt that the Sautrāntika school emerged out of the Vaibhāṣikas and accepted many of their doctrines as discussed by Vasubandhu II in his *AbkB.* Diṅnāga followed Vasubandhu II, and Dharmakīrti followed Diṅnāga in the formation of epistemology and new logical arguments. Thus,

**History of Indian Philosophy*, I, p. 394.

they are undoubtedly Sautrāntika rather than Vaibhāṣika, some of whose doctrines are criticized by all three of them.

D

This view is expressed by the German scholar Tilmann Vetter in his Int. of *PVin.* The ground is mainly the reference to the terms *śūnyatā* and *niḥsvabhāva* used by Dharmakīrti in his *PV.*, but that these terms have the same connotation as those of the Mādhyamikas is questionable for they may have another sense, as is obvious through Dharmakīrti's own usage. The reference (*PV.*, 2/205-10, *PVin.*, int., p. 10) cited as evidence establishes a different meaning. One *kārikā* reads:

tasmāt tadeva tasyāpi tattvaṃ yā dvayaśūnyatā. (*PV.*, 2/213cd).

[Therefore, the reality of it which is the emptiness of two (subject object=*grāhya-grāhaka*) is the same.] The term *tasmāt* indicates the concluding part of the discussion, and *tasyāpi* the view on cognition discussed before, and *tadeva* means similarity of points. There is no indication of the usage of the term *śūnya* in the Mādhyamika sense. Secondly. the view expressed in an earlier kārikā clarifies the whole picture. Dharmakīrti begins with the question:

sākṣācca jñānajanane samartho viṣayo' kṣavat,
atha kasmāt dvayādhīnajanma tat tena nocyate. (*PV.*, 2/191).

[When in reality the objects are, like the senses, capable of producing knowledge, why then is this production (*janman*) not called depending on two?].

Dharmakīrti answers that the senses are the indicator (*gamaka*); that is why sensation (*pratyakṣa*) is named accordingly. This line of reasoning is the same as that of Diṅnāga in *PS*, 1/4 and *AbkB.*, 1/45, which does not indicate any Mādhyamika mystical sense but the Sautrāntika sense. It proves the fact that the context as a whole is a discussion on the nature of sensation (*pratyakṣa*) not on any metaphysical or mystical nature of things. Then from 2/194-211, he deals with the problems of the assemblage of atoms (*anusañcaya*) as the object of the senses:

sañcitaḥ samudāyaḥ sa sāmānyaṃ tatra cākṣadhīḥ
sāmānyabuddhiścāvaśyaṃ vikalpenānubadhyate. (*PV.*, 2/194).

The later kārikās explain this point of *sañcitākāra* (form of an assemblage) by the example of the coherence of a picture (*citraikatva*) and in this context the terms *dvaya sūnyatā* (devoid of two) (213) and *lakṣaṇaśūnyatvāt niḥsvabhāvaḥ* (because of being devoid of this characteristic it is all naturelessness) are used. *Lakṣaṇa* here seems to be taken as a characteristic and *niḥsvabhāva* as *svalakṣaṇa*, or *vilakṣaṇa* (characterless), as is clear by previous *kārikās* where *śūnyatā* (selflessness or essencelessness) is described. Dharmakīrti wants to clarify the Buddha's intention of substancelessness of aggregates (*skandhādīnām*, 216). In other places Dharmakīrti also used it in the same sense of substancelessness. Previously, he himself has clarified five aggregates (*pañcaskandha PV.*, 1/55-56) and has described his view on *śūnyatā* in the sense of no-self:

muktistu śūnyatādṛṣṭeḥ (*PV.*, 1/255c).
virodhaḥ śūnyatādṛṣṭeḥ sarvadoṣaiḥ prasidhyati (*PV.*, 1/217ab).
nairātmyadṛṣṭeḥ śūnyatā dṛṣṭeḥ (*PVV.*, p. 75).

Similarly, the term *niḥsvabhāvatā* means characterlessness of five aggregates (*PV.*, 2/15-16). The concept of *śūnyatā* in this sense is well described in the Sautrāntika tradition, (*śese caturdaśākāre śūnyānātmavivarjite*, *AbkB.*, 7/12) and should not be confused with Mādhyamika interpretation.

The Sautrāntikas believed in the doctrine of causes, conditions, and the results (*hetu-pratyaya-phala*). There is no one seer or one thing to be seen, in this sense the distinction of external (*grāhya*) and internal (*grāhaka*) is sublated. What exists is the string of events undivided into the external and internal. (*AbkB.*, 1/42). In this sense, the term "*śūnya*" is used (which in early and Sautrāntika Buddhism originally meant 'empty of a soul', i.e. empty of the internal 'perceiver').

The burst of energy in the form of assemblage of atoms can only be described as an event which stimulates cognition. In this sense "objectivity" (*grāhyatā*) means the cause (*hetu*), as described by Dharmakīrti himself:

hetubhāvād ṛte nānyā grāhyatā nāma kācana,
tatra buddhiryadākārā tasyāstad grāhyamucyate. (*PV.*, 2/224).

[The name "objectivity" has no different meaning apart from the cause (*hetu*), whatever becomes the image in intellect is called the object (*grāhya*) of that (intellect).] It means the object, an event or cause, nothing else. Thus, there is no agent and no object to be perceived. What exists is only causes (*kāraṇa*), conditions (*pratyaya*), and results (*phala*). For example, the moment of light or sound of a bell (*AbkB.*, 1/45) is just a flow of events and the correspondence in between them. For example, when one expresses "the bell resounds" or "the light moves", neither the bell resounds nor the light moves but every following moment of sound or light is produced by the previous one. In this sense, Sautrāntikas refuted the theory of substance or self (*ātman*) either inside or outside. This is the real understanding of *śūnyatā* in the Sautrāntika sense.

Vetter's source of information was Prajñākaragupta's and Manorathanandin's commentaries which have taken this context in the sense of Mādhyamika-Yogācāra and the Yogācāra, respectively. They forget the fact that kārikā (223-225) clearly indicate the Sautrāntika concept of assemblage of atom as the cause (*hetu-grāhya*) of cognition.

E

C.D. Sharma's comment is interesting and reveals the ground on which he laid down the foundation of this conclusion. He does not agree with the name Sautrāntika-Yogācāra and calls this school Svatantra-Vijñānavāda (Independent Idealism). But, substantially, this will make no difference as he himself does not differentiate it from the Vijñānavāda of Asaṃga and Vasubandhu I. Firstly, no Buddhist philosopher claimed to be completely independent regarding either disciplinary rules or philosophical opinions, but belonged to one school or another. Secondly, Vasubandhu II followed the Sautrāntikas, Diṅnāga followed Vasubandhu II, and Dharmakīrti followed Diṅnāga. There may be changes in the line of argumentations, but they belong to the one school. If the term *svatantra* is taken in the sense of *svātantrika mādhyamika* of Bhāvaviveka, even then it is not consistent, because *svātantrika* means believing in independent logical proofs to prove the Mādhyamika doctrine, not being a completely independent, neutral, or freelance philosopher. Similarly, to call them Vijñānavādin is also against evidence.

One should also not make a hasty comparison with Western individual philosophers, or free thinkers. Buddhist philosophy as well as other Indian philosophy developed through schools, religious conviction, and monastic traditions initiated by one original philosopher. Sautrāntika tradition was strongly developed by Vasubandhu II, and Diṅnāga and Dharmakīrti were his followers and commentators. Even when not writing actual commentaries, they are still expounding some particular subjects not fully elaborated on or defended in their commentaries. Therefore, to call them independent Idealists (*svatantra vijñānavāda*) may create more confusion.

I have already discussed this point in the introduction. Dharmakīrti was not an idealist in any sense, because he believed in the doctrine of assemblage of atoms (*anusañcayavāda*). He was also not an independent (*svatantra*) philosopher but a commentator and defender of Diṅnāga's doctrines.

C.D. Sharma has been misled by Manorathanandin's interpretation of the opening Kārikā in a Mahāyāna sense.

F

The view that Dharmakīrti was a Sautrantika, expressed by Satkari Mookerjee and S.N Dasgupta, seems to agree with the facts, but nowhere are the grounds for this thesis described. It seems that the study of *NB* or of Vācaspati created a general impression of its being a Sautrāntika epistemological work. Other works like *PV* etc. were not discovered at that time. It is remarkable that these scholars expressed, contrary to Stcherbatsky and others, such a categorical opinion in that age of the beginning of such research. Mookerjee discussed in detail the Sautrāntika ontology, but very little epistemology. S.N. Dasgupta does not interpret history on the ground of his own personal philosophy in his *History of Indian Philosophy*.

These scholars (first Satkari Mookerjee, 1930, then Dasgupta, 1940) were the first to mention it, though neither of them explained it. Mookerjee's book, *Buddhist Philosophy of Universal Flux*, is as serious as Stcherbatsky's *Buddhist Logic*. He was the first modern scholar who called Diṅnāga and Dharmakīrti Sautrāntikas. Prior to him, among ancient commentators and critics Dharmottara, Durvekamiśra, Vācaspati, Pārthasārathi, Udayana, Mallavādin, Siṃhasūri has definitely called them Sautrāntikas.

Rāhula Sāṅkṛtyāyana, though doubtful about including Diṅnaga and Dharmakīrti under Vijñānavāda, on the occasion of personal discussion used to say the "concept of *svalakṣaṇa*" (sense-data) and causal efficiency (*arthakriyākāritva*) are quite different from Yogācāra. But he himself mentions Dharmakīrti as a Sautrāntika-Yogācāra, in accordance with Stcherbatsky's view.

A.K. Warder discovers the difference between the *viṣaya* (object of senses) and the *ālambana* (object of consciousness) and on that ground shows Diṅnāga's *AP* to be not an idealistic work and writes to me a note:

"Actually in *Indian Buddhism* and the *Outline of Indian Philosophy*, I made Diṅnāga break away from Yogācāra and found a new school, the 'Pramāṇa' school, because Diṅnāga and Dharmakīrti are both realists (sense-objects are real). My article on "Objects" further confirms that. Finally, I think that if Diṅnāga wrote the *Marmapradīpa* he was a Sautrāntika (I, of course, always believed Vasubandhu II was a Sautrāntika). If Diṅnāga was a student of Vasubandhu I he started as a Yogācāra. If, as now seems probable, he was a student of Vasubandhu II, then he started as a Sautrāntika and presumably remained one."

REFERENCES

1. Stcherbatsky, "The Buddhist idealistic school of Dignāga and Dharmakīrti developed a transcendental theory which exhibited some striking points of similarity with the transcendental theory of Kant." *The Central Conception of Buddhism and the meaning of the Term Dharma* (*CCB*), p. 54.
2. M. Hattori, "He became a pupil of Vasubandhu, and under the influence of that great scholar he came to obtain mastery of the Vijñānavāda theory and of logic." *Dignāga on Perception*, Introduction, p. 1.

   B.K. Matilal, "It is necessary to specify the sense of the term 'idealism' in which it is generally used to describe the Yogācāra-Vijñānavāda school of Buddhism. I shall apply this term here particularly to the philosophical school of Asaṅga and Vasubandhu, of which Diṅnāga and Dharmakīrti became later exponents." *Buddhist Studies in Honour of I.B. Horner*, p. 139.
3. Various views on Vasubandhu II :

   "The identity of this great master is shrouded in mystery. The traditional biography preserved in Chinese literature narrates that he was a Sarvāstivādi Vaibhāṣika in early days of his life and then he turned a Yogācāra Idealist under the influence of his elder brother Ācārya Asaṅga. He started his career as a Kāśmīra-Vaibhāṣika and composed the *Abhidharmakośa*. When he was convinced eventually of Yogācāra spiritualism, he composed the *Viṃśatikā* and other treatises. Therefore the ideological differences between his early and later writings are inevitable and logical. Without paying much credence to this tradition. Frauwallner sought out a solution to such ideological differences by propounding a theory of two Vasubandhus, older and younger. In this view the older Vasubandhu was a Yogācāra master while the younger one was a Sarvāstivādi-Vaibhāṣika. Though the theory appears to be convenient, it goes counter to internal evidence. It is a known fact that although Vasubandhu composed his *Abhidharma-kośa* from the viewpoint of the Kāśmīra Vaibhāṣika system (*Kāśmīra-Vaibhāṣika-nīti-Siddhakośa*, VIII, 40) he hardly accepted every tenet of Kāśmīra-Vaibhāṣika without questioning its validity. We often find him differing from the Vaibhāṣikas and at the same time, siding with such opinions as would lead him eventually to the idealistic viewpoint . . .

   One may entertain here the impression that Vasubandhu is siding, in this respect, with the Sarvāstivādi-Vaibhāṣika system. But it appears in fact that the above contention is an obvious forerunner of his mind's attitude towards the Yogācāra spiritualism rather than the Sautrāntika nominalism." *Viṃśatikā*, N. Aiyaswāmi Sāstri, Introduction, pp. 1-2.

Stcherbatsky mentions, "There remain the dates of the Chinese translations of Asaṅga and Vasubandhu, which alone, if correct, would be sufficient evidence to assign them to the fourth century. Otherwise one feels inclined to bring Vasubandhu nearer to Dignāga, whose teacher he was." *CCB.*, p. 3.

For details on this issue, see:

'The Date of Vasubandhu, the Great Buddhist Philosopher', J. Takakusu, pp. 79-88.

'The Date of Vasubandhu Seen from the Abhidarmakośa', Taiken Kimura, pp. 89-92.

'The Date of Vasubandhu seen from the History of Buddhist Philosophy', Genmyo Ono, pp. 92-94. *Indian Studies in Honar of Charles Rockwell Lanman*, 1929.

4. "Ācārya Dignāga, l'un des dix grands maîtres de la secte Vijñaptimātratā fondée en Chine par Hiuan-tsang et son éléve Kouei-ki, est l'auteur de l'Ālambanaparīkśā, l'un des textes principaux sur lesquels cette secte a ètabli le fondement de sa doctrine.

Bien que Dignāga soit trés célébre comme maitre et surtout comme fondateur d'une nouvelle logique (Nyāya), cette Ālambanaparīkṣā n'appartient pas en propre a la doctrine Nyāya, mais exprime la doctrine Vijñaptimātratā avec la même tendance que la Vimśativijñaptimātratā de Vasubandhu qui, s'appuyant sur les principes de Nāgārjuna, affirme dés le début que le triple monde n'eşt que pensée.

Il est donc indispensable de se reporter a ce traite et aussi a la Vijñaptimātratāsiddhi de Hiuan-tsang et au Mahāyāna-Sūtrālaṃkāra pour mieux pénétrer la pensée de Dignāga et la mieux situer dans l'évolution du bouddhisme mahāyāniste.

D'autre part, pour bien comprendre les thėses que notre auteur expose et réfute, il est necessaire d'etudier l'Abhidharmakośa de Vasubandhu qui développe les théories principales des Sarvāstivādin et qui donne quelques indications sur celles des Sautrāntika. Car Dignāga, de meme que la plupart des Mahāyānistes é partir de Nāgārjuna, édifie ses doctrines sur la critique des Hīnayānistes. et c'est seulement aprés avoir réfuté leurs diverses conceptions réalistes affirmant l'existence en soi (*bhāva*), qu'il affirme la necessite idealistique de l'object de la connaissance." Susumu Yamaguchi, *AP.*, (2), Introduction, p. 2.

B.K. Matilal also asserts, Although Diṅnāga belonged to the school of Buddhist idealism, he gave a complete reinterpretation of the older theories in such a way that it makes it difficult for us to call him an idealist without qualification. He wrote his *Ālambana-parīkṣā* unmistakably in an idealistic vein. But his logical and epistemological theories set forth in his greatest work, the *Pramāṇasamuccaya*, can be treated as belonging neither to idealism nor to realism." *Epistemology, Logic and Grammar in Indian Philosophical Analysis*, p. 34.

"According to certain interpretations, even Diṅnāga can be called a 'realist' (and no doubt an 'empiricist'), provided that unique particulars are regarded as external point-instants. But I think the Diṇnāga school betrays, in some essential respects, a Phenomenalistic attitude and a Nominalistic attitude as well." ibid, p. 51.

5. Umesha Miśra, *History of Indian Philosophy*, I, p. 393.
6. *Critical Survey of Indian Philosophy*, p. 12.
7. Satkari Mookerjee calls Dharmakīrti a Sautrāntika in regard to his theory of perception as a Sautrāntika theory. *Buddhist Philosophy of Universal Flux*, p. 119.
8. Rāhula Sāṅkṛtyāyana mentions Dharmakīrti as a Sautrāntika. *Bauddha Darśana*, p. 59.
9. In *Viṃśatikā-ṭīkā*, kārikā 50, Vinītadeva labels the *pūrvapakṣa* as Sautrāntika while according to Kwei-chi the 'Bāhyārthavādin' here meant the Vaiśeṣika. *Viṃsatikā*, p. 48.
10. It is surprising that Hattori has clarified the position of Diṅnāga in *AP*. as that of a Sautrantika:

"In Ālambanap., Dignāga mentions two necessary conditions which the object of cognition (*ālambana*) must fulfil: first, the object must be the cause (*kāraṇa*) of a cognition, and, second, it must possess the same form (*ākāra*) as that appearing in the cognition. That is to say, a cognition must on the one hand be produced by the object (*tad-utpatti*), and on the other hand have coordination of form with the object (*tat sārūpya*). To satisfy the first condition, the object must be a real entity (*dravyasat*), because what is unreal has no faculty of producing a cognition. To meet the second condition, the object must have a gross form (*sthūlākāra*), because a subtle invisible form is never represented in a cognition. Taking these two conditions into account, Dignāga examines the views of the realists (1) that the object of cognition is a single atom (*paramāṇu*), (2) that it is the aggregate (*saṁcita*) of atoms, and (3) that it is the gathering (*saṁghāta*) of atoms. According to the Sautrāntikas, any object which is constituted by many elements is considered as (*saṃvṛtisat*) or *prajñapti-sat*, empirically real or nominally existent, because it is no longer cognized when it is destroyed or analyzed by intellect into its elements. That which is neither destroyed or analyzed into elements is admitted as *paramārtha-sat* or (*dravyasat*, ultimate reality or real entity). See *AK*, VI, 4:

yasmin bhinne na tad-buddhir anyāpohe dhiyā ca tat
ghaṭāmbuvat saṁvṛti-sat paramārtha-sad anyathā. Dignāga adopts these Sautrāntika concepts of *saṃvṛtisat* and *paramārtha-sat* in examining the views of the realists." *Diṅnāga on Perception*, p. 118.

Dharmakīrti's account also is the same.

11. As the objects are in the state of flux the sensation (*pratyakṣa*) of the first moment is the only fundamental while inference (*anumāna*) is grounded on it. Dharmakīrti denies the possibility of recognizing the particular (*viśeṣa*) on this very ground.

viśeṣa-pratyabhijñānaṃ na pratīkṣaṇa-bhedataḥ (*PV.*, 2/118). Also see:

arthakriyāyogyaviṣayatvāt tadarthīnām pravṛtteḥ, arthakriyāyogya-lakṣaṇam hi vastu; tato'pi vikalpād vastūny eva tadadhyavasāyena pravṛtteh, pravṛttau vikalpasya pratyakṣeṇābhinnayogakṣematvāt. Hetu, p. 8;

12. Stcherbatsky pinpoints it.
"The information about the Sautrāntika theory of cognition conatined in the *Sarva-darśana-saṃgrahaḥ* and similar works (*bāhyārthānumeyatva*), reposes on a confusion by Brahmanical authors between Sautrāntika and Vijñānavāda not seldom to be met with." *CCB.*, p. 63.

CHAPTER 3

Evidence for Dharmakīrti's Position

There have been continuous controversies among ancient and modern scholars on Dharmakīrti's philosophical position. Different scholars in different ages applied his logic and epistemology by including his logic in their own systems. But his own internal epistemology and ontology remained unaltered. Therefore, I have taken his whole philosophical system in the form of internal evidence, viz., if he was a Sautrāntika, then his fundamental doctrines must agree with Sautrāntika tradition. Thus, the method of agreement (*sādharmya* or *anvayavidhi*) and method of difference (*vyatireka* or *vaidharmyavidhi*) is applied to judge whether Dharmakīrti's epistemological, ontological, and axiological doctrines are in harmony with Sautrāntika tradition or not.*

One question may strike the mind. In the case of the disappearance of Sautrāntika literature, how is it possible to know definitely their doctrines? Comparison will be impossible. Though most of the literature of the Sautrāntika seems to be lost, even then the discovery of Kumāralāta's fragments, *Abhidharmakośabhāṣya* of Vasubandhu, and the detailed commentary of Yaśomitra, provides us with the definite doctrines of the Sautrāntikas, which are sufficient to observe whether Dharmakīrti's doctrines are in agreement with them or not. Apart from this, non-Buddhist critics like Uddyotakara, Vācaspati, Udayana, and Pārthasāarthi clarify them and we have the Tibetan tradition which provides us with definite doctrines of Sautrāntikas.

The very definition of Sautrāntikas given by Yaśomitra** adduces sufficient proof of their doctrines: that they considered the *Sūtrapiṭaka* the only valid source, i.e., the old *Sūtra*, not the Māhāyāna *sūtras.* Fortunately, the whole *Sūtrapiṭaka* (in Pāḷi and some in Sanskrit),

**supra*, p. 18.
***supra*, pp. 8-10.

with some commentaries and sub-commentaries, has already been published.

In the case that Dharmakīrti nowhere calls himself a Sautrāntika, then how can one prove it? There is no doubt of the fact that Dharmakīrti used neither the term Sautrāntika, nor Yogācāra, Vijñānavāda, Vaibhāṣika, Mādhyamika or any other. Had he offered this kind of statement, no controversy would have taken place. It does not mean that he was a Sautrāntika in disguise. It seems that the general tendency of logician commentators in that age was not to mention their ontological positions or the schools they belonged to. For it was well understood by scholars of that period what the affiliation of a commentator or defender was. Uddyotakara, Vācaspatimiśra, Pārthasārathi, etc. were well acquainted with the fact that Diṅnāga and Dharmakīrti were commentators and defenders of Sautrāntika Vasubandhu II—that is why they call them Sautrāntikas.

There is no doubt or confusion about the ontological positions of Asaṃga and Vasubandhu I, as they are definitely consistent with their Vijñānavāda ontology and they mentioned it also. Vasubandhu II criticized the views of his predecessors (*Sarvāstivādin—Vaibhāṣikas*, etc.) who were not in conformity with logic and the *Sūtrapiṭaka*, a criticism started by Bhadantasthavira, Kumāralāta, etc. The ancient name of this trend of thought was *Dārṣṭāntikas*, or adherents of empirical (*dṛṣṭa*) examples. The method of *dṛṣṭānta* (empirical example) was itself adopted by the Buddha on almost all occasions of decision and argument. When Buddhist philosophers began to speculate about entities which had no empirical ground, a worse kind of confusion emerged among Ābhidharmikas themselves, as happened at the time when the *Kathāvatthu* was composed to decide the original teachings of the Buddha on the ground of Buddhist formal logic and internal consistency. The confusion of this age was not primarily on disciplinary problems, but mainly regarding reality.*

Vasubandhu II undertook the task of purifying Buddhist philosophy with the sharp razor of empirical logic, and Diṅnāga and Dharmakīrti continued this operation mainly with the weapons of logic and epistemology. The ontological position of Vasubandhu II, Diṅnāga, and Dharmakīrti can be called by the name Sautrāntika and their ontological position can be definitely determined. The only term which Dharmakīrti uses for Diṅnāga is "nyāyavādin", which is gene-

**supra*, pp. 21-22.

rally translated as "logician", but this term seems to connote something more than a logician. There were many other Buddhist and non-Buddhist logicians. Then why is this name (nyāyavādin) not used for them? There must be something particular which caused Diṅnāga and Dharmakīrti to be called Nyāyavādin and not others. The term *nyāya* though used generally for logic, connoted something more than logic, that is, correct logic or justice in logic which is acceptable to all reasonable minds. Gautama, Vātsyāyana, Uddyotakara were also logicians, but by believing in the authority of the Vedas and accepting twelve objects of cognition (*prameya*) they were rather one-sided and dogmatic. Diṅnāga and Dharmakīrti brushed aside authority, either Buddhist or non-Buddhist, as a separate means of right knowledge, and regarded the objects which are not perceived through the senses as doubtful. The method (*nyāya*) was rather objective and agreeable to all logical minds. It removes the possibility of any dogmatic subject-matters (*prameyas*) which contradict this criterion. Thus, the term "nyāyavādin" is suitable for them.

The Mādhyamikas and Vijñānavādins accept logic only from the worldly point of view and thus cannot be named Nyāyavādins. Some rules of formal logic were formulated by Moggaliputtatissa and empirical logic was developed by Vasubandhu II, Diṅnāga, and Dharmakīrti. The Vijñānavādins like Asaṃga also discussed logic, but they are nowhere called Nyāyavādins because they believed in authority (*āptāgama*) as a separate means of cognition. In fact they are called the 'learned' (*vidvas*) school, which is quite consistent with knowledge of authorities as opposed to logical studies. And Vasubandhu I criticizes the Sautrāntika theory of sensation (*pratyakṣa*) and relies on authority or intuition. Logic for them was only of worldly application. Some scholars who use the term "nyāyavādin" with Vijñānavāda and call Diṅnāga and Dharmakīrti by the name "nyāyavādino vijñānavādinaḥ" seem to be mistaken. Diṅnāga and Dharmakirti nowhere refer to Asaṃga or the Vijñānavādin Vasubandhu's writings for verification or clarification, but to the Sautrāntika Vasubandhu (either *Abhidharmakośabhāṣya* or *Vādavidhāna*).*

The Tibetan scholar Jigs med dbang po (1728-1881) in his work, *Grub pa'i mtha'i rnam par bzhag pa rin po che'i phreng-ba* (The Jewel Garland of the Dissertation on Philosophical Systems) brings into light this fact: "a Sautrāntika is a man following the Hīnayāna

**supra*, p. 29.

line of thought, recognizing self-cognition and external objects as existing in truth. The names Sautrāntika and Dārṣṭāntika are synonymous. There are two schools, the one following tradition and the other advocating logical investigation." Guenther holds, "In this Sautrāntika school the essential works on Buddhist logic originated. They are *Pramāṇavārttika*, *Pramāṇaviniścaya*, *Nyāyabindu*..."* All the seven works of Dharmakīrti are mentioned and 'Jigs-med-dbang-po himself concludes this section showing his reverence for logic:

"To sum up:
May logicians enjoy this banquet
Of the secrets of those who follow
Reason in their teaching which I have served up
For I have long and deeply studied logic."**

It implies that the Tibetan tradition assigned logical development fundamentally to Sautrāntikas, not to Vijñānavādins. Also that there were two branches of Sautrāntika; namely, those who simply followed the tradition (*āgama*, the *Sūtras*), writing commentaries on these and perhaps works like *AbkB.*, and those who developed logic, writing independent treaties like *Nyāymukha.****

The usage of the term "nyāyavādin" also removes the possibility of their formulating logic from a worldly point of view as believed by Stcherbatsky and followed by others. Had Dharmakīrti been a logician from a lower point of view, this term would never have occurred for him because names are given according to the fundamental differential characteristics, not according to lower or subsidiary ones. For example, the Mādhyamikas believed in logic from a worldly or lower point of view but can never be called Nyāyavādins. Similarly, a true Vijñānavādin can only believe in logic on a phenomenal level and cannot be named Nyāyavādin. Only the philosophers who believe in the fundamentality of logic are appropriately called Nyāyavādins. As the Sautrāntikas believed this, the name "nyāyavādin" is appropriate for them. The Jainas used the name "nyāyavādin" for Vasubandhu II. That is why the name "nyāyavādin" is consistent with Sautrāntika. (App. III)

**Buddhist Philosophy in Theory and Practice*, p. 218.

**ibid., p. 83.

****supra*, pp. 20-22.

There is no doubt that some later Vijñānavādins, known as "sākāravādin vijñānavādins", like Ratnakīrti, Jñānaśrīmitra, etc. also followed Dharmakīrti's logic to defend their systems, and attempted to bring harmony among all Ācaryas. But in doing so they have deviated from the original Vijñānavāda and have come closer to Sautrāntikas in many of their doctrines.

Vācaspatimiśra sometimes calls Diṅnāga and Dharmakīrti "Nyāyavādin bauddha" or sometimes Sautrāntika which implies the name "nyāyavādin sautrāntikas" for their system. They were epistemologist logicians (Pramaṇavādins or Nyāyavādins) which differentiates them from logicians of other systems. The following is the evidence which positively proves Dharmakīrti a Sautrāntika.

EPISTEMOLOGY

1: The very definition of right cognition (*samyagjñāna*) differentiates Dharmakīrti from Mādhyamika and Vijñānavāda, and proves him a Sautrāntika. Dharmakīrti in the very beginning of *PV* and *NB* defines precisely what he means by right knowledge; that is, knowledge which leads to successful activity.*

Stcherbatsky used the term "empirical knowledge" (*samyagjñāna*), understanding empirical in the sense of lower or phenomenal, as Absolutists contrast it with higher. The very term "*samyak*" (right) excludes this possibility. The Buddha used "*samyagjñāna*" or "*sammādiṭṭhi*" to denote right knowledge which consisted in understanding *duḥkha, anitya, anātman* as the characteristics of reality, discussed by Dharmakīrti in *PV*., 1/252-58. The Buddha himself, though indirectly, indicated that right knowledge is meaningful (*atthasahita*) and seen individually (*paccattaṃ veditabbo*). In *Kālāma-Sutta*, he gave fruitful or successful activity as a criterion of truth, and criticized wrong views (*micchādiṭṭhi*) on the ground that they are useless. Similar is the case with inexpressible problems (*abyākata*, sk. *avyākṛta*)as discussed also by Vasubandhu II and Yaśomitra.

Dharmakīrti has really followed the Buddha in defining right cognition and there is no possibility of calling it lower or phenomenal. No one can use the term "*samyak*" for lower or phenomenal. It appears that Vijñānavādin commentators like Vinītadeva and Manorathanandin got alarmed by this definition and attempted to interpret

**supra*, p. 53.

it differently. Manorathanandin tries to reconcile it with Vijñānavāda: "*etaccāvisaṃvādanaṃ bāhyārthetaravādayoḥ samānaṃ pramāṇalakṣaṇaṃ, vijñānanaye'pi sādhananirbhāsajñānāntaraṃ arthakriyānirbhāsa jñānameva saṃvādaḥ, ato vijñaptimātratve pramāṇetaravibhāgavyavahāro asaṃkīrṇaḥ*". *PV.*, 1/1).
[This definition of the means of knowledge, namely non-contradiction, is the same for the doctrine of the external object and the other (idealism). In the Vijñāna system also after the knowledge of the appearance of the means there is knowledge of the appearance of action towards an object. Therefore, there is agreement in the mere makings of consciousness; the usage for the analysis of the means and non-means is not confused].

Vinītadeva expressed similar views. Both of them sought to prove "non-contradictory" (*avisaṃvāda*) as the real meaning and overlooked successful activity (*arthakriyākāritva*), which apparently seems to be a partial and too narrow interpretation, and an apparent deviation from Dharmakīrti's own clear definition.*

The expression "*bāhyārthetara vādayoḥ samānaṃ pramāṇalakṣaṇaṃ*" (the definition of valid cognition is the same in the doctrine of the external object and the other) and *vijñānanaye'pi* (also in vijñāṇavāda) proves beyond doubt that they have attempting to reconcile it with Vijñānavāda. In the case Dharmakīrti was fundamentally a Vijñānavādin, there would then be no question of such reconciliation.**

In that case, one would have reconciled it with Sautrāntika. The usage "*api*" (Manoratha) or "*anyathā prakaraṇena yogācāranaya nirāsaḥ syāt*" (Vinīta). (If it is interpreted differently, then it will contradict the Yogācāra) clearly reveals this fact. Dharmottara, Durvekamiśra, and Mallavādin (the *Tippaṇakāra* on *NB.*), clearly indicate that the definition cannot be consistent with Vijñānavāda, which believes in (except the knowledge of Tathāgata) the doctrine that all knowledge is illusory (*tan matena tu sarvamālambane bhrāntaṃ muktvā tathāgatajñānaṃ, NB., Tipp.*, 17/1). Thus, his definition of *samyagjñāna* proves Dharmakīrti a Sautrāntika.***

2. Further evidence is Dharmakīrti's theory of validity of right cognition as depending on extraneous conditions; i.e., successful activity or causal efficiency (*arthakriyākāritva*). Such a criterion is

**supra*, p. 54.

***supra*, p. 64.

****supra*, pp. 106-07.

possible from a Sautrāntika or Vaibhāsika point of view and never from that of Vijñānavāda. The only consistent criterion of validity for Vijñānavāda is self-consciousness (*ātmasaṃvedana*) which does not depend on any extraneous (*parataḥ*) condition. Dharmakīrti's clear indications—

pramāṇamavisaṃvādi jñānam, arthakriyāsthitiḥ (*PV.*, 1/lab).
(Valid cognition is non-contradictory, the establishment (of it) is through action towards an object.)
prāmāṇyaṃ vyavahāreṇa (*PV.*, 1/7a).
(Validity of cognition depends on its application).
svalakṣaṇa-vicārataḥ (*PV.*, 1/8d).
(Taking own-characteristic into consideration).
arthakriyāyogyaviṣayatvāt tadārthināṃ pravṛtteḥ (*Hetu.*, p. 53).
(Because of there being a sense-object fit for action towards an object because of the starting (activity) of those who desire it).
sa pāramārthiko bhāvo ya evārthakriyākṣamaḥ (*PV.*, 3/166cd).
(Whatever is susceptible of action towards an object is ultimately real).
tadevaparāmārthasat, arthakriyāsāmarthyādvastunaḥ (*NB.*, 1/14-15).
(because of capability of sustaining action towards an object of reality it is called the ultimate reality).
idameva hi vastvavastulakṣaṇam (*PVSV.*, 1/168, p. 323).
(It is the characteristic of reality or unreality).
(*na hi ābhyāṃ arthaṃ paricchidya pravartamāno'rthakriyāyāṃ visaṃvādyate* (*PVin.*, I p. 30).
(For having distinguished the object by these two, the activity does not contradict action towards the object) etc. All this evidence proves that he believed in "*arthakriyākāritva*" as the sole criterion of judging validity (*prāmānyaṃ*) and invalidity of knowledge. That action towards an object is the fundamental criterion for validity removes the possibility of his belonging to the Vijñānavāda school, which believes in a mental reflex (*pratibhāsa=patibiṃbana*) based on the force of transcendental illusion (*avidyā-balāt*) springing forth from store-consciousness (*ālaya-vijñāna*) without any external object.

Dharmakīrti's standpoint is contrary to this, viz. that it is external reality (*vastu-artha*) which serves human purposes and removes the possibility of illusory cognition (*bhrānti-jñāna*). Illusory cognition, like a mirage, is undoubtedly a cognition but turns out to be illusory and loses its validity when it fails to fulfil human needs: such as, quenching thirst.

3. Dharmakīrti's solution of the problem of the identity between the object and its self-conscious image is grounded on the relation of correspondence (*sārūpya-saṃbandha*), which can never be consistent with Vijñānavāda, which believes in only mentality so that no question of correspondence arises. Correspondence is only possible when there are two things, or two aspects of one process. Dharmakīrti lays stress on "*sārūpya*" at various points in *PV*:

siddhaṃ sārūpye'sya svavedanaṃ (2/443d).

(Its cognition) self-consciousness is established in correspondence).

sārūpyāt vedanākhyā (2/444a).

(Because of correspondence it is called (self) consciousness). This description completely resembles that of *AbkB.* of Vasubandhu II who clarifies it through the examples of the movement of a flame and the ringing of a bell.* The representation (*ābhāsa*) or form (*ākāra*) implies "of what". If there exists nothing apart from the mental images, as the Vijñānavāda hold, no question of correspondence arises**. That is why Dinnāga and Dharmakīrti established two kinds of correspondence between objects and images, i.e., *tadutpatti* (caused by it) and *tatsādṛśya* (similar to it)[1] which can be clarified through a diagram:

flow of svalakṣaṇas — *flow of consciousness (citta saṃtāna)*

(*sāmarthya*)—— capacity to affect mind —— (consciousness-*vijñāna*)

tadutpatti — *tatsādṛśya*

☐ ——→ ☐ *viṣaya* ☐ ☐ *indriyavijñāna*

*supra, pp. 90-91.

***supra*, p. 95 ref. 10.

This treatment of this important point ranks Dharmakīrti as a Sautrāntika. From the Vijñānavāda point of view the process is quite the reverse.

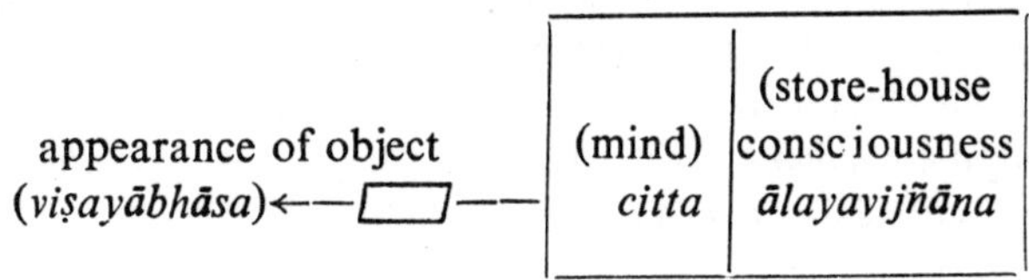

This diagram clearly indicates that the origin of cognition is different Vijñānavāda and Sautrāntika. The former believes in the existence of store-house consciousness which produces external object, like a dream, while the latter believes in the object (*viṣaya-anusañcaya*) as the cause of cognition. That is why the correspondence (*sārūpya*) by the way of cause (*tadutpatti*) and similarity (*tadsādṛśya*) is possible from the Sautrāntika point of view, not from the Vijñānavāda point of view.*

4. Dharmakīrti's emphasis on *pratyakṣa* as the most important means of knowledge and very ground of all valid cognition is in conformity with Sautrāntika. From the very beginning the Dārṣṭāntikas emphasized *dṛṣṭa* or "perceived" as the criterion of reality. Vasubandhu II criticized Vaibhāṣika metaphysical entities on the ground of not being perceived (*dṛṣṭa*)**

Diṅnāga, although he does not mention it clearly, having *svalakṣaṇa* as the object of sensation, Proves it to be the ground of all valid cognition. Diṅnāga and Dharmakīrti do not admit a thesis (*pakṣa*) which contradicts sensation (*pratyakṣaviruddha*). But, Vijñānavāda denies any real object of the senses and their reliability and emphasizes intuition or scriptural authority.

5. Dharmakīrti's definition of *pratyakṣa* (*kalpanāpoḍhaṃ abhrāntaṃ pratyakṣaṃ NB.*, 1/9) (sensation is devoid of imagination and illusion) also proves him a Sautrāntika, being from a fundamental (*paramārth*) standpoint and sole criterion of valid cognition.[2] It contradicts the Vijñānavāda position, which can only believe in it from the phenomenal point of view and can never believe in its being the sole criterion of valid cognition. The first term, or concept, "*kalpanā*", as defined by Diṅnāga and Dharmakīrti, is also in conformity with the Sautrāntikas.

**supra*, pp. 68-69.

***supra*, pp. 20-22.

Kalpanā or *vikalpa* is used in the sense of conceptual formation, or imagination in the Sautrāntika Abhidharma tradition. In Vijñānavāda, "*kalpanā*", is used in a specific sense of *grāhya-grāhaka kalpanā* (object-subject imagination), which is different from the sense of Diṅnāga and Dharmakīrti.

The *Tātparyanibandhana* throws light on the nature of *kalpanā* in the system of Vaibhāṣika and Yogācāra, which differs from Dharmakīrti's definition:

"*yāto bahvyaḥ kalpanāḥ santi, tathā—indriyavijñānānām. vitarkavicāra-caitasiksamprayuktānāmaudāryasūksmatayā svaviṣaye pravṛttiriti vaibhāṣikī kalpanā, vitarkavicārādaudāryasūkṣmate...Yogācārānām**.

[There are many types of imagination, as it is said—according to the Vaibhāṣika imagination is a sense cognition invariably connected with mental factors such as applied thought, sustained thought. Because of its grossness or subtleness it is the indulgence in its own objects. According to the Vijñānavāda (imagination), because of applied thought and sustained thought, is grossness and subtleness.] Similarly *Ṭippaṇa* mentions—*tathāhi vaibhāśika indriyavijñānam vitarkavicāra-caitasikasamprayuktam kalpanāmicchanti. Yogācāramatena ca tathāgatajñānamadvayam muktvā sarvajñānam grāhyagrāhakatvena vikalpitamkalpanā*, p. 21.[3] This difference between Vaibhāṣika and Yogācāra proves sufficiently that the definition of *kalpanā* is only agreeable with the Sautrāntika standpoint. Similarly, the term "*abhrānta*" is consistent only from the Sautrāntika point of view and not with that of Vijñānavāda. Dinnāga, however, did not use "*abhrānta*" (non-illusory) in his definition of sensation, which has created a great amount of controversy and dispute among the commentators, and Dharmakīrti also does not use it in *PV*. The explanation of this omission seems to be Dinnāga's dealing with the problem of illusion (*bhrānti*) in his chapter (K. 7-8) on *Pratyaksa*. Dharmakīrti, following him, discussed four kinds of illusory perceptions as not perception but imagining, in the end of his chapter on Perception (*PV*., 2/288-300). He reduced their numbers to two (sensory and mental). *Ṭippāṇṇa* on *NB* presents different views on this issue and expresses the opinion that this definition corresponds with Sautrāntika—*nanūktam Yogācāramatamasamgṛhītam syāditi. ucyate, bāhyanayena sautrāntikānusāreṇa lakṣaṇam kṛtamadoṣaḥ, Yogācāra-matena tu abhrāntagrahaṇam na kartavyam samvādakasya samyagjñānasya prastutattvāt.* (*NBTT.*, p. 19; *Pradīpa*, p. 264)

**Tātparyanibandhana Pradīpa*, p. 265.

[If it is said that the Yogācāra doctrine would be excluded (by this definition). It is answered. If (the illusion) is defined from the point of view of Sautrāntika's external object then it is faultless. But from the Vijñānavāda point of view the acceptance of non-illusion is not appropriate; because of the presence of non-contradictory correct knowledge].

We have also seen the observation of Durvekamiśra who criticized Vinītadeva and positively asserts that this definition conforms with Sautrāntika.*

In this context also Durveka differentiates the Sautrāntika viewpoint from the Yogācāra and supports Dharmottara's comment that "*abhrānta*" means non-contradiction of successful action (*abhrāntam-arthakriyākṣaṃe aviparyastaṃ yat taducyate*).[4] No one can overlook this observation. Thus, the definition of *pratyakṣa* as elucidated by Dharmakīrti corresponds to Sautrāntika not to Yogācāra.

6. The division of *pratyaksa* as classified by Dharmakīrti, is in conformity with Sautrāntika. Dharmakīrti based this classification on Diṅnāga, who had followed the Sautrāntika Vasubandhu on this point. The Vaibhāṣikas believed in the threefold division, viz. sensory, mental and Yogin-not in *svasaṃvedana* (self-consciousness). Vijñānavāda, being mentalist, can never accept this division, particularly the sole criterion of sense-perception (*indriya pratyakṣa*).

The fourfold division is: (i) sensory (*indriya*), (ii) mental (*mānasika*), (iii) self-conscious (*svasaṃvedana*) and (iv). Yogin (*pratyakṣa*). *Indriyapratyakṣa* is identified because of the dominance of the senses described in Sautrāntika tradition as *adhipati pratyaya* (dominant factor) Both Diṅnāga and Dharmakīrti, in confomity with Vasubandhu II, have clarified this fact. We find the detailed description of the senses as a physically operative factor in the Sanskrit Sautrāntika tradition as well as the Pāli Theravāda tradition. This differentiates them from the Vijñānavāda, which neglects it.**

The definition of mental sensation (*Mānasa pratyakṣa*) also differs from Vijñānavāda. *Mānasa pratyakṣa* is the immediately following moment, after the sensory act, of the mind being devoid of any mental conceptualization. It is a form of bare mental awareness and depends on the senses. Dharmakīrti has answered two objections of a Brahmanical logician, on this very ground. The Vijñānavāda may

**supra*, pp 54-5.
***supra*, p. 20.

speak of mental perception but cannot make it dependent on the senses.

Durveka has presented Śāntabhadra's account of "*mānasapratyakṣa*' according to the Sautrāntika view: *iha Śāntabhadreṇa Sautrāntikānāṃ mataṃ darśayatā pūrvaṃ cakṣūrūpe cakṣuvijñānaṃ tatastenendriya-vijñānena sahajakṣaṇasahakāriṇā tṛtīyasmin kṣaṇe mānasapratyakṣaṃ janyate*" *iti vyākhyātaṃ**.
[Here Śāntabhadra referrring to the doctrine of Sautrāntikas mentions "first the eye consciousness with reference to a visible object of the eye, then through that sense-consciousness the mental sensation is produced by simultaneous cause in the third moment" is described].

It proves that the theory of mental sensation was from the Sautrān-tika point of view.

Dharmotatra clearly indicates that the mind begins to operate when the operation of the senses is finished. If this is not accepted, then there is no sharp distinction between sensation and conceptualization except the difference of degree. In other words denial of the very pure sensation (*etacca manovijñanamuparatavyāpāre cakṣuṣi pratyakṣ-amiṣyate vyāpāravati tu cakṣuṣi yadrūpajñānaṃ tat sarvaṃ caksurāś-ritameva. itarathā cakṣurāśritatvānupapattiḥ kasyacidapi vijñānasya NBT.* (*D*) 1/9).

It is a well-known fact that the theory of four conditions (*catuḥ-pratyaya*) was, though common to all schools of Buddhism, particu-larly developed in the Vaibhāṣika and the Sautrāntika traditions (*AbkB.*, 2/62) as the basis of their explanation of the origin of cogni-tion, and Dharmakīrti has followed it.[5] The doctrine of the double method of cognition of five external objects known in two ways (*pañca-bāhya-dvivijñeyaḥ, AbkB.*, 1/48) is discussed by Vasubhandhu II on the ground of the Buddha's utterance "*dvābhyāṃ bhikṣavo rūpaṃ gṛhyate caksūrvijñānena tadākṛṣṭena ca manaseti*" (Ye monks, knowledge of form is received through two channels: by eye-conscious-ness and by its attraction through the mind). Thus, this account of mental cognitions is in correspondence with Sautrāntika tradition, not with Vijñānavāda. (*PV.*, 2/238-248),

Sva-saṃvedana pratyakṣa (self-conscious sensation) is accepted in both the systems, Sautrāntika as well as Vijñānavāda, but there are some fundamental differences regarding the nature of *sva-saṃvedana.* Dharmakīrti's definition of self-consciousness of all minds and mental

****Pradīpa*, p. 61.**

factors (*sarvacittacaittānāṃ ātmasaṃvedanaṃ*" *NB.*, 1/10) and (*PV.*, 2/249-87) reminds us of the treatment of *citta* and *caitaṣika* by Vasubandhu II who calls them *sva-viṣaya* (self-object) *AbkB.*, 1/29;2/23, 62) and *svālambana* (self-dependence). Vijñānavāda, though, accepts this doctrine in conformity with the general Buddhist doctrine of no-self (*anātman*) but they do not believe that the object of self-conscious sensation is *svalakṣaṇa* as explained by Dharmakīrti, who grounded all kinds of sensation on *svalakṣaṇa*, which can be true only on the Sautrāntika explanation.

Yogipratyakṣa, as defined by Dharmakīrti, is in agreement with the Sautrāntika Vasubandhu's account of mindfulness (*smṛtyupasthāna*, *Pāḷi-satipaṭṭhāna*) of a Yogin who becomes well established in reality (*bhūtārtha=anitya, duḥkha, anātman*) through the constant practice of *smṛti-upāsthana* or mindfulness, and as the net of imagination (*kalpanājāla*) is destroyed he lives moment to moment in bare sensations.*

This description is different from that of the Mahāyāna idea of the Bodhisattva who contemplates either *śūnyatā* or *vijñaptimātratā* and has no degree of gradation (*prakarṣaparyantajaṃ*) as mentioned by Dharmakīrti. Stcherbatsky's translation of Yogin as mystic intuition of a saint and his explanation of *bodhisattva* and of *bhūtārtha* as transcendental reality are not correct. The object of all these fourfold *pratyakṣas* is "*svalakṣaṇa*" or unique particulars which does not allow any mystical element in the empiricism of Dharmakīrti.

7. Diṅnāga and Dharmakīrti examined the problems of different means of valid cognition accepted in different schools and reduced their number to two only: sensation (*pratyakṣa*) and inference (*anumāna*). This division is based on the Sautrāntika tradition rather than Vijñānavāda, which accepts three sources of valid cognition including *āptāgama*. Dharmakīrti criticized *śabdapramāṇa* whether Buddhist or non-Buddhist and included *āptāgama* in inference. Asaṃga and Vasubandhu I on the contrary believed in the Buddhist scriptures as valid source of cognition. Dharmakīrti has gone to the extent of saying there is only one object of cognition (*meyaṃ tu ekaṃ svalakṣaṇaṃ*), known through sensation and inference (*anumāna*). The *anumāna* is not completely separate from *pratyakṣa* and depends on *arthakriyākāritva* (successful activity) which is only possible through a particular sensory object (*svalakṣaṇa*). Thus, it leaves no place for any mystical element. Dhamakīrti discovered that valid cog-

**supra*, pp. 46-57.

nition can be derived only through these two sources and thus established the limit of valid knowledge which had been duly explained by the Buddha himself.

All this epistemological evidence is in agreement with Sautrāntika and disagreement with Vijñānavāda. Thus, one can come to the definite conclusion that Dharmakīrti, along with Vasubandhu II and Diṅnāga, is a Sautrāntika.

Ontology

Another important question which calls for an investigation is the ontological views of Dharmakīrti and whether they are in agreement with Sautrāntika or not. This covers his views about the fundamental reality, about the external world and the internal world, or his metaphysics as a whole.

8. Dharmakīrti, after analyzing the instrument of valid cognition thoroughly, discusses the problem of reality and comes to the conclusion that two realities, viz. unique particular physical events and mind and mental events exist in reality (as *svalakṣaṇas*) and that the denial of either of them will lead to self-contradition. The further division of objects in two, viz. *svalakṣaṇa* (particular), and *sāmānya-iakṣana* (universal), is based on Sautrāntika tradition and is well explained by Vasubandhu II. The Vaibhāṣikas also believed in it and the Sautrāntikas accepted it with some modification from the Vaibhāṣika viewpoint. But it is quite different from the Vijñānavāda doctrine of three kinds of characters, i.e., *parikalpita* (imaginary) *paratantra* (dependent) and *pariniṣpanna* (real) which are nowhere mentioned by Dharmakīrti. The definition of *paramārthasatya* (ultimate reality) as the *svalakṣaṇa* (unique particular) object of sensation and of *samvṛrisatya* (*sāmāny*-general) as the object of inference is duly in agreement with Sautrāntika. On the other hand, Vijñānavāda has an entirely different conception of reality.*

9. Dharmakīrti's treatment of *paramāṇus* as distinct entities creating a gross form by coming closer, definitely differs from Vijñānavāda which denies their existence completely, and agrees with the Sautrāntika view of atoms as described by Vasubandhu II in detail in his *AbkB.***

10. Dharmakīrti's maxim "*yat sat tadanityaṃ*" (whatever exists is non-eternal) proves him a full-fledged Sautrāntika, as this doctrine was the very ground of Sautrāntika movement against the Vaibhāṣika

*supra, p. 34
**supra, p 62

which introduces eternal entities like *pratisaṃkhyānirodha apratisaṃkhyānirodha*, etc. accepted by Vaibhāṣikas and Vijñānavādins.*

The term "*anitya*" is used in Pāli Theravāda or Sanskrit Sautrāntika tradition which does not accept the durability of a flow even for a moment. The Vaibhaṣikas assumed three moments, origin (*utpāda*), staying (*sthiti*) and decay (*bhaṅga*). On the contrary Vasubandhu II criticized the Vaibhaṣika view of "*sthiti*" implying (durability) and explained the Sautrāntika view of a constant flow (*anityasaṃtāna*) of all existing things without any break. This doctrine of *anityavāda* is typical in the Sautrāntika tradition, and that is why Dharmakīrti selected the term "*anitya*" (non-eternal) instead of "*kṣaṇika*" (momentary).

The theory of universal flux, though other Buddhist Philosophical schools also accept it, is comprehensively discussed in the Sautrāntika tradition. Even *nirvāṇa* was not regarded as an entity, but as the cessation (*nirodha*) of aggregation like the disappearance of a lamp flame. Thus, we find complete agreement of Dharmakīrti with Sautrāntikas and difference from Vijñānavāda and other schools.

11. Dharmakīrti's whole ontological position can be expressed in a single word; "*svalakṣana*". *Svalakṣaṇa, anitya paramārthasatya, arthakriyākāritva anātman, śūnya*, are all different names of *svalakṣaṇa* which was duly explained by Vasubandhu II and epistemologically elaborated by Dharmakīrti. The term *svalakṣaṇa* is also used in Vijñānavāda, but it has a different connotation, i.e., the "mental moment" and thus neglects the objective part of it. Mādhyamika, particularly the Prāsaṅgika, refutes any *svalakṣana*. Stcherbatsky's interpretation of "*svalakṣana*" in the sense of the Absolute of Idealism is not logical at all. *Svalakṣaṇa* does not seem to be consistent with Yogācāra. The usage of the term "*svalakṣana*" is traceable in different systems of Buddhist philosophy. The Vaibhāṣikas used this term in a technical sense, and Sautrāntika on the ground of this very definition discarded some of the entities dogmatically assumed by them.

Vasubandhu II and particularly Dharmakīrti duly analyzed the nature of *svalakṣaṇa* in a full-fledged empiricist manner by calling it the object of the senses or sense-datum (*tasya viṣayaḥ svalaksaṇaṃ*), thus differing from Vijñānavāda.

12. The nature of illusion (*bhrānti*) as explained by Dharmakīrti differentiates his doctrine from Vijñānavāda. According to Dharmakīrti an illusion is not groundless but projected on the *svalakṣanas* by imagination. Contrary to this, Vijñānavāda holds that illusion is

supra, p. 20.

groundless and produced by one's own imagination only, (*ātmakhyāti*) which appears as though external. Dreams, according to Vijñānavāda, appear to be a manifestation of the projection of the external world: but Dharmakīrti regards dreams as unreal, because they have no causal efficiency (*arthakriyākāritva*) and are contradicted by awakening. This description is in agreement with Sautrāntika and different from Vijñānavāda.

12. The doctrine of non-causal destruction (*ahetukavināśavāda*) explained by Dharmakīrti is derived from the Sautrāntika Vasubandhu's *AbkB*. and thus differentiates him from Vijñānavāda where it is not mentioned.

Dharmakīrti explains in detail that destruction does not need any cause as everything, by its own nature, enters into cessation or destruction (*sattāmātra anubandhāt vināśasya*). Production itself involves destruction and waits not for any other agent, such as a hammer, etc. This doctrine was particularly expounded by the Sautrāntikas and Dharmakīrti has just explained it epistemologically.*

13. Regarding the Noetic condition Dharmakīrti follows the Sautrāntika tradition of unity of mind (*citta*) and mental factors (*caitasik*) and their being always self-conscious (*svasaṃvedana*). It marks a distinction from Vijñānavāda which does not contemplate this unity.

14. The negation of the eight kinds of consciousness marks the clear distinction of Dharmakīrti from Vijñānavāda, which apart from the six consciousnesses introduces two more, i.e., *kliṣṭa-manovijñāna* (complex-consciousness), and *ālayavijñāna* (stores-consciousness). The Sautrāntikas criticized it and Dharmakīrti also disbelieved in it. This negation of fundamental doctrines of Vijñānavāda in the system of Dharmakīrti proves without any doubt that to include him under Vijñānavāda is a blunder. One who discards the very foundation of a school, cannot be classified under it.**

15. The negation of *Ālayavijñāna* means the negation of Vijñānavāda. The only ground on which the reality of the external (material) world is condemned is the theory of store-consciousness (*ālayavijñāna*) which contains the seed (*bīja*) of all physical appearances. Dharmakīrti's denial of *Ālayavijñāna* and replacement of it by *samanantara-pratyaya* (*PV*., 2/522) implies a total difference from Vijñānavāda tradition. This fact was well noticed by Tibetan scholars. *PVB*. explains in detail why Dharmakīrti negated *Ālayavijñāna*, that the

**AbkB*., 4/2, pp. 571-76; *PV*., 31 193-97.

***supra*, p. 12.

homogeneous immediate dominant mental activity (*samanantara-pratyaya*) is the causal factor or condition, even for those who believe in *ālayavijñāna*.

Stcherbatsky seems to be aware of this fact and comments accordingly: "The term *kun-gzhi*=*ālaya* in this place has given rise to a great deal of controversy among Tibetan commentators. The majority are not inclined to interpret it as meaning '*ālayavijñāna*' in the sense in which that term is used by Asaṅga and Vasubandhu, i.e., as implying the doctrine of a 'store-house-consciousness' where all the traces of former impressions and all the germs of the future ones are stored. They, therefore, interpret here *ālaya* as meaning only *manovijñāna*, and the passage as meaning 'there is thus (in that moment) no other consciousness than mental sensation". It seems, however, possible to assign "*ālaya*" here the meaning of consciousness in general without referring to a special theory. "As a matter of fact, the *Pramāṇavārtika* never mentions the *ālayavijñāna* doctrine and there is evidence enough to maintain that Dharmakīrti rejected it as a soul in disguise".* Stcherbatsky translates the view of the Tibetan scholar Jam-yan Shad-pa who refers to Vimuktisena, Haribhadra and Śāntarakṣita rejecting the *ālayavijñāna* doctrine in Dharmakīrti's system. Stcherbatsky quoted the view of a Tibetan logician Jam-yan Shad-pa (his Sanskrit name is Mañjughoṣapāda (1648-1722) who declared that those who accept the view that Dharmakīrti believed in Ālayavijñāna are blind. Stcherbatsky translates:

"Further some maintain that it is wrong to hold that all six kinds of consciousness with the accompaying mental phenomena (*citta-caittā*) are locked up in a store-house-consciousness, because in this case, e.g. from the standpoint of the Svātantrikas, the "store-house" doctrine is not accepted...and also (Dharmakirti) in his seven treatises holds that the theory of a "store consciouness" is an arrow shot into darkness...And again *Pramaṇavartika* says 'Two ideas (*kalpanā-dvayaṃ*=*tog ñis*) cannot exist simultaneously'. The ornament of the Seven Treatises (by Gendundub) says 'those who maintain that in the system of the seven treatises the 'store consciousness' doctrine is admitted are blind men (living) in the darkness of their own ignorance".**

**BL.*, II, pp. 328-29.
***Ibid.* p. 329.

It proves beyond doubt that Dharmakīrti was not an Idealist, but a Sautrāntika who accepted only six kinds of consciousness as explained in *AbkB.**

Dharmakīrti does not favour the Idealistic view and maintains that Mind (*manas*) is a stream of thought, and in the stream every preceding moment is the substrate cause (*upādāna*) of the following one. This preceding moment is called homogeneously immediate condition (*samánantarapratyaya*). This mental sensation (*mānasa-pratyakṣa*) which appears in the second moment depends on the sensory sensation (*indriyapratyakṣa*) and in its absence the second moment also does not arise, i.e., in the case of blind (*andha*) and dumb (*badhira*). This is definitely a Sautrāntika viewpoint and to mix it with Idealism will lead to a blunder. (*PV.*, 2/239)

16. Dharmakīrti's demarcation from the Idealist school is well expressed by his treatise "*Santānāntarasiddhi*" (proof of the existence of other streams of thought, or refutation of Solipsism) which proves the existence of other minds. Those who think that Dharmakīrti was justifying Idealism are mistaken. As a matter of fact, he is criticizing the Vaibhāṣika view and defending the Sautrāntika position of proving the existing of other minds on the ground of "representation" which is not possible in Vijñānavāda, as it always implies: "representation of what?" In the case that there exists nothing but one mind the question of representation is futile. Thus, the whole ontological formation of Dharmakīrti is in agreement with Sautrāntika and different from Vijñānavāda.**

Axiology

17. Dharmakīrti believes in sixteen properties of four noble truths which are emphasized in Sautrāntika tradition. Mādhyamika and Vijñānavadins have neglected them (*PV.*, 1/149-259).

18. To discover the three cardinal characteristics, viz. *duḥkha* (disgust), *anitya* (momentariness) and *anātman* (non-self), and to become Arahat or Pratyeka Buddha is the goal of life, which consists in living mindfully (*smṛti-upasthāna* or *satipaṭṭhāna*), moment to moment with reality, without falling into the trap of imagination and illusion, up to the point where the four noble truths are well pene-

**supra*, p. 39.

***Ibid.*, pp. 51-58.

trated. Dharmakīrti, while defining "*Yogi-pratyakṣa*", has duly clarified its nature. All this description is in agreement with Sautrāntika viewpoints well discussed in *AbkB* and differs from the mystical path and goals of Viñājnavāda and Mādhyamika, the so-called Mahāyanā systems.*

19. Theories of caste system, purification through water, self-torturing, etc. were criticized by Dharmakīrti as the views of impaired intellect.** This kind of ethical radicalism was initiated by the Buddha (*Ang.* IV), Vasubandhu II (*AbkB.*, III, 85-88), and Diṅnāga (*PS.*) not by the Vijñānavādins who themselves fell into the grips of Brahmanical Mysticism (*ālaya*=soul; Ref. *VPV.*, IV-9) and Monism. Dharmakīrti revived Vasubandhu's II and Diṅnāga's critical attitude and attempted to put an end to ethical dogmatism.

Thus, all these three kinds of internal evidence prove that Dharmakīrti is a Sautrāntika, as every one of these viewspoints is in agreement with it and different from Vijñānavāda and other schools.

REFERENCES

1. There are, according to Dharmakīrti, two ingredients for the object of the cognition: (1) it must be a cause (*kāraṇa*), (2) it must possess the same form (*ākāra*) as that appearing in the cognition. Thus, an object must be real (*sat*) and must have gross form (*sthūla ākāra*).
   A cognition is produced by the object (*tadutpatti*), and must have coordination (*tad-sārūpya*). Dharmakīrti regards *svalakṣaṇa* (point-instant) or *arthakriyā-śakti* (active energy) as the object of cognition.
2. Dharmakīrti is more careful in defining *kalpanā* as "a cognition of representation which is capable of being associated with a verbal designation" (*abhilāpa-saṃsarga-yogya-pratibhāsa-pratīti kalpanā*). It also includes the conceptual construction of infants and dumb persons who have the potentiality of verbal expression although they do not utter an actual word.
   That *pratyakṣa* is free from conceptual construction is proved by *pratyakṣa* itself, that is to say, by *svasaṃvedana* (self-consciousness): (*pratyakṣaṃ kalpanāpoḍhaṃ pratyakṣeṇaiva sidhyati.*) (*PV.*, 2/123), see App. IV. Dharmakīrti gives the following illustration:
   saṃhṛtya sarvataś cīntāṃ stimitenāntarātmanā,
   sthito' pi cakṣuṣā rūpaṃ īkṣate sākṣaja matiḥ. PV. (2/124.)
3. According to the Vaibhāṣika, *kalpanā* is a sense-cognition intimately connected (*saṃprayukta*) with such properties of a mental state (*caitasika*) as applied thought (*vitarka*) and sustained thinking (*vicāra*). In the Yogācāra view, all cognitions except the cognition of Tathāgata which is devoid of

**supra*, pp. 46-47.
***PVSV.*, pp. 617-18.

duality (*advaya*) are constructions, for they are (falsely) conceived as comprising of two parts, namely, the cognizer and the cognised.

4. Dharmottara (*NBT.*, pp. 12-13) criticizes Vinītadeva for his interpretation of *abhrānta.* as identical with *avisaṃvādaka*, which is the view of Kamalaśīla (*TSP.*, 1312) also. Vinītadeva and Kamalaśīla were led to such an interpretation because of their conviction that this definition of perception is intended to be acceptable to both the Yogācāra and the Sautrāntika. Dharmottara's interpretation of *abhrānta* (viz. *arthakriyākṣame vasturūpe viparyastaṃ*) is in contradiction with the Yogācara view, for it involves the admission of the reality of *artha.* The author of the *ṭippaṇī* (p. 19) therefore solves the difficulty simply by stating that the definition given here is intended to conform to the Sautrāntika view only. Durveka clarifies the same confusion. (*Pradīpa*, p. 42.)
5. *AbkB.*, 1/45, p. 129; 7/12; *PS.*, 1/4.

CHAPTER 4

Critique of the Ultimate Reality
(*Svalakṣaṇa*)

The only ontological entity Dharmakīrti establishes in his seven treatises can be expressed in a single word, *svalakṣaṇa*, which is translated as "own nature", particular, stimulus, burst of energy, point instant, individual, thing in itself, etc.; and Stcherbatsky has interpreted it in the sense of *absolute of Yogācāra Vijñānavāda.* This viewpoint is examined in this chapter.

Stcherbatsky, while commenting on "*tasya viṣayaḥ svalakṣaṇaṃ*" (*NB.*, 1/12), brought into light a-strange viewpoint: "Dharmakīrti evidently uses the term 'thing in itself (*svalakṣaṇa*) in more than one sense. The same, as is well known, has happened in European Philosophy. It means: 1) existence absolutely indefinite, not even differentiated into subject and object, it is then *grāhya-grāhaka-kalpanā-apoḍha*—it is the Absolute of the Yogācāras, the *śūnyatā* in its idealistic conception (*buddhy-ātmā*),...2) the *extreme* concrete and particular, the *Hoc Aliquid*=*kiṃcid idaṃ*, the pure *ālambana*, existence localized in time-space (*kṣana*), the limit of all mental constructions (*nāma-jātyādi-kalpanā-apoḍha*, but not *grāhya-grāhaka-kalpanāpoḍha*), the point instant of efficiency capable of affecting our sensibility (*arthakriyā-samartha*); it then already contains what Kant would have called the a *priori* forms of our sensibility, the possibility of coordination (*sārūpya*), if not already some rudimentary coordination; such is the meaning here and on this score it is sometimes supposed* that Diṅnāga's school was partly Sautrāntika; 3) (metaphorically) every concrete and particular (=*vyakti*) object, since its substratum is the thing in itself."**

**Tipp.*, p. 19. 10.
***BL.*, II., pp. 34-35, ref. 6.

The first interpretation of Stcherbatsky, when investigated carefully, appears to be non-factual and illogical in nature. As far as Dharmakīrti's own position is concerned he does not seem to commit the fallacy of using a term in two contrary senses, viz. Yogācāra and Sautrāntika.

Stcherbatsky himself opposes this in the second interpretation and positively asserts "such is the meaning here" (Sautrāntika), but he calls it "partly Sautrāntika" and gives it a new name: "Yogācāra-Sautrāntika" which is evidently a confusing term.

Stcherbatsky does not explain the vague point: if such is the meaning here where is the first one to be found?[1] Dharmakīrti's definition of *svalakṣaṇa* does not seem to be deviated from in any of his seven works. Why has Stcherbatsky not referred to the place where Dharmakīrti called *svalakṣaṇa* "absolute of Yogācāra"?[2]

If "such" (Sautrāntika) is the meaning here, then why does he not put it forward first, rather than an undocumented vague view which is not intended here? It implies that he had no definite evidence except a general impression reinforced by his interest in Idealism, perhaps, derived from Vinītadeva's misleading commentary on SS and hasty comparison with European Idealistic Philosophy.*

However, a further investigation is made here, on the grounds of the following analysis:

historical analysis: to trace out the source of Dharmakīrti's definition of *svalakṣaṇa*.

physical analysis: to analyze the very nature of *svalakṣaṇa* as described by Dharmakīrti.

epistemological analysis: to investigate its epistemological consistency.

The Buddha's empirical formula (as found in the Paḷi texts and supported by the Sanskrit fragments) of *phassa* as a relation of three things (*tiṇṇaṃ saṃgati phasso*) viz. object, senses, and consciousness (*rūpa*, *indrīya*, *vijñāṇa*) clearly indicates the visible (*rūpa*) nature of the object of the sense. One important factor of this analysis is the usage of the plural term *rūpe* in his formula (*rūpe ca paṭicca cakkhuñca uppajjati cakkhuviññāṇaṃ*) which implies many visible objects (pluralism). The Buddha himself applies the term *rūpa* in the wider connotation of visible objects of the senses (*rūpa*, *rasa*, *sadda*, *gandha*, *phoṭṭhabba*).[3]

In the Sthaviravāda tradition, later on, the *peṭakopadesa* seems to

**supra*, pp. 11-12.

be the first work to use the terms *sabhāva* (own nature) and *parabhāva* (other nature). A.K. Warder brings this fact into light: "Besides this remarkable method of simplifying the interpretation of the *Tripiṭaka*, the *Peṭahopadesa* is important for mentioning some significant new points of doctrine in the school. In connection with conditioned origination (p. 104) it brings in the concepts 'own-nature' (*svabhāva*) and 'other-nature' (*parabhāva*), apparently not used earlier in Buddhism and afterwards single out for special criticism by Nāgārjuna as representing the misinterpretation of the Buddha's teaching by the early schools. In the *Peṭakopadesa* the 'cause' (*hetu*) of a phenomenon is its 'own-nature; which is internal to the series or sequence in question. Its 'condition' (*pratyaya*) on the other hand is an 'other-nature', external to the series".[4] Though this description is in another context it is significant for introducing a methodology. This methodology (*naya*) paved a way for Ābhidharmika analysis. The term '*Lakkhaṇa*" (characteristic), sometimes to be used for own-characteristics like "earth has the characteristic of hardness", an example cited by later commentators.

The seven books of *Pāḷi Abhidhamma* analyzed and classified objects according to their differential characteristics. In the *Vibhaṅga* the aggregation of matter is again sub-divided into internal and external (*ajjhattikabahiddha*). The term *dhātu* is defined in the sense of "own-nature" and altogether 18 *dhātus* are analyzed:

rūpadhātu (visible element)	*cakkhudhātu* (eye element)	*cakkhuviññānadhātu* (eye cognition element)
saddadhātu (sound element)	*sotadhātu* (ear element)	*sota* ,, ,, ,, (ear cognition element)
gandhadhātu (smell element)	*ghānadhātu* (nose element)	*ghāṇa* ,, ,, ,, (nose cognition element)
rasadhātu (taste element)	*jivhādhātu* (tongue element)	*jivhā* ,, ,, ,, (tongue cognition element
phoṭṭhabbadhātu (touch element)	*kāyadhātu* (body element)	*kāya* ,, ,, ,, (body cognition element)
dhammadhātu (mental object element)	*manodhātu* (mind element)	*mano* ,, ,, ,, (mind cognition element)

The later *Pāḷi* commentators such as Buddhaghosa[5], Dhammapāla[6], etc. seem to be well acquainted with the concept of own-nature and clearly defined "*dhātu*" in that sense. Pāḷi commentaries[7] indicate *tatha, sabhāva, atthadhamma, vatthu, dhātu, visaya*, etc. in the sense of physical sensory objects. Unfortunately, all these works were not consulted by Stcherbatsky, consequently, the fallacy of non-observation and partial judgment has occurred. Now, let us proceed to analyze the Sanskrit tradition on *svalakṣaṇa.*

In the Sarvāstivāda tradition we find the first application of the term "*svalakṣaṇa*" in the *Vibhāṣā* in the technical senses of the object of senses (*indriya-viṣaya*). Particularly, Dharmatrāta and Vasumitra explained it in detail.[8] *AbD.* and *VPV.* also clarified the Vaibhāṣika viewpoint on "*svalakṣaṇa*"[9].

The Sautrāntikas have critically accepted the Vaibhāṣika division of two aspects of *rūpa-dhātu.* Vasubandhu II applied Occam's razor and cut down some of the doctrines of the Vaibhāṣikas such as *kāla, dravya, nikāya-sabhāgatā, prāpti, āyu*, etc., as contradicting the fundamental doctrine of sensation and momentariness, and the *Suttapiṭaka.** Sautrāntika Vasubandhu II established, on the ground of logical reasoning, the nature of *svalakṣaṇa* as a constant flux (*anitya-saṃtāna*) of material and mental properties without any agent or soul.[10] He also divided reality, following the Vaibhāṣikas, into two: *paramārtha* (*svalakṣaṇa*=ultimate) and *sāmānya* (phenomenal or universal).[11] The first is apprehended in the first moment of cognition directly and the second through a judgment.

Vasubandh II discarded Vaibhāṣika Atomism which assumes the real combination of atoms (*aṇusaṃghāta*).[12] He explained that atoms are real, but they do not touch each other (*na spṛśanti te*), but by coming nearer together a gross form (*dausthulya=pracaya=atiśaya=puñja*) is produced which affects the senses (*āyatanas*) in a constantly unbroken succession of flow, without stopping even for a moment. He divided *svalakṣaṇa* into two categories *dravya-svalakṣaṇa* (substance=atom-*svalakṣaṇa*), and *āyatana-svalakṣaṇa* (sensory *svalakṣaṇa*)[13] on the ground of *Pañcavijñānakāya*, an ancient text on Sanskrit Abhidharma, and Yaśomitra has clarified it in detail.[14] Now allow me to analyze the Mahāyāna systems (*Mādhyamika and Yogācāra*) on the concept of *svalakṣaṇa.*

We do not find the term *svalakṣaṇa* in Nāgārjuna's *Mādhyamika Kārikas* or in any other of his works.[15] He uses *bhāva* or *svabhāva* for own nature and refutes it on the grounds that all existence is conditioned (*pratītyasamutpanna*), then there is no possi-

**supra*, p. 20

bility of "own nature" or *svabhāva*. Later on Candrakīrti, an expounder of the Prāsaṅgika Mādhyamika school, uses the term *svalakṣaṇa* and refutes it.[16]

On the other hand, Vijñānavāda does not reveal much interest in this term, except some occasional references. Asaṃga[17] himself seems to be familiar with the division of *svalakṣaṇa* and *sāmānyalakṣaṇa* as traditionally coming in Abhidharma tradition and occasionally mentions it in his *Abhidharmasamuccaya*, *Madhyāntavibhaṅga* and *Yogācārabhūmiśāstra*. But a difference appears when he calls *svalakṣaṇa* mere reflection of consciousness.[18] Vasubandhu I has shown no interest in this term in his *Triṃśika* and *Viṃśatika* and Sthiramati[19] refers to it only while defining intellect (*mati*). All these Idealist philosophers, particularly, explained a triple division of characters (*parikalpita*, *paratantra* and *pariniṣpanna*) and show no interest in this term. Later on the Chinese adherent of Idealism, Hsüan-tsang,[20] has described *svalakṣaṇa* and *sāmānyalakṣaṇa* in some more detail which only proves the considerable influence of Diṅnāga on Vijñānavāda tradition; because Diṅnāga came first and Hsüan-tsang later.

The fundamental position of Idealism is the denial of any reality apart from consciousness. Only thought is real. Thus, in *svalakṣaṇa* consciousness (*vijñānasvalakṣaṇa*), each moment of consciousness is unique, and the structure of consciousness can be described only by ignoring the uniqueness of its moments. But in this sense the unique reality will itself become common. Even the word "unique" is used generally for all instances of uniqueness. If reality is consciousness only, it is nothing but consciousness and so must have everything in common with itself. Thus, Vijñānavāda, though influenced by early and later Ābhidharmikas, has got a different connotation of the term *svalakṣaṇa* according to its fundamentally idealistic position.

A superficial observation can easily lead to an identification of Diṅnāga and Dharmakīrti's description of *svalakṣaṇa* with that of Vijñānavāda, as happened in the case of Stcherbatsky, who seems to have a predisposed interest in Idealism and got deceived by this superficial similarity. But in fact, Sautrāntika and Vijñānavāda, though they used the same term, have different connotations for it. The former takes it in the sense of visible object (*rūpa*), and the latter in the sense of Pure-Consciousness (*śuddhavijñāna*); one is Pluralistic and the other is Monistic. Stcherbatsky seems to be handicapped by the non-availability of the material on the Vaibhāṣika and the Sautrāntika doctrines of *svalakṣaṇa* and his interest in Idealism made him jump to a hasty conclusion.[21]

This historical analysis clearly manifests the fact that the problem of *svalakṣaṇa* and *sāmānyalakṣaṇa* originated, primarily, in the Vaibhāṣika tradition; in the sense of visible objects (*rūpadhātu*), not in the Vijñānavāda which does not exhibit much interest in this term.

Another piece of evidence which contradicts Stcherbatsky's first interpretation is provided by the physical description, presented by Diṅnāga and Dharmakīrti, of the *svalakṣaṇa*. Diṅnāga, following Vasubandhu II, described the *svalakṣaṇa* as an object (*viṣaya*) of the senses (*pratyakṣa*) in contrast with the common (*sāmānya*) which is the object of inference (*anumāna*).[22] One is particular, the other is general. Diṅnāga does not enter into a detailed discussion on this issue, because Vasubandhu II has already clarified it in *AbkB* and *Vādavidhāna*. Diṅnāga, in *AP*., has criticized the Vaibhāṣika and Vaiśeṣika views of atoms and accepted the Sautrāntika view as described by Vasubandhu II. He never denied the doctrine of "assemblage of atoms" (*aṇusamudāyavāda*). Diṅnāga definitely uses it in the sense of visible objects (*rūpadhātu*) as explained in the Sautrāntika tradition.*

Dharmakīrti, following Diṅnāga, defines *svalakṣaṇa* as being the object of the senses (*pratyakṣa*). It creates dim or clear images by its being near or far from the senses. When a material object is near to the senses it creates a vivid image; if far, then dim.[23] On the contrary, no question of dimness and vividness arises in the case of Vijñānavāda which can only believe in mental force appearing as external, such as in a dream state; where the distinction of dimness and vividness does not hold. Thus, the very definition of *svalakṣaṇa* refutes the Yogācāra position.

Dharmakīrti himself clarifies that *svalakṣaṇa* consists of the assemblage of atoms (*aṇusañcaya*), which was fundamentally a doctrine of Sautrāntikas. This fact is also established by the Jaina critics of Diṅnāga and Dharmakīrti. Mallavādin and Siṃhasūri criticized Diṅnāga's definition of sensation (*pratyakṣa*) on the ground that in the case when the assemblage of atoms (*aṇusañcaya*) is appearance (not real), then it cannot be devoid of concept (*kalpanāpoḍha*).[24] Thus, the very definition of *pratyakṣa* will not stand. Dharmakīrti, defending Diṅnāga's position, mentioned that this (*sañcaya*) is not something different (as in the case of Vaiśeṣika category of *sāmānya*)

**supra*, p. 60

from the assemblage itself.[25] Therefore, it is not conceptual. Manorathanandin[26] and Prajñākaragupta[27] both have clarified it by giving different examples of a swarm of flies, hair and a line (*paṅkti*). A line of blind people is not something different from the people standing in a particular way. Dharmakīrti himself cited the example of separate sesame seeds (*viyukteṣu tilādiṣu, PV.*, 2/197) to show that *sañcita* is not something like a "whole" (*avayavin*), but the particular mode of assemblage which is cognized through the senses. Therefore, it is neither conceptual nor illusory.

In spite of Dharmakīrti's answer to the Jaina critics, they remained firm in their objection and criticized Dharmakīrti again on the same ground.[28] Now, the question is, if Diṅnāga and Dharmakīrti had denied the existence of atoms in toto, like Vasubandhu I, then the objection of the Jainas would have never occurred, and Dharmakīrti would not have defended the doctrine. It clearly proves that Vasubandhu II, Diṅnāga, and Dharmakīrti believe in atoms having interspace between them, a doctrine from the tradition of the Sautrāntikas. It means *svalakṣaṇa* is visible object (*rūpadhātu*) made of an assemblage of atoms (*aṇusañcaya*) or a mass of energy, which contradicts Stcherbatsky's thesis of calling it the "Absolute of Yogācāra".

Furthermore, the evidence which strengthens the above explanation is provided by the commentators on Dharmakīrti such as Dharmottara and Durvekamiśra who defended his doctrine of atomism. Dharmottara, while explaining the term "non-illusory" (*abhrānta*) called it "causally efficient real matter" (*arthakriyāksamarthavasturūpa*).[29] Durveka comments on it: "by this only the assemblage of atoms has causal efficiency, not the whole; because it is mentioned as unreal." (*anena paramāṇupracayamātrasya eva arthakriyākāritvaṃ na avayāvinaḥ tasya asattvāt iti sūcitaṃ*). Again, he puts forward an objection: "In your view only this atom-object is an external reality and all cognition of gross-appearance is produced with reference to those very subtle (atoms), then how is it at all called non-illusory?" (*paramāṇvartha eva bhavanmate bāhyaṃ vastu, sarvaṃ ca vijñānaṃ tesu paramasūkṣmeṣu sthūlābhāsaṃ ajāyate tat kathaṃ kiñcidabhrāntaṃ nāma iti*?). Then, in detail, Durveka answers this objection, on the same grounds as Dharmakīrti, that "gross-form" (*pracaya or sthaulya*) is not something different (*sthaulyam nāparaṃ kiñcit*).[30] Thus, it leaves no place for doubt about what Dharmakīrti meant by *svalakṣaṇa*. Unfortunately, neither the books of the Jaina critics, nor the commentary of Durvekamiśra, were available at the time when Stcherbatsky presented his thesis. He forgets the fact that the Vijñānavādin Vasubandhu I[31] himself criticized this doctrine of atoms of the Older Sautrāntikas and denied the existence of the atom through and through; while Diṅnāga and Dharmakīrti criticized only the individual atom and combination of atoms (*aṇusaṃghāta*), but not the assemblage of atoms (*aṇusañcaya*). Thus, an obvious gulf appears between the Yogācāra and the Sautrāntika standpoints.

Stcherbatsky himself, in another place, explains: "External reality is only the force which stimulates imagination, but not the extended body, not the stuff, not the matter; the energy alone. Our image of an external thing is only an effect of, it is produced by, external efficient reality.

Thus, reality is dynamic, all the elements of the external world are mere forces ..According to this theory, physical bodies consist of molecules and a molecule consists at least of eight atoms..."*

This explanation is an obvious indication of the fact that Vasubandhu II, Diṅnāga, and Dharmakīrti used the term "*svalakṣaṇa*" to denote an active physical force or a mass of atoms, not in the sense of something non-active like an absolute.

Furthermore, important evidence is furnished by the epistemological criticism of the Sautrāntika doctrine of momentariness. Dharmakīrti also proves the momentariness of all existence (*yat sat tat sarvamanityaṃ...NB.* 3/9), which becomes the subject of severe criticism. If everything is momentary, then how is it possible to perceive a thing which has already been annihilated? How can one hold the view that we grasp a thing which is not there? Vasubandhu I[32] himself criticized the older Sautrāntika view on this very ground. There has been a constant intellectual struggle between these two camps on this very issue.**

Dharmakīrti logically answers it on the ground that an external thing causes its own perception.[33] It is the object of perception inasmuch as it has the power to leave behind, through the sense-channel, its own impression in consciousness and there takes place a correspondence (*artha-sārūpya*). The first moment of *pratyakṣa* is only valid because it is not known before (*anadhigata*) and fulfils human desire (*arthakriyākārin*). Dharmottara[34] also clarifies in detail how in a continuous string of events, the cognition derived through the senses becomes valid. This solution is based on the Sautrāntika

**BL.*, I, pp. 190-91.

***supra*, p. 75

Vasubandhu's explanation of *sārūpya* (correspondence). Stcherbatsky has himself translated this particular part of *AbkB.*[35] in his *BL.* and clearly indicates in other places the unique position of the Sautrāntikas.[36]

The Sautrāntikas admit the existence of an external object (*bāhyārtha*). Thus, the correspondence (*sārūpya*) of the form represented in the cognition to that of an object is held to be the *pramāna* of the resulting *viṣayādhigati* (knowledge of the object). The Yogācāras, on the other hand, maintain that the object is merely the appearance of an object (*viṣayābhāsa*) in the cognition and no question of *sārūpya* arises. Dharmakīrti admitted *sārūpya* between object and cognition, which definitely differentiates him from Yogācāras.

Thus, we arrive, by historical, physical, and epistemological evidence, at the conclusion that Dharmakīrti's *svalakṣaṇa* is not the "absolute of Yogācāra", but the assemblage of atoms (*anusañcaya*) of the Sautrāntikas. Therefore, to call Dharmakīrti a Yogācāra or Sautrāntika-Yogācāra is not justified. What is reproven is the fact that he is a Sautrāntika.

REFERENCE

1. Stcherbatsky's reference *grāhya-grāhaka-kalpanā-apoḍha* (devoid of subject-object imagination) is not factual, as it is nowhere found in any of the seven treatises of Dharmakīrti. Dharmakīrti's definition of *kalpanā* is well known and Stcherbatsky himself presents it in the second interpretation which contradicts the first one.
2. The term absolute has various implications in the history of Western philosophy. Hegel used it in the sense of logical wholeness, Hamilton as metaphysical completeness, Bosanquet as aesthetic completeness, Royce as moral prefection. None of these connotations are applicable for a Buddhist system. Stcherbatsky nowhere precisely defines in what sense he is using the term "absolute". It is also doubtful whether the term absolutism can be used for Yogācāra. The Buddha himself criticized the Upaniṣadic concept of an absolute soul, or *brahman*, and taught pluralism. Dharmakīrti's definition of *svalakṣaṇa* as the object of the senses implies six *svalakṣaṇas* of the six senses. That is why Dharmottara sometimes used it in the plural: (*sarvāṇi eva hi vastūni durādasphuṭāni dṛśyante, samīpe sphuṭāni. tāni eva svalakṣaṇāni*) (*NBT(D)*, 1/13, p. 74).
3. Chap. 4, p. 191.
4. A. K. Warder has described the occurrences of the terms such as *sabhāva* in *Petakopadesa* (*Outline of Indian Philosophy*, p. 98); and his analysis of *paramatthasacca* (fundamental reality), and *sāmaññascca* (common reality) in *Suttapiṭaka* and Pāḷi commentaries in 'The Concept of a Concept' *Jour-*

nal of Ind. Philosophy., 1971), pp. 181-96, which is also very important in order to understand this evolution. The application of the term *salakhaṇa* is also found in *Dhammasaṃgiṇi* in one of the characteristics of *vipassanā* (insight): *katamaṃ tasmiṃ samaye sampajaññaṃ hoti? yā tasmiṃ samaye paññā pajānatā vicayo pavicayo dhammavicayo salakkhaṇā upalakkhaṇā paccupalakkhaṇā paṇiccaṃ kosallaṃ nepuññaṃ . . . vipassanā saṃpajaññaṃ . . .* (*Dhs.*, p. 57).

5. Throughout the Pāḷi and Sanskṛit tradition, the term "*dhātu*" connotes the meaning of own-nature. Buddhaghośa clarifies it: *yathā titthīyānaṃ attā nāma sabhāvato natthi, na evaṃetā. etā pana attano sabhāvaṃ dhārenīti dhātuyo . . . api ca dhātu ti nijjivamattassevete adhivacanaṃ* (*VisM.*, p. 339). Buddhaghośa's explanation of *salakkhaṇa* in the sense of non-contradictory nature (*aviparīta sabhāva*) is also of logical significance: *paṭivedho ti tantivā tanti-atthassa ca yathābhūtāvabodho . . . paṭivedho tī abhisamayo, so ca lokiyalokuttaro. visayato asammohato ca atthānurūpaṃ dhammesu, dhammānurūpaṃ atthesu, paññattipathānurūpaṃ pāññattisu avabodho. tesaṃ tesaṃ vā tattha tattha vuttadhammānaṃ paṭivijjhitabbo salakhanasaṃkhāto aviparīta-sabhāvo.*. (*Atts.*, p. 19).

6. Dhammapālācārya clearly uses *sabhāvalakkhaṇa* (own-nature) in the sense of *salakkhaṇa*: *kiñ ca bhiyyo duvidhaṃ lakkhanaṃ paramatthadhammānaṃ sabhāvalakkhaṇaṃ sāmaññalakkhanañ cāti. tattha sabhāvalakkhaṇāvabodho paccakkhañāṇaṃ, sāmaññalakkhaṇāvobodho annumānañāṇaṃ . . .* (*DAT.*, pp. 191-92).

7. *Paramatthadīpanī* and *Vibhāvinī*, two important commentaries on *AbS.* also bring into light the meaning of "*dhātu*" as "own-nature" (*sabhāva*): '*attanā sabhāvaṃ dadhāti ti dhātu . . . kassa ca pana puggalassa vā sattassa vā manussassa vā devassa vā brahmaṇo vā vase avatiitva attano sabhāvam dhārentī ti dhātuyo.* (*PD.*, p. 314). *avisesena pana vidhati, dhīyate, vidhānam, vidhīyate. dāya ettha vā dhīyati ti dhātu* (*Vib.*, p. 78).

These commentaries, available in Sinhālese script, also reveal the meaning of "*sabhāvarūpa*" and *salakkhaṇarūpa*: *kakkhalattādinā attano sabhāvena upalabbhanato sabhāvarūpam.* (*Vib.*, p. 151).; *uppādādīhi aniccatādihi vā lakkhaṇehi sahitam ti salakkhaṇaṃ.* (*Vib.*, p. 151). *uppādādinā antccādinā ca samkhataiakkhaṇena sahitaṃ rūpaṃ salakkhaṇarūpaṃ.* (*PD.*, p. 240). *aññapadesarahitena kakkhalattādina attano bhāvena suddham rupaṃ sabhāvarūpam.* (*PD.*, p. 280).; PD. in another place clearly mentions *rūpakalāpa* like a round mass (*piṇḍa idha*) of matter:

eka-saddo cettha samkhāne pavatto, tasmā tena yāni rūpāṇi ekāya eva jātiyā jāyanti, ekāya eva aniccatāya nirujjhanti, tesam piṇḍa idha rūpakalāpo nāmā ti dasseti. (*PD.*, p. 264).

Abhidhammamūlaṭīkā applied the term *dhamma* for "own-nature" (*sabhāvo*):

dhammā nāma bhāvoti. sabhāvadhāraṇadinā atthena dhammāti vutto. so ca sabhāvasseva hoti. (*AMT.*, p. 26).

In Pali, own-nature was also clarified under *sabhāvanirutti*:

sabhāvanirutti aviparītanirutti. aviparītaniruttīti tassa atthassa bodhena sabbapatiniyakālam tasambandho avyabhicāravohāro . . . atthato panesā nāmapaññattīti ācariyā. yadāhu: nirutti māgadhibhāsā, atthato nāmasammutīti. apare:

yadi sabhāvanirutti paññattisabhāvā, paññatti abhilāpitabbā, nā vacananti āpajjati, evam ca sati "atthadhammaniruttābhilāpe ñāṇam niruttipaṭisamuccāret abbhida" ti idam na sakkā vattu ṃabhilāpoti, na hi vacanato aññaṃ abhilāpitabbaṃ uccāritabbam atthi; atthi phassādivacanehi bodhetabbaṃ abhilāpitabbaṃ. evaṃ ca sati atthadhammānampi bodhetabbatātesampi niruttibhāvo āpajjati. api ca aṭṭhakathāya "phassoti ca sabhāvanirutti; phassā phassam ti nasabhāvani rutti" ti vacanato viññattivikārasahito saddo niruttīti dassitamevetaṃ sabhāvaniruttābhilāpe pabhedagataṃ ñānaṃ niruttipaṭisambhidā, evamayam niruttipaṭisambhidā saddārammaṇā nāma jāta. na paññattiārammaṇāya sotaviññāṇavīthiya parato manodvāre niruttipaṭisambhidā pavattati. (*AVV.*, pp. 396-97).

The doctrine of *Ariyasacca* (noble truths) describes the concept of real-nature (*tatha*):

ken' aṭṭhena saccāni? tathaṭṭhena. ko'yaṃ tathaṭṭho nama? yo paññācakkhunā upaparikkhiyamānaṃ māyā va viparīto, marīcī va visamvādako, titthiyānam attā viya anupalabhasabhāvo ca na hoti, atha kho bādhanapabhavasanti-nīyānabhūtena tacchāviparīta-bhūta-bhāvena ariyañānassa gocaro hoti, ayaṃ tathaṭṭho saccaṭṭho ti veditabbo. vuttañ ca: "iti tacchāvipallāsabhūtabhāvaṃ catusv api dukhādisv avisesena saccṭṭham āhu paṇḍitā" ti. (*Moha.*, p. 130).

This Pāḷi tradition which remained inaccessible to Stcherbatsky, brings to light the longstanding tradition of the Abhidhamma analysis of *svalakṣaṇa*. The striking points of similarity between Pāḷi and Dharmakīrti's concept of *svalakṣaṇa* proves their mutual excange. It also implies the paramount importance, generally neglected by Sanskṛit scholars, of the Pāḷi tradition in determining the real nature of Sanskṛit terms and concepts.

The whole account of the Pāḷi tradition of *svalakṣaṇa* can be listed as follows :

salakkhaṇa	(own-nature)
dhātu	(intrinsic matter)
sabhāva	(own-nature)
sabhāvanirutti	(own-expression)
ariyasacca	(noble truth)
paramatthasacca	(fundamental reality)
bhūtabhāvam	(the nature of existence)
tatha	(truth)
aviparīta	(non-contradictory)
anaññaṭṭha	(not other meaning)
sacca	(truth)
avipallāsa	(non-illusory)
vatthu	(thing, ground, reality)
atthadhamma	(object)
dukkha, anicca, anattā	(frustration, non-eternal, non-self)
visaya	(object.)
rūpakalāpa	(accumulation of matter)
sabhāvalakkaṇa	(own characteristic)
Paccakkhañānam	(sensory cognition)

phassa (sensation)
apaññatti (non-conceptual)
avyabhicāri (non-contradictory)

8. The following Vaibhāṣika account of *svalakṣaṇa* has been translated from Chinese by Prof. C.D.C. Priestley, who has kindly supplied it to me.

The *Vijñānakāya*, an ancient treatise on Abhidharma (composed by Devaśarman), reads.

The eye-consciousness can only discern the blue colour; it cannot discern that it is a blue colour. The mind-consciousness also can discern the blue colour. But until it can discern its name, it cannot discern that it is a blue colour. If it is able to discern its name, at that time it can both discern the blue colour and discern that it is a blue colour (*T.* 1539), ch. VI, p. 559B).

Part of this passage is referred to by Diṅnāga (*PSV.*, 1/4), Manorathanandin (*PVV.*, 2/194), p. 159), and Mallavādin (*DNC.*, p. 61): "*cakṣurvijñānasamaṅgī nīlaṃ vijānāti no tu 'nīlaṃ' iti arthe arthasaṃjñī na tu arthe dharmasaṃjñī . . .*"

In the *Abhidharmasāra*, Dharmatrāta again clarifies it:

"The realm of the visible object (*rūpadhātu*) is cognized by two consciousnesses . . . These are the eye-consciousness and the mind-consciousness. The realm cognized by the eye-consciousness is the peculiar characteristic; the real cognized by the mind-consciousness is the peculiar characteristic and the common characteristic . . . For the five sense-consciousnesses have the peculiar characteristic as their sphere since they are devoide of thought, are in the sphere of the present, and are momentary." (*T.* 1552), ch. I, p. 880a.

Another work by Dharmatrāta, the *Pañcavastuvibhāṣā* reads:

"Thus, a visible object is cognized by two consciousnesses from among the six consciousnesses, that is, the eye and the mind. At first, with the eye-consciousness, only the peculiar characteristic is apprehended. Then, with the mind-consciousness, the peculiar and common characteristics are apprehended." (*T.* 1555) ch. II, p. 992a.

Vasumitra also explains the Vaibhasika view: "The five consciousnesses (*pañcavijñānakāya*), (that of) the eye and sofor th, (conduce to) passion (*sarāga*); (they) do not (conduce to) freedom from passion(*virāga*). (Their functions are) only to perceive (lit. to take the individual aspects (*svalakṣaṇa*) (of their external correlatives): (they have) no thinking (faculty) (*avikalpa*) at all." *Samayabhedoparacanacakra* (*T.* 2031), p. 16B; translated by Masuda in *Origin and Doctrines of Early Indian Buddhist Schools*, p. 48.

Dharmatrata, in another place, explains in detail the nature of *svalakṣaṇa* in question-answer form:

Q: What are the two characteritics:

A: The peculiar characteristic and the common characteristic. The peculiar characteristic is not common. It is only this and nothing else. For example, hardness is a characteristic of matter. The common characteristic is common. It is this and something else. For example, matter is impermanent.

Q: If hardness is the peculiar characteristic of matter, it is also a common characteristic. With regard to the other four groups (*skandha*) it is the peculiar characteristic. With regard to the two kinds of matter it is a common characteristic. Thus, the peculiar characteristic and the common characteristic depends on one's point of view. The two sorts, peculiar characteristic and common characteristic, are then unestablished.

A: Because it is one with matter itself, and because hardness is a characteristic of matter; it is called the peculiar characteristic of matter. The many kinds of matter can be distinguished; therefore, we speak of ten kinds. Your assertion, that the peculiar characteristic and the common characteristic are unestablished because they depend on the point of view, is false. Why? Because it does not refute our position. It is like father and son or like fruit and seed or like the truth of the accumulation of suffering, or like obeying the rules. If you regard it as the peculiar characteristic, then it is not the common characteristic. If you regard it as the common characteristic, then it is not the peculiar characteristic. It is like one man who may be called both father and son. Because of his father, he is called a son, and because of his son, he is called a father. If you regard him as a father, then you do not regard him as a son, and if you regard him as a son, then you do not regard him as a father. If you say that they are unestablished, it is false. Why? Because they are already established . . . Therefore, the meaning of father and son is established, and as it is already established, it cannot be established again. If it were established again when already established, there would be an infinite regression. Therefore, the meaning of peculiar characteristic and common characteristic is established. *Abhidharmasāra* (*T.* 1552), ch. I, p. 870B.

9. The recently discovered *AbD.* and *VPV.* also present the Vaibhāṣika view on *svalakṣaṇa*: *kāyaṃ svasāmānyalakṣaṇābhyāṃ parīkṣate. vedanā cittaṃ dharmāśca. "svabhāva evaiṣāṃ svalakṣaṇam". kaḥ svabhāvaḥ? kāyasya bhūtabhautikavaṃ vedanāyā anubhavatvaṃ. cittasyopalabhitvaṃ.* (*AbD.*, p. 270). *VPV.* refutes *ālayavijñana* and clarifies *svalakṣaṇa* in the context of *Śūnyatā*: *tadevaṃ sati sūtre asminmadhyamā pratipat pradarśitā. yaduta kenacitprakārena śūnyāḥ saṃskārāḥ mithyā parikalpitena puruṣālalayavijñānabhūtaparikalpādinā. kenacidaśūnyaḥ yadutasvalakṣaṇasāmānyalakṣaṇābhyāṃ iti. yathā kātyāyana-sūtre: "lokasamudayaṃ jñātvā yā loke nāsti tā sā na bhavati. lokanirodhaṃ jñātva yā loke'sti tā sā na bhavati itimau dvāvantau parityajya madhyamāya pratipadā tathāgato dharmaṃ deśayati.*" (*VPV.*, p. 270).

Unfortunately, none of these Vaibhāṣika missing links were available to Stcherbatsky.

10. Vasubandhu II accepted the Vaibhāṣika view of *svalakṣaṇa with alterations*; *jñeyasvalakṣaṇākāraṃ* (*Abk.*, 7/11).;*sāsravaṃ paracittajñānaṃ jñeyānāṃ cittacaittānāṃ yat svalakṣaṇaṃ tadākārayati*; *svalakṣaṇagrāhakatvāt.* (*Bhāṣya*, p. 1046).

11. Yaśomitra clearly mentions *svalakṣaṇa* as ultimate reality: *paramārthena sat. svalakṣaṇena sat ityarthaḥ.* (*AbkB*, 6/4; *Sphuṭārthā*, pp. 889-90).

12. Vasubandhu II criticized the Vaibhāṣika notion of *Mahābhūtas* (*AbkB.*, 1/12), and uses the terms *svabhāva* and *svalakṣaṇa* for own-characteristic. (*AbkB.*, 1/10; III/100).

13. *āyatanasvalakṣanaṃ pratyete svalakṣaṇaviṣayā na dravyasvalakṣaṇaṃ* (*AbkB.*, 1/10).

Ref. by Diṅnāga (*PSV.* 1/4), Siṃasūri (*DNCV.*, p, 79), Manoratha (*PVV.*, p. 176), Prajñākara (*PVB.*, p. 280).

14. Yaśomitra explains this division of *svalakṣaṇa*: *yathā cakṣuḥ-śrotra-ghrāṇa-jihvā-kāya-vijñānālambanāny abhisamasya mano-vijñānam gṛhṇātīti kṛtvā sāmānyalakśaṇa-viṣayam tad vyavasthāpyate. tathā nīla-pītalohitāvadātālambanānāṃ caturnāṃ cakṣurvijñānāṇāṃ tāni catvāri bahutarāṇi cālambanāny abhisamasya cakṣur-vijñānaṃ ekaṃ gṛhṇātīti sāmānya-lakṣaṇaviṣayam tat prāpnoti. rūpâyatana-sāmānya-lakṣaṇaṃ asyālambadaṃ iti kṛtvā. tathā śrotra-ghrāṇa-jihvākāya-vijñānāny api svaviṣayeṣu yojyāni āyatanasvalakṣaṇam pratiti, svaṃ laksaṇaṃ svalakṣaṇaṃ. āyatanānāṃ svalakṣaṇam āyatanasvalakṣaṇaṃ. cakṣurvijñāna-vijñeyatvādi. rūpāyatanatvādi vā. tat praty ete pañca vijnānakāyāh svalaksaṇaviṣayā iṣyante pravacane. na dravyasvalakṣaṇaṃ prati svalakṣaṇa-viṣayā iṣyante iti prakṛtaṃ. dravyāṇāṃ nilādikānām svalakṣaṇam nīlādyākāracakṣur-vijñānādivijñeyatvam. nilākārādi vā. na tat praty ete pañca vijñanakāyāh svalakṣaṇā viṣayā iṣyante ity adoṣaḥ.* (on *Sphuṭārtha,* I. II, p. 28 of Wogihara's edition).

It becomes quite obvious from this explanation that the Sautrāntikas critically developed the Vaibhāṣika concept of *svalakṣaṇa.* They brushed aside the Vaibhāṣika doctrine of *dravya* (*nīlādyākāra*) and laid stress on what we really receive through the senses (*āyatana*). This description reveals striking similarities with Diṅnāga and Dharmakīrti's account of *svalakṣaṇa.*

15. Nāgārjuna seems to use *bhāva* and *svabhāva* in the specific sense of "eternal nature" or "substance" not in the sense of "momentariness". His account of *pratītyasamutpāda* as the synonym (*ekārtha*) of *śūnyatā* is: *yah pratityasamutpādaḥ śūnyatām tām pracakṣmahe* (*MK.*, 2/5). *yaḥ śūnyataṃ pratītyasamutpādāṃ madhyamāṃ pratipadaṃ ca ekārthaṃ nijagāda praṇamāmi tamapratimabuddhaṃ* (*VV.*, 70).

It means that the own-nature of all *dharmas* is to be conditioned. In other words, the own-nature means "no-own-nature" (substancelessness) and vice versa. Nāgārjuna definitely is not a nihilist. He nowhere criticizes momentariness (*anityasaṃtāna*). On the contrary, his fundamental thesis of *śūnyatā* implies momentariness as well as a substancelessness; because every conditioned thing has to be changeful and substanceless.

16. Candrakīrti refutes "*svalakṣaṇa*":
kiñca yadi svasāmānyalakṣaṇadvayānurodhena pramāṇadvayaṃuktaṃ. yasya tallaṣkaṇadvayaṃ kiṃ lakṣyamasti. atha nāsti . . . (*Prasannapadā*, pp. 59-61).

Candrakīrti's main criticism is of Bhāvaviveka (the founder of the Svatantrika-Mādhyamika-Sautrāntika school) and Diṅnāga. It seems that he has not properly understood the meaning of *svalakṣaṇa.* He interprets it on the basis of his grammatical skill, in the sense of *sva*+*lakṣaṇa* as though own (*sva*) is an adjective of characteristic (*lakṣaṇa*), a meaning which neither Bhāvaviveka nor Diṅnāga intended. It seems like refuting a self-imposed interpretation.

17. The following account of occurrences of the term *svalakṣaṇa,* in the Yogācāra tradition, is sufficient to prove that it has no particular interest, as the Vaibhāṣikas and Sautrāntikas have, in the term *svalakṣaṇa*:

dhātvartha katamaḥ? sarvadharmabījārthaḥ, svalakṣaṇadhāraṇārthaḥ, kārya-kāraṇabhāvadhāraṇārthaḥ . . . (*AbSam.*, p. 15). *ko viśeṣo'sti sallakṣaṇasvalakṣaṇayoḥ? sallakṣaṇaṃ hi sāmānyaṃ, svalakṣaṇaṃ tu viśeṣaḥ.* (*MV.* p. 14). *alakṣaṇa-nairātmyaṃ, vilakṣana-nairātmyaṃ, svalakṣaṇanairātmyañca.* (ibid. p. 89).

yathāpratītysamutapādavibhaṅge evaṃ svalakṣaṇaṃ paryeṣite (*Yogāsthāna-Śrāvakabhūmau naiṣkarmya-bhūmi*, p. 382). raṅ gi mtshan ñid med la kun tu rtog pa tsam du dmigs pas kun brtags pa zes byaḥe (Asaṃga, *Mahāyānasaṃgraha*, I, fasc. 1, p. 31).

"Parce qu'elle n'a pas de caractére propre (*svalakṣaṇa*) et qu'elle se présente comme une pure imagination (*parikalpamātra*),, elle est nommée imaginaire." (translated by Lamotte in *La Somme du Grand Véhicule d'Asaṅga*. II, fasc. 1, p. 107).

18. *iti svalakṣaṇaṃ* . . . *arthasattvātmavijñapti pratibhāsaṃ prajāyate vijñānaṃ.* (*MV.*, p. 35).

19. *dhīḥ prajña, sā api upaparīkṣya eva vastuni pravicayo* . . . *yaḥ samyakmithyā vā saṃkīrṇasvasāmānyalakṣaṇesu eva dharmesu vivekāvabodhaḥ* . . . (*TrimB.* p. 26).

20. L'expression pari-niṣ-panna . . . indique:
1. L'universalité . . . ,le "nulle-part-elle-ne-manque" de cette nature; 2. son éternité, sa non-naissance non-destruction . . . ; 3. sa réalité, sa non-fausseté Elle se différencie du *svalakṣaṇa*, "caractére propre du Dharma," qui n'est pas universel; du *sāmānyalakṣaṇa*, "caractére commun", qui n'est pas éternel; de l'espace et de l'Ātman que ne sont pas réels. *La Siddhi de Hiuan-tsang*, trans. by La Vallée Poussin, p. 257.

He further explains:

"La donnée réele, d'un autre nom, le *svalakṣaṇa*, l'individu, (étant connue seulement par la "perception directc" (*pratyakṣapramāṇa*), genre de connaissance affranchie des mots et de toute démarche intellectuelle (*jñāna-vikalpa*) n'est pas l'object (*viṣaya*) du "savoir du plan relatif (*saṃvṛta*)" et de l'expression. Ce savoir et l'expression n'atteignent pas le svalakṣaṇa; ils se meuvent dans le domaine du général, des caractéres communs, *dharma-sāmānyalakṣaṇa*.

Mais, en dehors de ce savoir et de l'expression, il n'exist aucun moyen (*upāya*) de ḍésigner (*prajña*) le *svalakṣaṇa*. On dit. par consequent, que le *svalakṣaṇa* est le point d'appui du savoir relatif et de l'expression.

Par le fait, le son met en oeuvre, repose sur des similientités, nous entendons des caractéres (*lakṣaṇa*) imputés (*adhyāropita*) la donneé réelle (svalakṣaṇa) et qui ne sont pas absalument existents (*dravyasat*), qui ne sont pas des "choses". *La Siddhi de Hiuen-tsang*, trans. by La Vallée Poussin, p. 86ff.).

It should be kept in mind that Hsuan-Tsang studied in Nālandā at the time when Diṅnāga's logic had been included in the Yogācāra and the legend of Vasubandhu II turning to Mahāyāna became well established. Later Buddhist philosophers (Prajñākara, Ratnakīrti, Jñānaśrīmitra, Sāntarakṣita, Kamalaśīla, etc.) had been usinϱ his logic and epistemology to explain their own doctrines.

In China, Hsuan-Tsang did the same. Hence, they can never be considered as the standards of determining Diṅnāga and Dharmakīrti's own position. At least, not without committing a fallacy of Hysteron Proteron (putting the cart before the horse).

21. Stcherbatsky himself seems to be aware of the difference between the Sautrāntika and Yogācāra views on epistemological and ontological issues, and has translated part of the *Nyāyakaṇikā* of Vācaspatimiśra, who called Diṇnāga and Dharmakīrti, categorically, Sautrāntikas and their opponents Yogācāras (*BL.*, II, pp. 360-72). Stcherbatsky himself comments: "Hence Dharmakīrti and Digṅāga are represented here as Sautrāntikas. Although in their own opinions they are Yogācāras. Their opponents are the old Yogācāras of Asaṅga's school and the later Mādhyamika Yogācāras" (ibid, p. 370, fn. 3). It is definitely a confusing statement and a misrepresentation of Vāçaspati's own learning. The reason is quite apparent: how can they belong to the school of their opponents? If Diṅnāga and Dharmakīrti have been criticizing Asaṃga and Vasubandhu I's Yogācāra, then what kind of Yogācāra are they representing? Historically, at that time, there were not any other types of Yogācāras.

It appears that Stcherbatsky's interest in Idealism and Vinītadeva's *SSTI.* convinced him that they were idealists, and later when he found other material (Vācaspatimiśra's account), he could not really change his previous opinion, even at the cost of committing a logical fallacy.

22. Diṅnāga clearly describes *svalaksaṇa*:
na hi svasāmānyalaksaṇābhyāmanyatprameyamasti. svalaksaṇavisayaṃ hi pratyaksaṃ sāmānyavirayamanumānamiti pratipādayisyāmaḥ. (*PSV.*, 1/2), and believes that they are the cause of cognition in the collective (*samuditā*) form: *pratyekaṃ ca te samuditāḥ kāraṇaṃ.* (*PSV.*, 1/15). Quoted in *DNCV.*, p. 101.

23. *tasya* (*pratyakṣasya*) *viṣayaḥ svalakṣaṇaṃ. yasyārthasya sannidhānāsannidhānābhyām jñānapratibhāsabhedastat svalakṣaṇaṃ. tad eva paramārthasat, arthakriyāsāmarthyalakṣaṇatvastunaḥ. anyat sāmānyalaksaṇaṃ. sa anumānasya visayaḥ.* (*NB.*, 1/12-17).

This description nowhere differs from Diṇnāga's view, except in its clarification.

Dharmottara also clarifies the same fact: *svaṃ asadhāraṇaṃ lakṣanaṃ tattvaṃ svalaksaṇaṃ. vasturo hi asādhāraṇaṃ ca tattvaṃ asti sāmānyaṃ ca. yad asādhāraṇaṃ tat pratyakṣagrāhyaṃ.* (*NBT.* (D), p. 75)

Arcaṭa also comments on Dharmakīrti's assertion: *tatrādyaṃ asādhāraṇavisayaṃ.* (Hetu., p. 53).;

asādhāraṇavisayaṃ svalakṣaṇaviṣayaṃ. (*HBT.*, p. 25, referred to by Durvekamiśra in his *Pradipa*, p. 75).

For Dharmakīrti's description of *svalakṣaṇa* in his other treatises *supra*, p. 81

It is the same everywhere, except that it has different implications in different contexts.

24. For details see the criticism of Diṅnāga's *paramāṇusañcayavāda* in the *DNC.* of Mallavādin and Siṃhasūri's *vṛtti* (pp. 59-101). They have concluded:

nanu ca pratyekameva te samuditāḥ kāraṇaṁ, tathāsanta eva samuditāḥ paramāṇavaḥ caksurādijñānotpattihetuttvāt ālambanaṃ . . . na hi eka indriyaparamāṇurvisayaparamāṇurvā vijñānamutpādayitulaṃ, na tatsamudāyāh prajñaptisativāt. (p. 101).

25. Dharmakīrti put forward an objection that "the assimilation of atoms cognized through eye cognition, called *sāmānya,* must be then conceptual: (*sañcitaḥ samudāyaḥ sa sāmānyaṃ tatra cākṣadhīḥ. sāmānyabuddhiścāvaśyaṃ vikalpenāunbadhyate?* (*PV.*, 2/194.)

Dharmakīrti answers it: "Because of the nearness of the atoms, non-different other are produced; they are called the collection, and the cause of origin of cognition (sensation). And this peculiarity of atoms is not possible without the different atoms having interspace between them (they are never seen individually, but always collectively); because of taking it in this very different connotation the cognition of the universal is described (by Diṅnāga)".

arthāntarābhisambandhājjāyante ye'ṇavo'pare,
uktāste sañcitāste hi nimittaṃ jñānajanmanaḥ. (*PV.*, 2/195).
aṇūnāṃ sa viśesaśca nāntareṇāparānaṇūn,
tadekaniyamājjñānamuktaṃ sāmānayogocaraṃ. (*PV.*, 2/196). (Also see *PV.* 2/123-29).

26. Manorathanandin has, taking Diṅnāga's view into consideration, clarified it: *nanu 'sañcitālambanāḥ pañca vijñānakāyāḥ' iti siddhānataḥ, "tatrānekārthajanyatvāt svārthe sāmānyagocaraṃ".* (*PS.*, 1/4). *iti coktaṃ, tathā ca paramāṇūnāṃ samudāyaḥ sañcita ityucyate, sa eva ca sāmānyaṃ mataḥ, tatra ca sāmānye akṣadhīrjāyate, sāmānyabuddhiścāvaśyaṃ vikalpenānubadhyate, tat kathaṃ avikalpaṃ pratyakṣaṃ ucyate ?* (2/194) ; and clarifies the answer of Dharmakīrti :

. . .na hi pratyekaṃ aṇavo dṛśyāḥ, kintu sahitā eva. . .na tu paramāṇu atiriktasāmānyaviṣayaṃ, tat kathaṃ sāmānyaviṣayatvāt savikalpatvaprasaṃgaḥ. (2/196, p. 159).

27. Prajñākaragupta has rightly commented on and defended Dharmakīrti's doctrine of the collection of atoms (*anusamudāyavāda*), and clarified it by an example : as a single hair is never seen from a distance, but only in assemblage form. Similarly, though atoms are gross in form, by their special capacity (*sāmarthyaviśeṣa*) in a collective form, they produce sensory cognition :

sārūpyanti tat kena sthūlābhāsañca te aṇavaḥ (*PV.*, 3/322)

he comments :

aṇava eva yadi viṣayastataḥ sthūlābhāsavijñānamiti sārūpyābhāvātkathaṃviṣayo vijñānasya. vṛksādipiṇḍagrahaṇavad bhrāntameva bhavet. varṇākāratayā sārūpyantīti cet, na . . . atha sthūlatā grahaṇadharmaḥ. . . (p. 350)

Earlier, he presents an example of a bunch of hair :

yathaiva keśā davīyasi deśesamsktā api ghanasanniveśāvabhāsinaḥ paramāṇavopi tatheti na virodha, tadapi sūksmāḥ kathañjanayanti. kevalavad eveti cet. kevalānāmasāmarthyāt, asāmarthyamevahetubhāvavirodhi na sūksmatā, keśavadeva na cendriyādīnāṃ sthūlatādiviśesa upajāyate sāmagryāvasthāyāṃ. atha ca sāmarthyaviśeṣādeva janakatvaṃ. (*PVB.*, 3/224, p. 296)

28. *niraṃśaparamāṇunāmābhāse sthaulyavedane, pratyakṣam kalpanāyuktaṃ pratyakseṇaiva sidhyati.* (*Nyāyāvatāra* 2/28, p. 82). This śloka is an answer of Dharmakīrti's *kārikā : pratyaksaṃ kalpanāpoḍhaṃ pratyakṣeṇaiva sidhyati* (*PV.*, 2/123).

Similarly, Ratnākara, while criticizing the different views of atomism, refers to Dharmakīrti's view on atoms and criticizes it; *anityāścetakaṇikāḥ, kālāntararasthāyino vā? ksaṅikāścet. kimekasmād bhavanti, kāraṇād vā kuto api? ākasmāccet. nanu kimiha kāraṇa pratisedhamātraṃ, bhuvanapratisedhaḥ, svātmahetukatvaṃ, nirupākhyahetukatvaṃ vā vivaksitaṃ? ādye, bhavanasyanapekṣatvena sadā sattvasya asattvasya va prasaktiḥ:*
"nityaṃ sattvaṃasattvaṃ vā ahetoranyānapeksanāt." (*PV.*, 1/82).
ityuktaḥ. . .(*Ratnākara*, 1/16, p. 79).

29. *NBT*(*D*), pp. 41-42.
30. *Pradīpa*, pp. 41-44.
31. *Viṃśatikā*, 11-16. Also see *TrimB.* of Sthiramati, pp. 30-31.
32. Vijñānavādin Vasubandhu (I) criticizes the Sautrāntika theory of *Pratyakṣa* on the ground that the object which is perceived has already disappeared: *na so'rtho dṛśyate tasya pratyakṣatvam kathaṃ mataṃ.* (*Viṃśatikā*, 16.) *yadā ca sā pratyakṣabuddhirbhavatīdaṃ me pratyakṣamiti tadā na sā artha dṛśyate* (*sva-vṛtti*).
33. *bhinnakālaṃ kathaṃ grāhyaṃ iti ced grāhyatāṃ viduh, hetutvaṃ eva yuktijñā jñānākārārpaṇakṣamaṃ.* (*PV.*, 2/247).
34. . . . *darśanaṃ ca arthasākṣātkaraṇākhaṃ pratyakṣavyāpāraḥ. utprekṣaṇāṃ tu vikalpavyāpāraḥ. tathāhi parokṣaṃ arthaṃ vikalpayanta utprekṣāmahe na tu paśyāma iti utprekṣātmakaṃ vikalpavyāpāraṃ anubhavād adhyavasyanti. tasmāt svavyāpāraṃ tiraskṛtya pratyakṣavyāpāraṃ ādarśayati yatrārthe pratyakṣapūrvako' dhyavasāyas tatrā pratyakṣaṃ kevalaṃ eva pramāṇaṃ iti.* (*NBT.*, 1/21).
35. "(Sautrāntika). A conformity between them, the fact owing to which cognition, although caused (also) by the activity of the senses, is not something homogeneous with them. It is said to cognize the object and not the senses. (It bears the reflection of the objective element, which is its corollary) and again the expression "consciousness apprehends" is not inadequate, inasmuch as here also a continuity of conscious moments is the cause of every cognition. ("Consciousness apprehends" means that the previous moment is the cause of the following one). The agent here also denotes simply the cause, just as in the current expression "the bell resounds" (the bell is doing nothing, but every following moment of sound is produced by the previous one). We can give another illustration: consciousness apprehends similarly to the way in which a light moves." (*BL.*, II, p. 347). (*AbkB.*, IV).

It also implies that the term *kṣaṇa* as used by Stcherbatsky in his second interpretation is not appropriate for the Sautrantika system, but *anitya* or "*santati*" as clarified by Vasubandhu II, by the example of the flame and the sound of a bell.

36. "It is certainly not the naive realism of Nyāya-Vaiśeṣika. For the Brahmanical writers it was different from the later, more definite idealism . . . It has, in any case, a position of its own, very far from ordinary realism, resemb-

ling perhaps some modern theories which accept the reality of external as well as internal facts and a certain "coordination" between them, without the one "graspings" the other. The cinematographic representation of and the converting of all the facts of inner and outer world composing an individual stream of life into complex play of interconnected momentary flashes, is anything but realism". (*CCB.*, pp. 65-66).

"The curious result has been attained in the way of a compromise between the early extreme pluralism and the later extreme monism. The monists developed into a school of Idealism. From Mādhyamikas, were born the Yogācāras. The pluralists, Sarvāstivādins, developed into the critical school of Sautrantikas. The latter were apparently the first to assume the reality of a thing-in-itself behind the outward phenomenon." (*BL.*, I, p. 529).

He further asserts:

"Roughly speaking, a real external world is assumed in Hīnayāna, denied in Mahāyāna and partly reassumed in the logical school". (ibid, p. 525).

Thus, Stcherbatsky's first interpretation (Vijñānavādin) is incorrect and the second interpretation (Sautrāntika) is correct.

CHAPTER 5

Conclusion

Finally, we come to the end of our enquiry which is directly connected with Dharmakīrti's philosophical standpoint; and that is all we are actually concerned with in this book. Let us stop here with a short summary of our conclusion.

The prevalent *controversy* regarding Dharmakīrti's philosophical standpoint indicates the doubtful nature of the issue. The *examination* of the controversy reveals the invalid, inconsistent, contradictory and illogical nature of wrong views. The three fold (epistemological, ontological and axiological) *evidence* drives the author to the following conclusion.

Firstly, the *epistemological evidence*: the definition of right cognition, criterion of right knowledge, theory of correspondence, means of right cognition, importance of direct cognition, definition of direct cognition, division of direct cognition, two means of valid cognition and limit of valid cognition; secondly, the *ontological evidence*: two realities, atomism, non-eternalism, nature of reality, illusion, non-causal destruction, unity of mind and mental factors, negation of eight kinds of consciousnesses, store-house consciousness and solipsism; and thirdly, the *axiological evidence* the theory of the four noble truths, three intrinsic characteristics of reality, ethical radicalism, positively prove that Dharmakīrti's Philosophical standpoint is that of Sautrāntika.

The other conclusions which follow by implications are as follow:

1. Diṅnāga who followed the philosophical doctrines of Sautrāntika Vasubandhu, also belonged to the Sautrāntika School.

2. Vasubandhu II who wrote *Abhidharmakośabhāṣya* was a Sautrāntika and did not change his position till death.

3. Some of the ancient commentators of these three Sautrāntika philosophers have misled some modern scholars of high repute.

Other conclusions by implications have already been mentioned in the introduction.*

It is essential to clarify the fact about this critical research. All these conclusions are historical and therefore probable and relative, depending on different causes and conditions. The definitive conclusions are derived at because of the strength of the evidence and logic as an attempt to remove doubtful, controversial and uncertain situation, but, the thesis is not beyond the laws of probability and relativity. Therefore, these polemic issues are left open for future investigations and discussions.

**supra*, pp. 15-17

APPENDIX I

Sāṃvyavahārika

As mentioned in Chapter 1, one of the causes of misconception is the misinterpretation of the term *sāṃvyavahārika* or *vyavahāra* in the sense of lower or worldly. Tilmann Vetter recently produced evidence from *PVin.* in support of the prevalent interpretation that Dharmakīrti's logic is from the worldly point of view:

=*sāṃvyavahārikasyaitat pramāṇasya rūpaṃ uktaṃ atrāpi vimūḍhā visaṃvādayanti lokaṃ.* (*PVin.*, I, p. 100).

[The formulation of valid source of cognition is described on the basis of its applicability, even here deluded minded (dare to) contradict the world]

Damit ist die Natur des für die Praxis (des Alltags) verwendbaren Erkenntnismittels gelehrt. Auch hinsichtlich dessen nāmlich enttäuschen aussenstehende Toren die Leute. *PVin.*, p. 101.

It appears as though Dharmakīrti is contradicting himself by taking back whatever he has said before. But it is not true. The term *sāṃvyavahārika* or *vyavahāra* is used in the specific sense of 'practicability' or successful activity' by Dharmakīrti;

vyavahāropanīteṣu vyavacchedo'sti kaścana (*PV.*, 3/125; *PVSV.*, pp. 244-48).

vyavahārādau pravṛtteśca siddhastadbhāvaniścayaḥ. (*PV.*, 2/68.

vyavahāre'pi tenāyamadoṣa iti cet. PV., 31/118; *PVSV.*, 1/120, p. 236; *PVSVT.*, pp. 235-36).

anirākaraṇe teṣāṃ saṅkete vyavahāriṇāṃ. (*PV.*, 3/116; *PVSV.*, 3/118, p. 235; *PVSVT.*, pp. 235-36).

vyavahārastadāśrayaḥ. (*PV.*, 4/184).

vyavahāropanito'tra. (*PV.*, 4/185).

anādirvāsanodbhūtaṃ bādhante' rthaṃ na laukikaṃ (*PV.*, 4/234; *PVV.*, pp. 440-41; *NB.*, 2/28, 3/35-36).

Dharmottara also comments on *samyagjñāna*:
puruṣārthopayogi samyagjñānaṃ. (*NBT*., (*D*), p. 1).
upayogo=vyāpāraḥ (*Pradīpa*, p. 10).
avisaṃvādakaṃ jñānaṃ samyagjñānaṃ. (*NBT*.(*D*), p. 17).
avisaṃvādakaṃ pravṛitiviṣaya vastu prāpakaṃ samyagjñānamiti. (*Pradīpa*, p. 17).
tato'rthakriyāsāmarthavastupradarśakaṃ samyagjñānaṃ (*NBT*., p. 23).
ayamāśayo yathā loke satyavādiśabdapravṛttinimittasyopadarśitārthaprāpaṇasya puruṣe sa sambhavāt sambhavādakaśabdaḥ pravartate, tathā jñānepi tat sambhavāditi (*Pradīpa*, pp. 17, 20, 27).
See the understanding of the term by other critics also. Udayana refers to the Buddhistic view of *lokavyavahāra*: "*lokavyavahārasiddhamiti cet*". *siddheva tarhi, na hyanyato'pi kiñcit siddhayati*. (*ATV*., pp. 240-41, 200-1).
The Jaina scholar Hemacandra also presents a criticism: that if you (Dharmakīrti) assume the definition of the valid source of cognition grounded on its applicability (*sāṃvyavahārika*), then knowledge can never be non-conceptual (not capable of application (*vyavahāra*): *yadyavikalpakaṃ jñānaṃ tadā na tad vyavahāra janana samarthaṃ. sāṃvyvahārikasya caitat pramāṇasyalakṣaṇamiti ca bhavantaḥ*... (*PM*., 1/1/8, p. 6).
Akalaṅka also indicates contradiction on the ground of this theory. *sarvavijñānānāṃ sva-saṃvedanaṃ pratyakṣamavikalpakaṃ yadi, niścayasyāpi kasyacit svata eva niścayāt kutaḥ tatsamvyavaharasiddhiḥ*- (*Akalaṅkagranthatrayaṃ*) pp. 6-7,

Yaśomltra while explaining and meaning and purpose of *Abhidharmaśāstra* has clarified this problem.
Dharmakīrti, following the same tradition asserts:
Śrutamayena jñānenārthān gṛhitvā yukticintā-mayena vyavasthāpya bhāvayatāṃ tanniṣpattau yad avitathaviṣayaṃ tad eva pramāṇaṃ (*PVin*., I. p, 74).

Both Yaśomitra (*Sphuṭārthā*, pp. 8-9), and Dharmakīrti *PV*., 1/7) have been explaining *sāṃvyavahārika* in the sense of *Abhidharmaśāstra* or *pramāṇaśāstra* which leads to the realization of the ultimate truth, not in the sense of lower or worldly as understood by Tilmann Vetter and others.

Tilmann Vetter himself analyzed, in his work entitled "*Erkenntnisproblem Bei Dharmakīrti*", the Sautrāntika ontology (pp. 13-25) where he explains the Soutrāntika doctrines of Dharmakīrti. The subject of "*sāṃvyavahārika*" should also be interpreted in thesame manner.

APPENDIX II

Ālambana

The confusion, as mentioned above, is created by non-discrimination of the connotations of the terms *ālambana* and *viṣaya. Ālambana,* in the Sautrāntika tradition, means the object of consciousness (*citta-caitta*) which is self-object (*svālambana*) and does not need any corresponding reality. *Viṣaya,* on the contrary, is the object of the senses which needs a corresponding reality. It is proved by the following references:

AbkB., 1/29:

kaḥ punarviṣayālambanayorviśeṣaḥ? *Yasmin yasyakāritraṃ ṣa tasya viṣayaḥ yaccittaihgrhyate tadālambanaṃ*). *AbkB.*, 2/23, 2/62; *Sphuṭārthā* (.*supra* ch. 4, ef. 14).

Diṅnāga *AP.*, *PS.*, *Dignāga on Preception.* on pp. 32-35. Dharmakīrti *PV.*, 3/451; *PVB.*, p. 438.

Even Vijñānavādins used this term in the same sense:

saṃjñā viṣayanimittodgraṇaṃviṣaya ālambanaṃ...nimittam tadviśeṣo nīlapītādyālambana-vyavasthākāraṇaṃ (*TrimB.*, p. 21).

The whole Pāḷi Abhidharma tradition reveals the same meaning. I collected the references which are available only in Sinhālese character: *dubbalapurisena daṇḍādi viya citta-cetasike hi ālambīyati, amuñcamānehi gaṇhiyatīti ālambanaṃ ārammaṇasadde pana sati cittacetasikaṃ āgantvā ramantīti ārammaṇaṃ* (*PD.*, p. 110).

tadeva dubbalapurisena daṇḍādi viya citta-cetasikehi ālambīyati, tāni vā āgantvā ettha ramantīti ārammaṇaṃ ti. (ibid, p. 98).

taṃ taṃ upādāyā'ti paramatthadhammānaṃ taṃ taṃ pavatti visesaṃ upādāya, upanidhāyā ti olimbiya. (ibid., p. 357).

parikappiyatīti parikappabuddhiyā parikappetvā gāyhamānā ettha pana evamādippabheda ālambanabhūtaparikappīyamānā sabbā paññattī paññāpiyatīti atthena paññattītiyojanā. (ibid., p. 35).

See an important paper by A. K. Warder on 'Objects', *Journ. of Indian Phil.*, 1975, pp. 355 ff.

APPENDIX III

Nyāyavādin

The term *nyāyavādin* clearly indicates the connotaation epistemologist logician and Sautrāntika. Thus, Vasubandhu II, Diṅnāga and Dharmakīrti were Nyāyavādin Sautrāntikas.

The Jaina logician Siddhasenadivākara refers to Vasubandhu II as *nyāyavādin*:
antarvyāpaiva sādhyasya siddherbahirudāhṛtiḥ
vyarthā syāttadasadbhāve 'pyevaṃ nyāyavido viduḥ. (20).

Dharmakīrti calls Diṅnāga a *nyāyavādin*:
śeṣavad vyabhicāritvāt kṣiptaṃ nyāyavideḍṛśaṃ. (*PV*., 3/333).
īdṛśamanumānaṃ śesavadanaikāntikaṃ vyabhicāritvannyāyavādin ācāryadiṅnāgena pratiṣiptaṃ. (*PVV*., p. 360).
nyāya udāhṛta. (*PV*., 3/20). In *Vādanyāya* Dharmakīrti holds:
nyāyavādināmapi vādeṣu asadvyavasthopanyaṣaiḥ śaṭhā nigṛhnanti tanniṣedhārthamidamārabhyate (p. 1).

Jainas also call Dharmakīrti a *nyāyavādin*:
nyāyavādineṣṭameva kāraṇasyahetutvaṃ yadāha- "ekasamagryādhīnasya rūpade rasato gatiḥ, hetudharmānumānena dhūmendhanavikāravat. (*PV*., 1/10; *PM*., 1/2/12, p. 43).
kathamayamābālagopālavipalānganādiprasiddho'pi. nopalabdhaḥ sūkṣma-dṛśināpi nyāyavādinā" (*PM*., 1/2/12, p. 42).
"nānvayasandeha iti nyāyavādināpi vyatirekabhāvādeva hetvābhāsāvuktau" *PM*., 1/2, p. 44.

The term *nyāya* here connotes right or justice in logic. Also see *Nyayaśāstra*-rigs pahi hastar ba chos, the science of right judgment *Mahāvyutpatti*, p. 133; 1/17; *Pradīpa*, p. 78).

APPENDIX IV

Dharmakīrti on Sensation

(*pratyakṣa*)

The following is translation of some kārikas of *Pramānavartika* Pratyakṣapariched, 1-7, 123-133.

1. The means of knowledge is of two kinds, because there are two kinds of objects, as there is or is not a capacity for action towards an object. Hair and such things are not objects, because there is no reliance on them of the kind that occurs towards objects.
2. And (also) because of similarity and non-similarity, because of being and not being within the scope of language, and because, when other signs (than the object) are present, intellect occurs with respect to one but not with respect to the other.
3. That object with respect to which (purposeful) action is possible is called the ultimate real, whereas the other is the conventionally real. These are respectively the unique particular and the universal.
4. If it is argued that nothing has a causal capacity, (we point out that) the causal capacity of seeds, etc. towards sprouts, etc., you may argue that the capacity is regarded to be merely conventional. So be it.
5. If it is argued everything has causal capacity, we reply that there is none in universals, because of the not seeing of the cognition of logical agreement and non-agreement like the cognition of a visible object through the eye.*
6. By this (absence of causal capacity in the universal, its effect being mere knowledge) the notions of such things as a pot, up-

*Text with Prajñākaragupta reads;..it is not seen of the cognition of agreement and non-agreement in the universal characteristic like the cognition of a visible object through the eye.

ward motion, general characteristic and number are explained due to conformity with such things of the mind as convention, enjoyment, etc.

7. Hair, etc. are not universals, because there is no desire for them of the kind that occurs towards real objects. In the case of absent things, there is no fault (of their having the features of a universal), because they are grasped as knowables.

× × × ×

123. Sensation, which is free of conceptualization (imagining), is established only by means of sensation itself. The conceptualization (imagining) of all (beings), which is cognized individually (subjectively) is dependent on names.
124. One who remains with a tranquil mind, having withdrawn his thought from all (concepts), looks at a visible object with his eye: that thought is born of sensation.
125. Then, forming a judgment he knows "There was something like my (present) imagining". There is no access of the sense-organ to the situation just stated.
126. For a particular observed in one place is never seen elsewhere. Therefore, it is not the case that owing to a non-difference in cognitions there exists another, a universal which is separate (from the particular).
127. Therefore, every thought born of sensation has a particular as its object. There is no possibility of the functioning of words with respect to particulars.
128. Particulars have no agreement (with words) because no convention functions: and the object of words may be connected with them (with words, not with particulars).
129. For when there is a relationship of the form "this (expression) is of that (object)", the relationship is between only those two objects, which are imaginings; then it is not within the range of the senses.
130. Then, because there is no (longer) a discovery (as in sensation) of an object with a clear image, a difference of form in consciousness is what distinguishes objects.
131. Even when an object appears through the eye of which one says: "It is other than that" only that (conception, imagining) is connected with words, surely not the range (object) of the senses.
132. Because there is no discovery, that which is not engaged with the senses merely through the other word and an unexpressed

relationship (between word and object) itself is not connected with cognition.

133. (If) there were a simultaneous functioning of without-imagining (sensation) and with-imagining (sensation), affecting the mind, (then) there would be bewilderment. Or (If) their functioning were extermely rapid their unity would tend to result (they would appear in the mind to be the same, resulting in the same confusion).

APPENDIX V

Prabhāsvaraṃ Cittaṃ

Ruegg (*La Théorie du Tathāgatagarbha et du gotra*) has referred to the doctrine of Dharmakīrti that, by nature, the mind is clear but defilements come from the outside, and has taken it as referring to the *Amalavijñāna* of the non-traditional Vijñānavādins. This view is examined in this appendix.

The examination proves that Dharmakīrti has not used *citta* here in the Vijñānavādin sense, but in the sense of the Sautrāntikas. The following were the grounds which led Ruegg to present such an interpretation:

1. Taking for granted (pp. 433-435) the view of a 10th century Buddhist Idealist Philosopher, Jñānaśrīmitra, who mentions the unanimity of different Buddhist Philosophers, such as Maitreyanātha, Asaṃga, Vasubandhu, Kumāranātha, Diṅnāga, Dharmakīrti, Prajñākaragupta, etc., in one of his monographs (*Sākārasiddhiśāstra*, p. 506);

2. Taking for granted the interpretation by Manorathanandin of the term "*āśraya*" in the sense of *Ālayavijñāna*; and

3. Taking for granted some Tibetan traditions on this issue.

Now, here is an examination of these grounds:

i. Jñānaśrimitra is following the legend of only one Vasubandhu, which has already been examined (Chapter 1). Moreover, one can definitely say that almost all of these philosophers mentioned by him had different philosophical viewpoints. Jñānaśrīmitra attempted to include all of them under the Sākāravijñānavāda school. It may be a good attempt at synthesis, but it is not evidence for facts. The legend of Mañjuśrī's conversion of Diṅnāga is contradictory in nature as *PS.*, which was written after the conversion, is a Sautrāntika work, and not a Vijñānavādin work.

ii. The term "*āśraya*" (basis) does not mean here *ālayavijñāna*, but the *cittasaṃtāna* (series of consciousnesses) as described by Ruegg, himself (pp. 435, 481, 489), on the basis of the Sautrāntika doctrine (*Abk.*, 1/20), and he also refers to Tilman Vetter's (*Erkenntnis...*) view of the denial of Asaṃga's theory in this context (p. 43, fn. 2). The present author has already adduced strong evidence showing that Dharmakīrti never accepted the *Ālayavijñāna* doctrine in his seven treatises, and has used the term "*āśraya*" (basis) in the sense of a series of consciousnesses (*cittasaṃtāna*) in other places (*PV.*, 2/449, 3/138), which indicates the pure (*prabhāsvara*) nature of the flow of consciousness without any self or ego (*satkāyadṛṣṭi*), which gets defiled by *caitasikas*, such as ignorance (*avidyā*), which creates an idea of ego or self (*ātman*), which is the root-cause of all defilements (*tanmūlāśca malāḥ sarve sa ca satkāyadarśanaṃ, PV.*, 1/215cd).

In the context (*PV.*, 1/207) of describing the path (*mārga*) to get rid of disgust (*duḥkha*), Dharmakīrti mentions that, by nature, the mind is clear, and defilements (*malāḥ*) are extraneous (*PV.*, 1/210). It does not mean that the mind never gets defiled, as in the case of the Vijñānavādin, but on the contrary, Dharmakīrti indicates self-love (*ātmarāga*), or belief in ego (*satkāyadṛṣṭi*) as the root-cause of all defilements. It means that, in the first moment of mental performance, the mind is devoid of imagination and illusion; in other words, it is tabula rasa (*prabhāsvara*), but gets defiled because of ignorance (*avidyā*), which can be destroyed by true knowledge (*vidyā*). It has nothing to do with the inactive absolute of Vijñānavādin.

Dharmakīrti criticizes the concept of eternal liberation (*nitya mokṣa*) in the previous Kārikās on the basis that it would not require a technique to achieve it. "Scholars describe eternal in the sense that it does not change its nature" (*nityaṃ tamāhurvidvāṃso yaḥ svabhāvo na naśyati, PV.*, 1/206cd). In this case, the problem of bondage and liberation will not arise. "The cause of origin of disgust is bondage—how is it possible of an eternal (entity)? The case of no origin of disgust is liberation—how will it be possible of an eternal (entity)?" (*duḥkhasyotpādahetutvaṃ bandho, nityasya tat kutaḥ* (*PV* 1/20,4 ab.) and *aduḥkhotpādahetutvaṃ mokṣaḥ, nityasya tat kutaḥ* (*PV.*,1/205, ab.).

The problem of bondage and liberation (*bandha-mokṣa*) is only possible when one accepts the doctrine of non-eternality of self or *cittasaṃtāna* (*anityaḥ sa ucyatāṃ PV.* 1/207d). After dealing with the problem of cessation of disgust (*duḥkha-nirodha*), Dharmakīrti now proceeds (*PV.*, 1/207) to describe the Sautrāntika doctrine of the four-fold path of cessation of disgust. He also mentions in this context that the cause of illusion is ignorance, which causes an illusory appearance, such as: because of a rope, there appears a snake, but when the cognition which makes the rope apprehended emerges, the illusory snake disappears and never comes back again. Similarly, by nature, cognition reveals the true nature of a thing, but, because of the idea of an ego (*satkāyadṛṣṭi*), illusory things appear. Also, by nature, mind is free from the defilements of the idea of self or ego, but gets defiled because of self-love (*ātma-rāga*). On the other hand, by meditation on no-self or *śūnya*, one gets rid of these defilements. The same meaning is expressed in the Sūtra (*Aṅguttaranikāya*, I, 5, 9-10), referred to by Ruegg (p. 412) and by Tilman Vetter (p. 85). Ruegg (p. 412) has dealt in detail with the concept of "*prabhāsvaraṃ cittaṃ*" in different systems of Buddhist schools. He is quite aware of the fact that different schools have used this concept in different senses. How can one, in this circumstance, make an absolute assertion that Dharmakīrti has used this term in the sense of Vijñānavāda, who considered mind as being absolute and blissful light?

3. The term *prabhāsvara* (*tib.'odgsal*) is a purely operational term. Ruegg has referred to a Tibetan scholar who has quoted Dharmakīrti under the Vijñānavādin's doctrine, and on this basis, concluded that Dharmakīrti is, or is similar to, Vijñānavādin. But one should not forget the fact that, even in Tibetan tradition, this term is used in different senses by "Gam-po-pa" (xvii, 3b) who clearly indicates two meanings vis-a-vis Sautrāntika and Vijñānavādin. Formerly, he takes it in the sense of light as valid mental performance (*rig pa'odgsal*), and later in the sense of light as being in itself (*raṅ odzin gyi-odgsal*), which means "nothing" (*ston-pa=śūnya*), or "something absolute in nature" or "*Ālayavijñāna*". But, in Sautrāntika tradition, it is simply "an encased light" or "quietism" or "pure series of consciousness" or *bhavaṅga* in Theravāda Abhidhamma.

Ruegg has indicated in his article entitled 'On Ratnakīrti' in the *Journal of Indian Philosophy* 1, 1970, p. 304) that Diṅnāga and Dharmakīrti had affinities with the Sautrāntikas:

> "The importance thus attached to the ontological status of the term of an inference is indeed quite understandable in view of the well-known affinities of the classical school of Buddhist logic with the Sautrāntika School, which had concerned itself with the absolutely real (*paramārthasat*) defined as causally efficient (*arthakriyāsa-*

martha), and of the fact that its *pramāṇavidyā* "theory of knowledge" was intimately bound up with praxis.

In other words, while usually counted as Vijñānavādins (of the 'non-traditionalist' variety), Dignāga and Dharmakīrti were concerned in their theory of knowledge not only with concepts, but also with things (*artha*) and our behaviour to them; and, in this respect, their position appears to be closely connected with that of the Sautrāntikas."*

Therefore, Ruegg might also have considered the issue of *prabhāsvaraṃ cittaṃ* in the sense of the Sautrāntika's doctrine of a series of pure consciousnesses (*cittasaṃtāna*), devoid of the idea of an ego or self (*ātman*).

*D. Seyfort Ruegg, *Journal of Indian Philosophy*, 1, 1970. p. 304.

APPENDIX VI

Dharmakīrti's Works

Dharmakīrti's seven works and two auto-commentaries which are used in this book are as follows:

1. *Pramāṇavārttikaṃ* (*PV*), *kārikās* only, Sanskṛit verse, discovered and edited by Rāhula Sāṅkṛtyāyana, *JORS*, Paṭna, 1948.
   with Manorathavṛtti, Sanskṛit, discovered and edited by Rāhula Sāṅkṛtyāyana, *JORS*, Paṭna, 1949.
   with Prajñākarabhāṣya, Sanskṛit, discovered and edited by Rāhula Sankṛtyāyana, *JORS*, Paṭna, 1953.
   with Manorathavṛtti, Sanskrit, edited by Dwarikadass Shastri, Vārāṇasī, 1969. (Generally used here.)
2. *Pramāṇaviniścaya* (*PV in.*), with Sanskrit references, Chap. I, *pratyakṣa*, Tibetan and Sanskrit prose and verse, edited by Tilmann Vetter, Wien, 1966.
   Chapter II, *Svārthānumāna*, with Sanskrit references, Tibetan and Sanskṛit, prose and verse, edited by E. Steinkellner, Wien, 1972.
   Chapter III, *Parārthānumāna*, Tibetan, prose and verse Bstan-hgyur, Tibetan *Tripiṭaka*, 130. no. 5710, pp. 102-07, Tokyo-Kyoto, 1957.
3. *Nyāyabindu** (*NB.*), with Dharmottaratīkā, Sanskrit prose, edited by Prof. Th. Stcherbatsky, St. Petersburg, 1918.
   with Hindi translation of Sūtras, Sanskṛit prose, edited by Candraśekhara Shastri, Varanasi, 1954.

The *Nyāyabinduṭīkā* by Dharmottara, edited in the *Bibl. Ind.* ed. of the *Nyāyabindu*, P. Peterson; also a *tippaṇi* edited in the *Bibliothica Buddhica*, St. Petersburg, 1909, Peterson, who discovered and published the *Nyāyabindu* in 1889, did not know that Dharmakīrti was its author. This was established by Pathak in *JBRAS*, 1894, XVIII, p. 88f. and p. 213ff. Cf. Jacob in *JRAOS*, 1905, pp. 361-62.

with Pradīpa of Durveka, Sanskṛit prose, edited by Dalasukh Bhai Malavaniya, Paṭna, 1955.

4. *Hetubindu* (*Hetu*), with Ṭīkā of Arcaṭa and Āloka of Durveka, Sanskrit restoration from the Tibetan by Rāhula Sāṅkṛtyāyana, one śloka, the rest prose, edited by Sukhalāljī Saṅghavī and Jinavijayaji. *GOS*, CXIII, Baroda, 1949.
   with German translation, Sanskrit and Tibetan, edited by E. Steinkellner, Wien, 1967.
5. *Vādanyāya*, with commentary of Śāntarakṣita Sanskṛit, prose edited by Rāhula Sāṇkṛtyāyana, *JBORS*, XXI, XXII, Patna, 1935-36.
   with commentary of Śāntarakṣita ed. by Dwarikadass Shastri, Varanasi, 1972.
6. *Santānāntarasiddhi* (*SS.*), with ṭīkā of Vinītadeva, Tibetan, one verse, the rest prose edited by Th. Stcherbatsky, St. Petersburg, 1916.
   with Ṭīkā of Vinītadeva, Russian translation, edited by Th. Stcherbatsky, St. Petersburg *Bibliotheca Buddhica*, XIX, 1922.
   A Study of Indian Classical Logic, English translation, ed. by H. Kitagawa, Tokyo, 1965.
   Papers of Stcherbatsky, English translation from Russian edited by H. C. Gupta, Calcutta, 1971.
7. *Sambandhaparīkṣā* (*SP.*), text and sva-vṛtti, Tibetan, prose and verse, ed. by E., Frauwallner. Wien, 1934.
   (collection of 22 kārikās from *Prameyakamala* mārtaṇḍa (Int. *PVB.*), Sanskrit verse, ed. by Rāhula Sānkṛtyāyana, *JORS.*, Patna, 1953
   with commentary of Prabhācandra, Sanskṛit prose and verse, edited by Swāmi Dwarikadass. Vārāṇaṣī, 1972.

Sva-vṛttis (auto-commentaries)

1. *Pramāṇavārttikasvavṛtti* (*PVSV*), with ṭīkā of Karṇakagomin, commented on only one chapter Svārthānumāna, Sanskṛit prose, ed. by Rāhula Sāṅkṛtyāyana, Allahabad, 1943.
   (only vṛtti), Sanskṛit prose, edited by Dalsukh Bhai Malvania, Varaṇasī, 1959.
   only vṛtti, Sanskṛit, prose, ed. by R. Gnoli, Roma, 1960.
   Translation 1-51 only, by S. Mookerjee and H. Nagasaki, Nālandā, 1964.

2. *Sambandhaparīkṣāsvavṛtti* (*SPSV.*), See. *supra*, p. 150, 7)

Other works of Dharmakīrti as listed in the Tibetan colophon may not be authentic as discovered by Prof. Th. Stcherbatsky, "The Tibetan colophon contains some other works ascribed to Dharmakīrti, viz., a collection of verses, comments on *Śūras Jātakamālā* and on the *Vinayasūtra*, but whether really belong to him is not sure."

He also writes a note on it:

"He is also reported by Tārānatha to have written a work on tantrika ritual and tantrists of Jāvā reckoned him as a teacher of their school. But probably this was only their belief sprung from the desire to have a celebrated name among their own school. The work is found in Tanjur." (fn. 2).

[1]*BL.*, I, p. 37.

Glossary*

abhidharma	higher dharma analysis
abhidharmabhājaniya	analysis according to Abhidharma
adhimokṣa	determination
adhipatipratyaya	dominant condition (sense)
adhvan	time
advasaṃkara	intermixture of time
adveṣa	aversion
ahetukavināśavāda	doctrine of non-causal destruction
ahiṃsā	non-violence
ahrī	lack of self-respect
akuśala	immoral
alobha	non-greed
amalavijñāna	pure consciousness
anāgata	future
anapatrāpa	shamelessness; no fear of blame
anātman	no ego or self
anityasantāna	non-eternal flow

*One important point regarding translation is to be clarified. Sometimes, it is hard to find an English equivalent for a Sanskrit term. The technical terms such as Vaibhāṣika, Sautrāntika and Vijñānavāda translated as realism, critical realism and idealism respectively, should not be confused with the terms used in the Western Philosophy. The author has sometimes applied them according to Professor Stcherbatsky with minor changes. Often, one Sanskrit term is translated variously by different scholars, For example, *svalakṣaṇa* is translated as particular point-instant, unique, things in itself, burst of energy, assemblage of atoms, own characteristic, etc; and the term *sārūpya* as correspondence, conformity, and coordination, etc. The English alphabetical order is adopted for the convenience of the English readers.

anityavāda	non-eternalism
anumāna	inference
anupalabdhi	non-apprehension
aṇu	atom
aṇusaṃghāta	combination of atoms
aṇusamudāya	collection of atoms
aṇusamudāyavāda	doctrine of assemblage of atoms
aṇusañcaya	assemblage of atoms
aṇusañcayavāda	doctrine of assemblage of atoms
anvaya	agreement
anvayavidhi	method of agreement
anyathānyathika	change of relation
apatrāpa	shame, fear of blame
apramāda	non-negligence
aprāpti	non-possession
apratisaṃkhyānirodha	intellectually non-discriminative cessation
artha	object
arthakriyā	causally efficient, successful activity, action toward an object
arthakriyakāritva	causal efficiency
arthasaṃveda	cognition of the object
asaṃskṛta	uncomposed
asaṃprajanya	non-deliberation
aśrādhya	disbelief; lack of confidence
aṣṭavijñāna	eight types of consciousness
audhatya	vanity or pride
avasthānyathika	change of position
avayavin	whole
avidyā	ignorance
avidyābalāt	by the force of illusion (ignorance)
avyākṛta	indeterminate
ayogaśūnyatā	inconsistent voidness
ābhāsa	appearance
āgama	scripture
ākāra	form
ālambana	object or support of consciousness
ālayavijñāna	store consciousness
āntarikaliṅga	internal reason
āptāgama	authority

āśraya	basis
ātmakhyāti	self-appearance
ātmasaṃvedana	self-consciousness
āyatana	sense
āyatanasvalakṣaṇa	sensory particulars
āyu	age
bāhyaliṅga	external reason
bāhyārthapratyakṣavāda	theory of direct cognition (sensation) of the external object
bāhyārthānumeyavāda	representationalism, inference of the external object
bhāṣya	commentary
bhāvānyathika	change of state
bhrānti	illusion
bīja	seed
buddhi	intellect
caitasika	mental factor
caturāryasatya	four noble truths
chetanā	volition
candas	will
citta	mind thought-moment
cittamātra	mere consciousness (idealism)
cittasantāna	flux of consciousness
dharma	event; element; mental object
dhātu	element
dīpaghaṭa	lamp-pitcher
dravya	substance
dravyasvalakṣaṇa	particular substance
dṛṣṭa	seen
dṛṣṭi	wrong view
dṛṣṭānta	empirical example
duḥkha	disgust
dveṣa	aversion
gaganagañjasamādhi	a stage of concentration
gaṃbhīra	deep
gocararūpa	visible matter
grāhaka	subject
grāhya	object
grāhyatā	objectivity

hetu	reason
heya	undesirable
hrī	self-respect
indriya	sense
īrṣyāmala	defilement of jealousy
jāti	universal
jñāna	knowledge
kalpanā	imagination
kalpita	imagined
kāraṇa	cause
kāritrānyathika	change of action or efficacy
kārya	effect
kaukṛtya	anxiety
kauśīdya	indolence; laziness
krodha	anger
lakṣaṇa	characteristic
lakṣaṇāyathika	change of characteristic
laukika	mundane
lokottara	super-mundane
mada	intoxication
mādhyamika	adherent of Mādhyamika school
malaḥ	defilement
māna	pride
mānasapratyakṣa	mental sensation
mānasika	mental
mandadhīḥ	weak intelligence
mātsarya	selfishness
māyā	trickery
mukti	liberation
mūlakleśa	fundamentally complex
mūrta	manifested
naya	method
nikāyasabhāgatā	universal
niḥsvabhāva	unsubstantial
nirodha	cessation
nyāya	logic: science of correct judgement
nyāyavādin	epistemologist-logician
pakṣa	minor term
pakṣadharma	minor premise
pañcaskandha	five aggregates

paṅkti	line
parabhāva	other nature
paracita	other stream of thought
paracittānumāna	inference of other stream of thought
paramāṇu	atom
paramārtha	fundamental
parataḥ	depending on extraneous condition
paratantra	dependent
parikalpita	imaginary
pariṇāma	transformation
pariṇāmavāda	doctrine of transformation
parinispanna	real
phala	result
prabhāsvaraṃ cittaṃ	mind as pure or clear light
pradāsa	envy
prakāśaka	illuminator
prakāśya	illuminated
pramāda	negligence
pramāṇa	source of valid cognition
pramāṇabhūta	manifested valid source of cognition
pramāṇaphala	result of valid cognition
paramārthasatya	fundamental truth
prameya	object of cognition
praśrabdhi	tranquility
pratibhāsa	reflection
pratibimbana	reflection
pratisaṃkhyānirodha	intellectually discriminative cessation
pratītyasamutpāda	dependent origination
pratyakṣā	sensation, direct cognition
pratyakṣaviruddha	contradictory to sensation
pūrvikā	preceded
pūrvapakṣa	prior thesis, opponent's view
sādharmya	similar
śāṭhya	cheating
sahabhūhetu	co-existing cause
sāmādhi	concentration
sāmānya	universal
samantabhadra	all round beneficence
sāmarthya	capacity

saṃjnā	perception
saṃprayuktahetu	applied cause
samucāya	accumulation
saṃvṛti	conventional
sāmvyavahārika	practical, applicable
samyagdṛṣṭi	right view
samyagjñāna	correct knowledge
sañcita	assemblage
sañcitākāra	form of assemblage
sandigdhanekāntikahetvābhāsa	doubtful-contradictory fallacy of reason
santānavāda	doctrine of flux
sāra	essence
sārūpya	correspondence; conformity; coordination
sārūpya-sambandha	relation of correspondence
sarvapurṣārtha	all human goals
sarvatraga	all-pervading
satkāyadṛṣṭi	ego
sautrāntika	adherent of sūtrapiṭaka (critical realist) of a school
siddhānta	principle: established conclusion; accep ted view
skandha	aggregation
smṛti	memory
smṛti-upasthāna	mindfulness
sparśa	sensation; contact
sthiti	duration
styāna	stupidity
sūkṣmapariṇāma	subtle transformation
sūtra	dialogue; aphorism
svābhāsa	own appearance
svabhāva	own nature
svalakṣaṇa	particular, own characteristic, unique, peculiar, thing in itself, burst of energy
svasaṃvedana	own consciousness
svasaṃvedanavāda	doctrine of own consciousness
svasaṃvitti	cognition of own self

svatantra	independent
svatantravijñānavāda	independent idealist
śabdapramāṇa	authority
śakti	force
śāstra	science, source books of Vaibhāsikas (such as Mahāvibhāṣā)
śloka	verse
śraddhā	confidence
ṣaḍvijñāna	six consciousnesses
tādātmya	identity
tadutpatti	caused by it
tathatā	thusness
tatsādṛśya	corresponding to it
tāyin	protector
tri-kālasvabhāva	triple nature of time
tri-svabhāva	triple nature
ubhaya-nyāyavādin	adherent to both
udāra	benevolent
upādāna	material cause
upādeya	desirable
upakleśa	sub-complex
upamā	simile
upanāha	hatred
upekṣā	equanimity
uttarapakṣa	anti-thesis; author's own view
vaibhāṣika	adherent of Mahāvibhāṣā (realist)
vaidharmya	dissimilar
vaitulika	sophist
vicāra	reflection
viciktsā	doubt
vidyā	knowledge
vihiṃsā	violence
vijñapti	making or manifestation of consciousness
vijñānavādin	idealist
vikṣepa	confusion
viniyata	limited
vipākahetu	resultant cause
viṣaya	object
viṣayābhāsa	appearance of object

vitarka	reasoning
vyakti	individual
vyatirekavidhi	method of difference
vyavahāra	application, practical activity
vyavahārika	applied, practical
yogi-pratyakṣa	sensation of a Yogin
yogyatā	capacity

Select Bibliography

Primary Sources

Abhidharmakośa of Vasubandhu II, ed. Rahula Sāṅkṛtyāyana, Vārāṇasī, *Saṃvat* 1898.

Abhidharmakośabhāṣya of Vasubandhu II, Varaṇasī, 1972.

Abhidhammatthavikāsinī, a commentary on *Abhidhammāvatāra*, by Ven. Sumaṅgala Mahasāmi, ed. A.P. Buddhadatta Nāyakathera, Colombo, 1961. (Sinhālese).

Abhidhammamūlaṭīkā, Nāma Aṭṭhasālinī Linatthapadavaṇṇanā, by Bhadanta-Ānanda Vanaratna Thera, ed. Paññāsāra Thera and Vimaladhamma Thera, Colombo, 1938. (Sinhālese).

Abhidharmadīpa with *VPV.*, ed. by P.S. Jaini, Paṭna, 1959.

Abhidharmasamuccaya, ed. by Śāntibhiksu Shāstri, Santiniketan, 1950.

Alambanaparīkṣā and *vṛtti*, recon. trans and ed. by N. Aiyaswāmi Śāstri, Madras, 1942. (Examen de l'Object de la Connaissance), textes Tibétain et Chinois, par Susumu Yamaguchi en collaboration avec Henriette Meyer, Paris, 1929.

Ātmatattvaviveka Udayana, Banaras, 1936.

Arthaviniścaya-sūtra and its commentary (*nibandhana*) ed. N.H. Saṃtāni, Paṭna, 1971.

Dīghanikāya-aṭṭhakathāṭīkā a sub-commentary of Sum., by *Dhammapālācārya*, ed. by Lily de Silva, London, 1970.

Dvādaśāraṃ-nayacakraṃ-vṛttiḥ of Mallavādin-Siṃhasūri, ed. by Muni Jambūvijaya, Bhāvanagar, 1966.

Hetubindu, with *Ṭīkā* (See Appendix VI, Dharmakīrti's Works, note 4).

Madhyānta-vibhāga of Asaṃga, ed. by R.C. Pandey, Delhi, 1971.

Mahāyānasūtrālankāra, of Asaṃga, (exposé de la doctrine du grand vehicule selon le systéme Yogācāra), ed. par. S. Lévi, Tome I, Texte, Paris, 1907.

Mohavicchedanī of Abhidhammamātikaṭṭhavaṇṇanā, by Kassapa Thera of Cola, ed. by A.K. Warder and A.P. Buddhadatta Thera, *PTS*, London, 1961.

Mādhyamikakārikā of Nāgārjuna, ed. by Louis de la Valleé Poussin, *Bibliotheca Buddhica*, St. Petersburg, 1910.

Nyāyabindu with Tikā by Dharmottara *and Dharmottarapradīpa*, by Durvekamiśra, ed. by Dalasukh Malvania, KPJRI, Patna, 1971.

Nyāyabindutīkā of Vinītadeva, ed. by Mṛināl Kānti Gaṅgopādhyāya, Indian Studies, Past and Present, Calcutta, 1971.

Nyāyabinduṭīkā of Dharmottara, (See Appendix VI, note 3).

Nyāyāvatāra-vārttika-vṛtti of Śāntisūri, ed. by Dalasukh Malvania, Bombay, 1949.

Pramāṇasamuccaya-vṛtti of Diṅnāga, recon. into Sanskṛit (some parts only), See App., *DNCV*., [(pp. 97-134), trans. chap. I, *Pratyakṣa* by M. Hattori (See *Dignāga on Perception*)

Pramāṇavārttikaṃ with vṛtti of Manorathanandin, ed. by Swāmi Dwarikādass, Varaṇasī, 1968.

Pramāṇaviniścaya, (See Appendix VI note 2).

Pramāṇavārttikavṛtti, (See *PV*),

Pramaṇavārttika-Bhaṣya of Prajñākaragupta, ed. by Rāhula Sāṅkṛtyāyana, KPJRI, Patna, 1953.

Pramaṇavārttika svavṛtti, (See Appendix VI, note 1).

Pramāṇavārttikasvavṛttiṭīkā, (See Appendix VI, note 1).

Mādhyamikavṛttiḥ de Nāgārjuna avec la Prasannapadā commentaire de Chandrakīrti Public par, Louis de la Vallée Poussin, St. Petersburg, 190?.

Pramāṇamīṃāṃsā of Hemacandracārya, ed. by Sukhalal Sanghavi, Ahmedabad, 1939.

Dharmottarapradīpa (See Appendix VI, note 3).

Abhidharmakośavyakhyā of Yaśomitra, ed. by Unrai Wogihara, Tokyo, 1971.

Sambandhaparikṣā, (See Appendix VI, note 7).

Santānāntara siddhi, (See Appendix VI, note 6).

Ślokavārttikakāśikā of Sucaritamiśra, *Trivandrum Sanskrit Series*, XC, XCIX, Trivandrum, 1926-1932.

Śāstradīpikā of Pārthasārathimiśra, Varaṅasī, 1970.
Ślokavārttikavyākhyā of Bhaṭṭomveka, ed. by S.K. Rāmanātha Śāstrī, Madras University no. 13, Madras, 1940.
Triṃśikābhāṣya of Sthiramati, with *Viṃśatikā* and *Vṛtti* of Vasubandhu I, Varaṇasī, 1967.
Tattvasaṃgraha of Śāntarakṣita, with *Pañjikā* of Kamalaśīla, ed. by E. Krishnamācārya, and trans. by G. Jha, 2 vols., *GOS.*, XXX, XXXI, Baroda, 1926.
Visuddhimagga, of Buddhaghosa, ed. Dharmarakṣita, Mahābodhi Publications, Sarnath, 1962.
Vibhāvinī, ed. Revatadhamma, A commentary on *Abhidhammaṭṭha-saṃgaho*, Colombo, 1956. (Sinhālese).
Vibhāṣāprabhāvṛtti, (See above *AbD*).
Vigrahavyāvartanī and vṛtti, of Nāgārjuna, ed. by Johnston and A. Kunst in *Mélanges Chinois et Bouddhiques*, Vol. IX, 1951.
Viṃśatikā I, ed. by N. Aiyāswāmi Śāstri, Namgyal Institute of Tibetology, Sikkim, 1964.
Śrāvakabhūmau Naiśkarmya Bhūmi, ed. by Karunesha Shukla, KPJRI, Paṭna, 1973.

Secondary Sources

Akalāṅka's Criticism of Dharmakīrti's Philosophy, Nagin J. Shah, Ahmedabad, 1967.
An Analysis of the Śrāvakabhūmi Manuscript, Alex Wayman, Berkeley, 1961.
Buddhist Philosophy, Theory and Practice Herbert V. Guenther, Hammondsworth, 1971.
Buddhist Logic, Th. Stcherbatsky, 2 vols, St. Petersburg, 1932, reprinted, New Delhi, 1984.
Central Conception of Buddhism and Meaning of the term Dharma, Th. Stcherbatsky, London, 1923.
Critical Survey of Indian Philosophy, C. D. Sharma, Delhi, 1964.
Die Philosophie des Buddhismus, E. Frauwallner, Berlin, 1969.
Dignāga on Perception, Masaki Hattori, Cambridge (Mass.), 1968.
Epistemology, Logic, and Grammar in Indian Philosophical Analysis, B.K. Matilal, The Hague, 1971.
History of Indian Philosophy, 2 vols. Umesha Miśra, Allahabad, 1948.
Indian Buddhism, A.K. Warder, Delhi, 1970.

Early Buddhist Theory of Knowledge, K.N. Jayatilleke, London, 1963.
Erkenntnisprobleme Bei Dharmakīrti, Tilmann Vetter, Wien, 1964.
Journal of Indian Philosophy, ed B.K. Matilal, Dordrecht, Holland.
La Theorie du tathāgatagarbha et du gotra, David Seyfort Ruegg, Paris, 1969.
'Landmarks in the History of Indian Logic', E. Frauwallner, *WZKSO*, Wien, 1961.
Outline of Indian Philosophy, A.K. Warder, Delhi, 1971.
Papers of Stcherbatsky, trans. by H. C. Gupta, Calcutta, 1967.
'The Earliest Indian Logic', A.K. Warder, *Trudi dvadtsat pyatogo mejdunarodnogo kongressa vostokovedov*, Moscow, Izdatelstvo Vostochnoi Literaturi Vol. IV, 1963.

Index

General

Philosophical Schools

Proper Names